D0948559

MICHEL TOURNIER'S METAPHYSICAL FICTIONS

PURDUE UNIVERSITY MONOGRAPHS
IN ROMANCE LANGUAGES

William M. Whitby, Editor Emeritus

Howard Mancing, General Editor

Enrique Caracciolo-Trejo and Djelal Kadir, Editors for Spanish

Allen G. Wood, Editor for French

Associate Editors

Volume 37

Susan Petit

Michel Tournier's Metaphysical Fictions

SUSAN PETIT

MICHEL TOURNIER'S METAPHYSICAL FICTIONS

JOHN BENJAMINS PUBLISHING COMPANY
Amsterdam/Philadelphia

1991

PQ
2680
.O83
284
1991

Cover illustration:

Self-portrait by Michel Tournier. Reprinted by permission.

Library of Congress Cataloging in Publication Data

Petit, Susan.
    Michel Tournier's metaphysical fictions / Susan Petit.
        p.   cm. -- (Purdue University monographs in Romance languages, ISSN 0165-8743; v. 37)
    Includes bibliographical references and index.
    1. Tournier, Michel -- Criticism and interpretation. 2. Metaphysics in literature. I. Title.
    II. Series.
    PQ2680.O83Z84   1991
    843'.914 -- dc 20   91-40887
    ISBN 90 272 1759 9 (Eur.) / ISBN 1-55619-302-5 (US) (alk. paper) (hardbd.)

248718/6

To Jack

A book does not have one author, but an indefinite number of authors. For to the writer must be added, as part of the creative act, all those who have read it, are reading it, or will read it.

Michel Tournier
Le Vol du vampire

Table of Contents

Preface

In "Pierre Menard, autor del *Quijote*," a short story masquerading as biographical criticism, Jorge Luis Borges imagines a minor French Symbolist poet whose principal lifework was writing two chapters of *Don Quixote*. Menard did not copy from Cervantes's text; rather, he re-created it, going through numerous rough drafts, which he then burned. According to Borges's narrator, Menard's *Quixote*, though identical to the original, is more subtle because phrases which are merely seventeenth-century platitudes coming from Cervantes's pen become laden with irony and insight when produced by a twentieth-century mind. Borges's *jeu d'esprit* shows, in the words of Emir Rodríguez Monegal, that "reading is more decisive than writing because it always writes the text anew" (346): though the imaginary Menard's words are the same as Cervantes's, the reader interprets them differently because of the assumptions he or she makes about the author's intentions and beliefs.

This paradox is central to the fiction of Michel Tournier, who is well aware that the meaning of works changes with their readers' interpretations and whose fiction, by using a modern narrative voice to tell seemingly old-fashioned, realistic stories, explores the meaning of past *genres* and beliefs for today's world. Because he uses traditional forms, one could see him as a Realist or a Naturalist who was born too late, and he has often expressed admiration for such earlier authors as Jules Renard, Jean Giono, and Maurice Genevoix, whom he admires for their ability to capture the physical world (*Vent* 179). Tournier's ability to create realistic-seeming narration contributes to his great popularity with the French reading public.

But, as Roger Shattuck wrote in an essay first published in 1983, Tournier is hardly the "French equivalent of James Michener" (208); in fact, Shattuck judged him "the most exciting novelist now writing in French" (218). Tournier's complex *œuvre* is exciting precisely because it is a variant on

Menard's *Don Quixote*: rather than literally reproducing the works of past centuries, he reconceives them from a contemporary point of view so that a reader is confronted simultaneously with a late twentieth-century style and a traditional literary work. The resulting fiction, like Borges's story, is immensely playful and inventive, and deeply thought-provoking.

In order to create this dualistic literature, Tournier relies heavily on borrowings and adaptations, many of which come from philosophy, Tournier's original field. Small appropriations include inserting "a whole passage"* from Leibniz's *Monadology* into *Vendredi ou les limbes du Pacifique* (Rambures 163) and altering a scene from Alain-Fournier's novel *Le Grand Meaulnes* to put it into *Le Roi des aulnes*, an act Tournier justifies on the grounds that the scene is more important in *Le Roi des aulnes* than in *Le Grand Meaulnes*, so Alain-Fournier's priority of time does not stand up against Tournier's priority of theme (*Vent* 55). Tournier's larger borrowings reveal his deeper concerns. *Vendredi ou les limbes du Pacifique* is not only a revision of Defoe's *Robinson Crusoe* but also a two-person version of the Bible; *Le Roi des aulnes* imagines, among other things, Saint Christopher as a prisoner of the Germans during World War II; *Les Météores* is *The Divine Comedy* reconceived as a realistic novel set in the 1930s, 1940s, and 1950s; *Gaspard, Melchior et Balthazar* could be called a version of the Gospels by Flavius Josephus in collaboration with Flaubert; *La Goutte d'or* is Hans Christian Andersen's "The Snow Queen" with an Algerian Berber taking the role of Kai.

Uniting such disparate elements—and the list above is far from complete, for each novel is based on multiple inspirations—results in fiction which shows the beliefs of past centuries through the veil of more recent doubt. William Cloonan calls Tournier's protagonists romantics because Cloonan thinks that they pursue self-delusions and refuse to develop (*Michel Tournier* 100); Colin Davis says that they look for interpretations "which seek to exclude the human reality of doubt" (*Michel Tournier* 203). Both of these readings tend to assume that Tournier is usually ironic in his fiction and to reflect a twentieth-century belief that because ultimate knowledge is impossible, anyone who looks for it must be deluded. It is possible, however, to believe with Françoise Merllié that "a reading crediting Tournier with sincerity can be as rich as one suspecting him of Machiavellianism" (*Michel Tournier* 10). Although I cannot agree with all of Tournier's statements about his works,

---

*Throughout this work, all translations not otherwise credited are my own.

whenever it is possible I find it most fruitful to assume that he is sincere at bottom, however much wit appears on the surface. Simultaneously present in Tournier's fiction are both a skeptical attitude characteristic of the twentieth century and the conviction that the world can be known through faith and logic, which is the view he adopts explicitly. Having been attracted to philosophy by its ability to imagine coherent systems, he now creates fictional worlds where system is the driving force and where the seemingly random pattern of life reveals a hidden destiny.

Despite his serious purpose, joking is central to Tournier's fiction. Unfortunately, his humor often does not translate well into English, perhaps because it is subtle, being both straightfaced and whimsical. His fiction might be more popular in England and America if readers were sure that humor is intended when God forgives Cain because He would rather live in a city than be carried around in the smelly Ark of the Covenant ("La Famille Adam") or when a fourth, unknown Wise Man finds himself in Bethlehem at the Nativity because he is looking for a recipe for pistachio candy (*Gaspard, Melchior et Balthazar*). One can contrast Tournier's understated French humor with Tom Stoppard's more obvious English comedy in *Dogg's Hamlet*, a play in which, among other things, a group of schoolboys who know no English perform a fifteen-minute version of *Hamlet*, followed by an encore which is a two-minute *Hamlet*. As Tournier often does, Stoppard bases his plot on a philosophical idea, Wittgenstein's theories of language (Stoppard 7-8; Brassell 235-36); Stoppard's use of *Hamlet* is somewhat like Tournier's incorporation of well-known works of the past; and both Stoppard and Tournier create a realistic surface. Stoppard's play, however, is farce; Tournier's humor is almost always subtle.

His humor is becoming more obvious, though, for in the more than 20 years he has been publishing, he has gradually come in his fiction to rely less on his intellect and education and more on his feelings and sensations. Tournier actually based the plot of his first novel, *Vendredi ou les limbes du Pacifique*, more on philosophy, religion, anthropology, history, and psychology than on its most obvious source, Defoe's *Robinson Crusoe*. Because of its intellectual playfulness, and despite its overt celebration of physical life, the book clearly owes more to the library than to the beach, and Tournier has often expressed his unhappiness with its too explicit philosophical content. In each successive novel he has relied less on intellectual fireworks and more on a story line that engages a reader through apparent realism, as well as on simpler language and more accessible sources.

Nevertheless, Tournier has remained faithful to the aim he had when he abandoned philosophy for fiction: to "make a novel by Ponson de Terrail come out of Hegel's typewriter," or "to play checkers with a chess set" (*Vent* 180). Telling a story was not enough, though it was essential; he wanted his fiction to be a profound and complex exploration of the nature of existence. Borges's imaginary Pierre Menard makes one see Cervantes's well-known story anew; to achieve a similar binocular vision, Tournier also tells familiar stories, borrowing his plots from literature, myth, and religion and expecting his reader to recognize the sources and to have ideas about them before beginning to read. To make sure the reader is aware of the ideas he is using, Tournier does not hesitate to explain background, sometimes in the text of the book, sometimes in footnotes, sometimes in postscripts. It is in this sense that Tournier says that his books "must be recognized—reread—at the first reading" (*Vent* 189). If, as "Pierre Menard" implies, "reading is more decisive than writing," we should remember that Tournier is a reader first, reinterpreting his sources before rewriting them. His use of familiar materials is reinforced by a realistic, chronological narration intended partly to destroy suspense so that the reader can focus on the fictional journey, not the destination of the plot.

Important as it is, the plot is just a framework supporting an ideational structure which is Tournier's true subject matter. His works constantly invite the reader to join him in exploring the nature of the world, the interpretation of art, or the relationship of God to man, under cover of telling realistic tales. In deriving his fiction primarily from intellectual exploration of the meaning of life rather than from character and incident while preserving surface realism, Michel Tournier has radically reconceived the nature of contemporary fiction: his revision of myths is a re-vision of literature. But he is also returning to the origins of fiction, for the great myths and folk tales of the past use a realistic surface (if they use one at all) only to keep a reader's or listener's attention while they explore psychic and spiritual life.

In the study that follows, I have found that plot structure is the best key to meaning, for the arrangement of incident always shows what ideas Tournier's fiction is examining. His frequent use of religious themes implies their importance to understanding the *œuvre*, so I focus often on them, showing the development of Tournier's conception of Christianity and frequently referring to his expressed beliefs and values, because he has always wanted his writing to promote his ideas; for, as he told me in the interview included in this book, he writes because he has something to say. But that something depends also on the reader's participation, on "co-creation" between reader and author, providing Barthian *jouissance*. Tournier's criterion of a masterpiece is that it "give its reader participation in the joy of creation" (*Vol* 19); by that standard, all of his works invite readers to bring their own creativity to the act of reading and become co-creators of the work. I hope that this study will help other readers join in that "co-creation."

SUSAN PETIT
PALO ALTO, CALIFORNIA

Acknowledgments

Many more people than I could thank here have contributed to this work, but some cannot remain unacknowledged. To Michel Tournier I am indebted not only for the time he gave me for the interview which appears at the end of the book and for the self-portrait he has provided for the cover, but for producing a body of work so rich and moving that years of studying it have only increased its appeal. I thank also Hélène Laroche Davis, who guided my initial analysis of many of these works when I was her student, and Ronald Gerald Smith, who showed me how to approach Sartre's philosophy.

I am grateful to the journals where the following articles appeared for permission to use in this book ideas which first appeared in quite different form in their pages: "Psychological, Sensual, and Religious Initiation in Tournier's *Pierrot ou les secrets de la nuit,*" *Children's Literature* 18 (1990): 87-100; "The Bible as Inspiration in Tournier's *Vendredi ou les Limbes du Pacifique,*" *French Forum* 9 (1984): 343-54; "Joachim de Fiore, the Holy Spirit, and Michel Tournier's *Les Météores,*" *Modern Language Studies* 16.3 (Summer 1986): 88-100; "Fugal Structure, Nestorianism, and St. Christopher in Michel Tournier's *Le Roi des aulnes,*" *NOVEL: A Forum on Fiction* 19.3 (Spring 1986): 232-45, copyright NOVEL Corp. © 1987, reprinted with permission; "Salvation, the Flesh, and God in Michel Tournier's *Gaspard, Melchior et Balthazar,*" *Orbis Litterarum* 41 (1986): 53-65; and "*Gilles et Jeanne*: Tournier's *Le Roi des aulnes* Revisited," reprinted by permission from the *Romanic Review* 76.3 (May 1985): 307-15, copyright by the Trustees of Columbia University in the City of New York.

My greatest debt is to my husband, John M. Gill, for his unwavering encouragement, and for his willingness to read and criticize successive drafts of the manuscript with intelligence, insight, and love.

1

Vendredi: Tournier's Utopian Vision

Michel Tournier's first published novel, *Vendredi ou les limbes du Pacifique*, which won the Grand Prix du roman of the Académie Française in 1967, is probably his best-selling novel, partly because it is often read in schools, and it has inspired a stage play for children and a five-hour television version starring Michael York. The success of *Vendredi* is somewhat ironic, because Tournier has long proclaimed his dissatisfaction with the book and in 1971 published a simpler and briefer version of the story, *Vendredi ou la vie sauvage*, in Gallimard's "Folio Junior" series for adolescents. But although he insists that the "children's version"—a label he rejects—is the superior book, the original is much richer. Tournier himself cannot be so displeased with *Vendredi ou les limbes du Pacifique* because, rather than simply prohibiting its continued publication, in 1972 he put out a revision of it which incorporated material that had first appeared in the children's version. It is this 1972 edition, which has become the standard version of *Vendredi*, that I will discuss here. (The English translation, by Norman Denny, was published in 1969 in Great Britain as *Friday, or The Other Island* and in the United States as *Friday*, and is based on the first published version of *Vendredi*.)

The novel, whose title means "Friday, or The Limbo of the Pacific," is erudite, witty, and playful. Although the intellectual aspects of the book overwhelm the purely novelistic ones, it was precisely the mental agility Tournier displayed in the novel which charmed its first French readers, though it tended to put off the English and American reviewers, who often had little idea of what Tournier was attempting. Ironically, Tournier did not want to provoke a purely intellectual response; in an interview shortly after the book's publication, he insisted that he wanted above all for readers of the book to shake with laughter (Gorin). But that laughter would have to be provoked mainly by intellectual jokes. Even the novel's plot comes from art rather than life, for the book retells and revises the story of Daniel Defoe's *Robinson Crusoe*, thus reversing Defoe's process, for Defoe took his plot from a true story, not from literature.

Robinson Crusoe was a fitting choice of model, for it is considered by many critics to be the first true novel, and Tournier wanted *Vendredi ou les limbes du Pacifique* to be equally innovative. In it he attempted to meld the essay and the novel in a book whose adventures would be intellectual rather than emotional or physical, as he explained some years later in his spiritual autobiography, *Le Vent paraclet* (231). Tournier's specific goal was to remove all trace of civilization from his protagonist and create an entirely new world in place of the old one (*Vent* 229). The novel is amazingly ambitious in its attempt to revise psychology, Christianity, history, and philosophy and to present Tournier's ideas on those subjects in the form of a novel which he hoped would provide the "literary equivalent" of metaphysics (*Vent* 179). As a result, *Vendredi* is a strange but fascinating book. Although it appears to be a realistic adventure novel, from another point of view it can hardly be called a novel at all. Its complexity is indicated by the fact that Tournier was writing fiction using the ideas he had learned as a student of philosophy and anthropology and that he was, in his own words, "stuffed full of Jean-Paul Sartre and Claude Lévi-Strauss" ("Writing" 33).

Because of Tournier's ambitious goals in this first novel, *Vendredi* does many things at once. It rewrites the familiar story of Robinson Crusoe, imagines a non-Oedipal path to psychological wholeness, reinterprets Christianity, sums up a historical dialectic, replies to a famous debate between Lévi-Strauss and Sartre, and develops a philosophical theory of knowledge, all in the format of a novel. I will consider each of these threads in turn.

REWRITING *ROBINSON CRUSOE*

The revised Robinson Crusoe story is the most obvious and least original thread, for revisions of the Crusoe story are so common that in French they have a name, *robinsonnades*. (The French always refer to Crusoe by his first name.) In *Le Vent paraclet*, Tournier points out various changes he made to the story and shows how some of them, such as putting the island in the Pacific rather than the Atlantic, bring *Vendredi* closer to the popular idea of the story and to Defoe's sources than to Defoe's tale. Tournier has often explained that he wants to make use of "mythic" elements, those real or fictional situations and characters which seem to possess lives of their own, because they carry psychological power. A myth, for Tournier, is a "story that everyone already knows" (*Vent* 189), and it is, by definition, a compelling fiction which speaks to our inner lives. The general plan of such a myth is also usually quite simple; the popular idea of Crusoe's story could easily be summed up in a sentence or two, so that Tournier's story has a classically simple line which he fleshes out with a series of adventures, some modeled on Defoe but most not.

Tournier relies on a reader's presumed knowledge of the general outline of Crusoe's story but supplements that knowledge with an opening section which predicts later events. In this introductory episode, set in italic type, the twenty-two-year-old Robinson is on a ship, the *Virginie*, which is struggling to stay afloat in a storm off the west coast of Chile. It is September 29, 1759, one hundred years to the day after Defoe set the shipwreck in *Robinson Crusoe* and a time Tournier associates with the "English Puritans" who "invaded and colonized, Bible in hand, the virgin land of the New World" (*Vent* 233). Tournier's calling the ship the *Virginie* suggests not only the English colony of Virginia and the virgin lands of the Western Hemisphere generally but, more important, Robinson's "virginal" nature, for although he is not literally a virgin (he has left a wife and two children in York), he is something of a blank slate, a very young man who knows little of his real self.

The Dutch captain, Van Deyssel, is in the ship's cabin with Robinson, telling Robinson's fortune with tarot cards. Van Deyssel predicts a fortune for Robinson which will all come true in the course of the book—Robinson's organizing a kingdom which resembles a tidy, well-stocked cupboard; his retreat into a cave; the "twin" who will rescue him; and the "Solar City" and "solar sexuality" (12) which will lead toward the "god of heaven" incarnated in a "golden child" (13). As Van Deyssel tells him, Robinson's destiny is set, but it is revealed in a code that can be read only through the key, or "grid," of future events (13). Lynn Salkin Sbiroli's study of the meaning of the tarot cards for Robinson's mental and spiritual development explores these relationships in detail.

After the shipwreck and a period when Robinson succumbs to despair and lives in a pig wallow, the action of the novel's first half closely follows that of *Robinson Crusoe*. Tournier has said that his novel has two main parts, one before the arrival of Vendredi (Friday) and one after his arrival, which are given dialectical energy by the short section at the start of the novel portraying Robinson's despair (*Vent* 232-33). (There are actually two other short sections: the introductory section with Van Deyssel already mentioned and a coda at the very end, after Vendredi's departure.) After the shipwreck, then, Robinson lives in the pig wallow, an action not found in Defoe. When he turns away from the sloth and bestiality represented by that kind of existence, he civilizes his island, doing all the things we expect him to (because of our general knowledge of the Crusoe story) and a few we do not. Robinson lets his civilizing impulses run riot because he fears sinking back figuratively into despair and literally into the wallow.

Robinson re-creates the civilization he has left behind because he can give himself a reason for existing only by hyperactivity—he is not, as in Defoe's book, restoring a necessary and superior order of existence, that of European civilization, but merely doing things that keep him from feeling useless. This extreme reaction is the result of the dialectic; to escape the wallow, he must do the exact opposite of living slothfully. The exaggerated lengths to which Robinson goes in re-creating civilization, such as building a courthouse and writing a penal code, are at the root of the mainly satiric humor in this part of the novel, and both the specific events and the fact that they are funny are deviations from *Robinson Crusoe*, which is not a humorous book.

After Vendredi's arrival, in the book's second half, events begin to deviate more and more from those in *Robinson Crusoe*, beginning with the ironic circumstance that Robinson has no intention of rescuing Vendredi when he first sees him. When the cannibals bring Vendredi to the island, Robinson actually tries to shoot him, because Vendredi is running right toward the foliage concealing Robinson. He becomes Vendredi's rescuer only because his aim is spoiled and he shoots one of the cannibals by accident.

Unlike Defoe, Tournier presents Robinson ironically, especially in the passage following the rescue, where he is described as "dressed in nanny-goats' skins, his head in its fur hat stuffed with three millennia of Western civilization" as he receives the grateful Vendredi's homage (144). Like Defoe's Crusoe, Robinson "civilizes" Vendredi, but unlike him he has qualms about doing so. The major changes from *Robinson Crusoe* come after Vendredi accidentally touches off an explosion which destroys everything Robinson has created. Their roles change, and Vendredi teaches Robinson how to live on a tropical island, enjoying nature's bounty and playing diverting games. Finally, when a ship comes, Robinson refuses to leave, but Vendredi goes away. The desertion of the ship's cabin boy, however, gives Robinson a new companion on the island at the book's end.

It is this rewriting of *Robinson Crusoe* which interested Gérard Genette, who, in his study of intertextual relations, takes *Vendredi* as an example of *transvalorisation*, rewriting a text so that the values of the original work are reversed (418-24). Margaret Sankey, who has explored the specific changes Tournier made from Defoe's narrative, sees Tournier's revision as consisting mainly of an attack on the eighteenth-century idea of individuality which she finds in *Robinson Crusoe*.

THE PSYCHOLOGICAL DEVELOPMENT

Changing the plot of *Robinson Crusoe*, however, was the most minor of Tournier's revisions. Another and more interesting revision is in psychology. Georges Cesbron, who has considered the psychology and the philosophy of the "telluric" phase of Robinson's development, which takes place in the novel's first half, sees in Robinson's relations with the earth something approaching complete happiness, but this reading seems somewhat simplified. The philosopher Gilles Deleuze, who had been a schoolfriend of Tournier's, also considers Robinson's psychology in an essay which serves as postface to the inexpensive Gallimard "Folio" edition of the novel. It is Robinson's psychosexual development which most interests Deleuze, who emphasizes the sexual "perversion" which he finds to be the core of Robinson's development of an entirely new kind of existence.

The main changes in psychology which Tournier develops are revisions of Freudian Oedipal theory. Unlike Defoe's Crusoe, Robinson suffers more from psychological than technological problems; he must find not so much a way to survive physically as a way to forget his emotional isolation. He needs to create a new psychological self. He does this partly by creating an imaginary society, even wearing different costumes salvaged from the wreck as he carries out his various duties as magistrate, priest, and general, and the absolute seriousness with which he assumes the different roles and costumes is a major source of ironic humor in this part of the novel. The situation is serious, however: by assuming these different roles, by writing laws that refer to all inhabitants of the island, and by constructing public buildings, he is figuratively peopling his island and trying on different personalities.

This creation of imaginary others is not entirely successful, and Robinson must entirely re-create his own psychology to cope with his new situation. Giving himself a new (symbolic) biological heritage, he comes to think of the island as his mother, naming it "Speranza," a name suggesting both hope and a beautiful woman (45), and he goes through psychological rebirth by symbolically returning to the womb, descending into a tiny grotto deep inside a cave at the island's center, after undressing and coating himself with milk so he can slide down the narrow passage leading to a tiny cavity, in which he must assume a fetal position. There he finds a kind of "nonexistence" (106) suggestive of life in the womb, in which Speranza takes on "all the attributes of motherhood" (107). Shortly after, on the island's surface, he even drinks at a spring which comes out of a *mammelon*, a word which means both "knoll" and "nipple" (113): the newborn is now suckling at his mother's breast. Robinson's symbolic rebirth—and subsequent infancy—mean that he now can re-create his personality. The book's language insists that Robinson is now "telluric," or earth-born, and presumably his personality is now being shaped in relation to the island around him rather than by human society. Although he obviously has not cast off all of his doubts, fears, and inhibitions, he is much more ready than before to construct a new psychological self, particularly in regard to his sexuality.

Robinson returns several times to the grotto but fears that to continue to regress to infancy is harmful, especially when he has a sexual climax in the rock-womb and fears the incest of polluting his "mother" with his semen (114). Instead, he embarks on new psychological growth. He soon passes into an active sexual phase, but the absence of women (and his refusal to consider copulating with the animals on the island) leads him into two sexual experiments in which he goes progressively lower on the scale of existence. His first experience is with vegetable matter: he tries sexual relations with a fallen tree. This "liaison" ends in comic failure when, after several honeymoon months, he is bitten on his penis by a spider hidden in the tree and his "wounded member began to look like a tangerine" (122).

His second experiment, with inanimate matter, is more successful and more meaningful psychologically. He literally has sexual relations with the island, in a "coomb" where the soil is adequately loose and where the form of the gentle slopes reminds him of a woman's lower back (127). In a nice touch, he thinks that the mandrakes he sees growing there later are the result of his lovemaking. Although acting like a mature man in creating and supervising what he thinks of as the "administrated island," or the imitation civilization he has created (125), Robinson is also fulfilling childish Oedipal desires by sleeping with the island, his symbolic "mother." The important, non-Freudian point in this development is that Robinson has no Oedipal conflict because there is no father figure to compete with him for his "mother's" attentions. He does not have an Oedipus complex, for he is happily fulfilling his Oedipal desires; there is no guilt and no fear. Rather than finding maturity through resolving an Oedipus complex, he is developing a new, unprecedented, and guilt-free psychology based not on repressing but on expressing his Oedipal desires.

Robinson's psychological situation changes with Vendredi's arrival. Robinson becomes a sort of father, for Vendredi is only an adolescent, and Robinson, who is now probably in his forties, treats Vendredi like a child. Yet sometimes Robinson recognizes Vendredi as a brother (177). To further complicate matters, Vendredi presumably learns that Robinson is having sexual relations with Speranza, and he too copulates in the coomb with the island. Robinson is outraged when he surprises Vendredi in the act, especially as he has discovered that striped mandrakes are now growing where only pale ones had sprouted. This mixture of what seems to be incest and miscegenation, comic as it is for a reader, is excruciatingly painful for Robinson. Nevertheless, his reading of the Bible persuades him that Vendredi's copulation with the island is unimportant, a sort of incidental fact on the same level as the false accusation of rape Potiphar's wife made against Joseph in Genesis (179). Robinson feels that he is moving more and more into a world unlike the past and that the period of the island-wife is soon to be over, as are those of the island-mother and the administrated island (180).

After the explosion which destroys everything Robinson has built and Vendredi's assumption of the leading role in their relations, Robinson's psychological development continues to deviate from the Oedipal stages Freud considered necessary, and his sexual development stabilizes at an adolescent, pregenital level, as Tournier has explained elsewhere (*Vent* 121). He leaves the genital phase—his sexual activities in the coomb—and goes on to one in which his entire body is sexualized, and, experiencing what he considers "Uranian love" which makes him feel like the "wife of the heavens" (230), he realizes that differences of gender no longer matter to him. Robinson seems to be experiencing something like nongenital sexual climax in which he feels he has relations with the sun and stars. He reasons that he was never sexually attracted to Vendredi because, by the time of Vendredi's arrival, Robinson's sexuality had become "elementary"—that is, both simple and elemental—but he has now learned how to enjoy his entire body through play (229-30). Robinson has achieved a kind of sexuality which could be considered either regressive or advanced, preadolescent or postadult, and which is definitely no longer connected to his male sexual organs.

When the ship comes and Robinson has the chance to leave the island, he must decide whether to remain at his stage of development, freed of the oppressive demands of the superego (because he did not have to resolve his Oedipal relationship with the island by identifying with the father, rejecting the mother), or to return to his previous "normal" psychological condition. He chooses to remain on the island in a "perpetual present" (246). He finds, though, that this decision will force him to develop still further, when Vendredi leaves with the ship, while Jaan, the ship's mistreated cabin boy, deserts. Robinson must develop by becoming a Vendredi to the boy's Robinson; that is, he must teach the boy what he himself has learned, including presumably what he calls his Uranian "coitus" with the sun (230), a mystical union which is at once sexual and religious.

In later novels Tournier will expand further on the theme of nongenital sexuality, but here already one sees sketched the idea that a person's entire body is a source of eroticism and that ordinary genital sexuality is a limitation of one's erotic possibilities. One may be amused or shocked by Robinson's sexual development, but the book insists that his creation of new erotic paths is crucial to his fulfillment.

REVISING CHRISTIANITY

Besides changing Crusoe's story and undoing Robinson's normal Oedipal development to replace it with guilt-free polymorphous sexuality, *Vendredi* also rewrites the Bible and thus reinterprets Christianity, as I have shown in detail elsewhere ("The Bible as Inspiration") and as Catherine Glenn also points out. In recounting Robinson's story, Tournier retells the Old Testament in a comic vein, revises the New Testament, and briefly sketches a third, idyllic period following both testaments.

The Old Testament part of the story is essentially satiric because Robinson here represents the entire Jewish people, and what may be reasonable for a nation becomes ridiculous when applied to only one person. Beginning with his first moments on the island, Robinson's actions retrace the story of the Bible. As Cain killed his brother Abel, Robinson kills the first living thing he finds on the island, a ram (17), and later he imitates Noah, whose story inspires Robinson to build an ill-fated ship which he cannot even transport to the ocean (27). Like Moses, he has a pillar of smoke and one of fire when he tries to escape his exile (40-42), and he quotes Solomon's songs to his own "love," Speranza (135-36). The whole process by which Robinson keeps written records, constructs buildings, writes laws, and develops the island's resources imitates the development of the Kingdom of Israel and follows the same sequence.

Robinson has become a diligent reader of the Bible—the verses cited in *Vendredi* always correspond to the particular point of Robinson's development from the beginning to the end of the Old Testament—but that activity both helps and hurts him. It gives him a way to keep his sanity because he thinks that God is speaking directly to him, but following the Bible blindly becomes less and less satisfying. His Quaker training to listen to the voice of God speaking in him and his mother's insistence that the Bible's word is "deformed" by human transcription have tended to make him question the Bible (107-08), but he has nothing to substitute for its teachings because he cannot bring himself to trust his own feelings, although he believes that they may be the voice of the Holy Spirit.

Robinson's problem is neatly summed up in his relationship with Tenn, the ship's dog, which survives the shipwreck but does not join Robinson until he has begun to live in a "civilized" way by writing laws and regularizing his activities. Tenn represents the Ten Commandments, as suggested by his name and the fact that he appears at the early stages of Robinson's created civilization. (This is no doubt the reason it is Tenn that spoils Robinson's aim as he is trying to shoot Vendredi when the latter first appears; Tenn prevents him from committing murder.) The fact that Tenn is only a temporary substitute for human companionship echoes Tournier's idea that the Ten Commandments are only a temporary substitute for true knowledge of God. Tenn stops being necessary when Vendredi assumes the leading role on the island, and so Tenn dies in the explosion which ends Robinson's rule, just as the restrictive laws of the Old Testament (though not necessarily the Ten Commandments) are superseded, in Christian belief, by Christ's teachings. Robinson stops making and obeying written laws to live freely as Vendredi teaches him in response to his own innocent, playful impulses.

Before Vendredi's arrival, Robinson has reached a religious dead end to which Vendredi provides the solution, for Vendredi, with his "aerian soul" (161), represents Christ. He saves Robinson as the Messiah saved the Jews, in Christian theology, but only after a period of apprenticeship to Robinson's regime parallel to Jesus' education in Jewish law. Vendredi's relationship with Tenn is revelatory: they are immediately on intimate terms, to Robinson's chagrin (145), but not in a way Robinson approves, for Vendredi and Tenn are not so much man and master as equals who nevertheless have no sentimentality toward each other (171-72). Like Christ who came to fulfill the law, not to destroy it (but who in fact did overturn most of the legalistic aspects of Judaism), Vendredi even saves Tenn's life once (161-62), but later accidentally sets off the explosion which kills him.

After the explosion, events on the island are shaped in part by a correspondence to the New Testament, but it is much looser than the earlier correspondence to the Old Testament, for here Tournier is representing his own idiosyncratic conception of true Christianity, not that of established churches. In his role as Christ-figure, Vendredi must symbolically destroy sinful man, the Old Adam—or in terms of the novel, the Old Robinson. This Old Robinson is represented by the he-goat Andoar, which Vendredi kills. There is no question that Andoar represents Robinson; Robinson actually says "I was Andoar" (227), and he sees in both himself and the ram, with their patriarchal beards, symbols of the Old Testament. Just as Robinson's much earlier killing of a ram represented Cain's murder of Abel, so Vendredi's life-and-death struggle with Andoar is the novel's equivalent of Christ's death on the cross, for it redeems Robinson from his old self. In later novels, Tournier will return to the idea that Christ did not have to die for mankind to be saved; here he suggests it by the death of a literal scapegoat reminiscent of the goat which took the Israelites' sins with it into the wilderness (Lev. 16.7-10). This death is followed by Vendredi's resurrecting the goat in the form of a wind harp and a kite, both made from Andoar's remains, both representing rebirth into heavenly forms.

The religion which Vendredi teaches to Robinson by example is not literally Christian, and it does not even involve any overt worship of God. But Robinson explores the religious implications of the events as he writes in his logbook. The formerly earth-born and earth-bound Robinson sees the sun as a god and himself as its knight (215-16). He does not think that he is really worshiping the sun (225-26) but, presumably, God through His creation. Robinson sees in Vendredi the incarnation of an angel (221) and recognizes his old self as having been killed in Andoar's death (227). He now writes in his logbook not as before with red ink and a vulture's quill (144) but with blue ink and the quill of an albatross, both supplied by Vendredi (214-15): heavenly symbols have replaced symbols of death, as he writes his equivalent of the New Testament.

Robinson links Vendredi in his thinking with both Venus and Christ, thinking that Friday (*vendredi*) is not only the day named for Venus but the day of Christ's death: "Birth of Venus, death of Christ" (228). This apparent coincidence suggests that Vendredi's guidance will take Robinson to a world beyond Christianity (where Christ is dead) even as it revives the pagan deities represented by Venus, who suggests sensuality. Robinson's confusion adds to the ambiguous presentation of Robinson's new religion, which could be considered either paganism (an idea Robinson rejects) or a new kind of Christianity.

The last changes in Robinson's spiritual state are brought about by the arrival of the ship. The *Whitebird* is aptly named because the ship's arrival marks the novel's movement out of the Gospels as inspiration and into the period in which the Holy Spirit must give man guidance, and the Holy Spirit is usually symbolized by a dove, a white bird. Vendredi's departure on the ship suggests Christ's Ascension to Heaven, but the Holy Spirit in the form of the cabin boy has come to comfort Robinson, as it comforted the disciples after Christ's Ascension. The cabin boy, an Estonian, tells Robinson he is named Jaan Neljapäev; Robinson renames him Jeudi, or Thursday, explaining that *jeudi* is named for Jupiter and that the day is also "a Sunday for children"(254). (Thursday used to be a holiday for schoolchildren in France.) Tournier is making a joke, for "Neljapäev" means "Thursday" in Estonian (Hayman, "Grand Scale" 41), but the joke is serious: the boy is already an incarnation of Jupiter, as his original name shows.

Like the psychological theme, the religious one is clearly revisionist: Tournier posits a new Christianity which attunes the believer to the physical world and gives peace and joy while endowing the Holy Spirit with a more active role than Christ. It is based not on Christ's Crucifixion but on acceptance of the body as well as the mind and on harmony with nature, deriving from both the Bible and love of humanity. Later novels will explore these themes more clearly and will directly address the issue of Christianity as Tournier conceives of it.

DIALECTICAL HISTORY

One can also read *Vendredi* as being, in part, a response to a famous disagreement between the existentialist philosopher, playwright, and novelist Jean-Paul Sartre, whom Tournier has always revered, and Claude Lévi-Strauss, under whom Tournier studied anthropology at the Musée de l'Homme in Paris. In the *Critique of Dialectical Reason (Critique de la raison dialectique)*, which presents a dialectical reading of history heavily influenced by Hegel and Marx, Sartre attacks certain kinds of thinking as mere *robinsonnades* (678). He uses the word to mean any thinking which tries to justify and reproduce existing conditions as Defoe's Robinson Crusoe re-created English civilization on his island. In the *Critique* Sartre also claimed to be creating the foundation for a new anthropology and ethnology, partly because he thought that anthropology did not take into account how societies develop historically.

Sartre's belief that societies evolve dialectically—that is, through the clash and synthesis of opposite impulses—is illustrated in the first half of *Vendredi*. The opening section in which Robinson takes refuge in the pig wallow gives the novel a dialectical impulse, for its dialectical opposite, Robinson's frenetic activity in constructing his civilization, is motivated by his fear of sinking again into lethargy. Later events, such as Robinson's development of agriculture, are specifically said to reproduce the early technological development of humanity (47), and his fortification of his dwelling area and construction of a drawbridge suggest the Middle Ages (78). After Vendredi's arrival, the island reflects the coming of capitalist society and the colonization of the New World: there is division of labor based in part on racism, in which Vendredi, who is part Araucanian Indian and part African, represents the entire exploited Third World. In a delightfully right touch, Robinson decides to pay Vendredi's labor with coins salvaged from the shipwreck (149-50) so Vendredi can buy time off and trinkets of various kinds. The "historical" developments on Speranza, by imitating the historical and economic development of the world, reflect Sartre's dialectical conception of history.

However, the novel's treatment of this theme, too, is revisionist, and there is certainly no suggestion of the Marxist society Sartre and others would have imagined. The story line no longer follows world history in its second half, in which Vendredi teaches Robinson how to live. Here, the state has not so much withered away as vanished in the blink of an eye because of the explosion, and a utopian society has emerged. No one needs to work, for the island produces naturally everything necessary for life. And if Vendredi is the leader, he is far from being a master or governor of the island; he and Robinson live essentially on terms of equality, and there is no government. Work has been replaced by fruitful play, including sunbathing, walking on one's hands, preparing amusing meals, and play-acting. Tournier has diagrammed the dialectics of the last stage of this change like this: "earthly Robinson + Vendredi = solar Robinson" (*Vent* 235). With Vendredi's departure and Jaan's arrival, the only change is that Robinson will now be the guiding spirit of the activity on the island.

Developing his dialectical theory of history in the *Critique*, Sartre had ventured into the territory of Claude Lévi-Strauss, and Lévi-Strauss, who was a philosopher before he became an anthropologist, defended his ideas and attacked Sartre's view of society and history in the last chapter of his book *The Savage Mind (La Pensée sauvage)*. Lévi-Strauss says there that Sartre is wrong to think that societies can be understood only in terms of their dialectical historical development; he claims that they can also be understood analytically, or in relation to each other at a single period of time (256). He also objects to Sartre's implied attitude toward primitive societies, which he clearly feels is patronizing. Lévi-Strauss says that "primitive" societies do not lack history, as Sartre claims, but simply do not see themselves as changing historically (234), in contrast to modern Western societies, which are very conscious of the changes they undergo. The "primitive" societies, he says, realize that there are changes, but they refuse to see meaning in them (235). He denies, however, Sartre's claim that people in primitive societies are less capable of reasoning than those in technologically advanced societies (251); they simply think differently.

It may be that this debate between Sartre and Lévi-Strauss helped provide the germ of Tournier's novel. (The *Critique* was published in 1960, *La Pensée sauvage* in 1962, and *Vendredi* in 1967.) In any case, Tournier has said that he wished to put into *Vendredi* the essence of what he had learned from Lévi-Strauss at the Musée de l'Homme (*Vent* 194). So although Robinson's society develops dialectically over time in the book's first half, the second half shows a "primitive" society in which there is no more dialectic: it is a society beyond time. It is one of Tournier's jokes to write a *robinsonnade* which is the opposite of Sartre's concept; rather than showing Crusoe repeating the past by re-creating England on a deserted island, as Defoe's Crusoe does, Tournier's *robinsonnade* creates a new society.

Vendredi's attitudes reflect Lévi-Strauss's belief that the thought of primitive tribes aims both at interpreting the entire world through symbols and at understanding it in every concrete detail (220). In addition, Lévi-Strauss says, the "savage mind" exists in its "untamed state as distinct from mind cultivated or domesticated for the purpose of yielding a return" (219)—that is, Vendredi's thinking, unlike Robinson's or our own, has not been channeled purely or mainly toward achieving practical results but rather aims at understanding the entire world through symbols.

But when the *Whitebird* arrives, the primitive world in which Robinson has learned to live is face to face with the world of history. The timelessness of life on Speranza is indicated in part by Robinson's inability to believe that he has been living on the island for 28 years and by his conviction that he will not age if he remains there. Neither Robinson nor Vendredi likes the greed, selfishness, and insensitivity of "civilization" represented by the sailors, but Vendredi is attracted by the technology represented by the graceful schooner, seeing in it an airy being like himself. Robinson chooses the "primitive," timeless world of harmony with nature which Lévi-Strauss saw in tribes close to the earth, rather than the Sartrean dialectic of modern civilization. Time does not literally stand still on the island, for Robinson has indeed aged, but the passage of time has no more meaning for Robinson as long as he remains on his island.

SUBJECT, OBJECT, AND THE OTHER: *BEING AND NOTHINGNESS*

Sartre did not influence only the novel's dialectical theme, for in *Vendredi* Tournier is responding also to a number of psychological and philosophical theories Sartre developed in *Being and Nothingness (L'Etre et le néant)*, which the teenaged Tournier and his friends found wildly exciting when it appeared in 1943. They were completing their final year at the *lycée*, when philosophy is the principal subject studied, and were delighted to find themselves present at the birth of a new philosophical system (*Vent* 159-60). Since then, Sartre has been a major influence on Tournier's thought, even after Tournier abandoned his plans to become a professional philosopher and even though he disagrees with certain of Sartre's beliefs and rejects his attitude to life.

The philosophical and psychological theory Tournier most wanted to explore in *Vendredi* derives from Sartre's *Being and Nothingness* and concerns how others influence our view of ourselves and our world. The negative side of this influence is probably best known through Sartre's nonphilosophical writings. One of his most famous statements about "the Other" is the phrase "Hell is other people" (167), spoken by a character in his play *No Exit* (*Huis clos,* 1944). And Sartre's biography of the writer Jean Genet, *Saint Genet: Actor and Martyr* (*Saint Genet: Comédien et martyr*, 1952), makes much of a perhaps imaginary moment when Genet decides that he is a thief because his foster parents think he is one: other people's views of us can take away our ability to see ourselves clearly.

In *Being and Nothingness*, the Other is also generally presented in a negative way. Sartre says there that we learn that we have a personal identity primarily by realizing that we are not someone else, and specifically by realizing that we are not some other person who is looking at us. Even after that discovery, we may forget that we exist and be entirely absorbed in an action until we are recalled to awareness of self by the unexpected appearance of someone else. It is thus the Other who both gives one the possibility of conscious existence and freezes one's personality by imposing a judgment on it—a judgment, nevertheless, that one is free to reject, for Sartre emphasizes each person's responsibility for his or her actions and ideas.

In response to this question of one's relation to Others, Tournier shows in *Vendredi* how a man with no Others around him tries to create imaginary Others in order to give his world meaning and then, failing at least partially in that attempt, creates a personality largely independent of Others. Thinking at first that the island is inhabited, Robinson imagines the presence of Others; later, with this "key element" missing from his universe (53), he begins to doubt his senses and the reality of the physical world (54). To compensate for the missing Others, Robinson both imagines himself observed by God and creates his society of one, with its written laws, invariable customs, and public buildings. The lack of Others does not cause Robinson's sense of selfhood to vanish, as Sartrean theory might hold; on the other hand, it does make Robinson question his sanity, his morals, and the reality of the world around him.

This questioning leads Robinson to a view of reality similar to that in *Being and Nothingness*. Both Sartre (*Being* lxiv) and Tournier propose a position somewhere between realism and idealism. Sartre accepts both physical reality ("being," or the world of physical presence) and thought ("nothingness," or the world of humanly conceived possibles and lacks), and he places people in both categories. That is, people have a physical reality in the form of their bodies, which make them partly what Sartre calls "in-itselfs," or objects which coincide entirely with themselves, as everything nonhuman does. But people have also desires, which make them partly "for-itselfs," or consciousnesses which refuse to be merely what they are and which project themselves toward something different.

In *Vendredi*, Robinson's solitude drives him to become a philosopher who records his speculations in his logbook. He there develops Tournier's theory, which, like Sartre's, accepts both the world and consciousness as real. However, Robinson—or Tournier—insists strongly on a phenomenon similar to Sartre's "prereflective cogito." In this state, a person is conscious not of self but merely of the world. Robinson writes that when he is unaware of himself, "Then Robinson *is* Speranza" (98, emphasis in original). But suddenly something happens and Robinson becomes conscious of himself, and "An object [Robinson] has suddenly been degraded into a subject" (98). The idea of loss is crucial: Robinson sees himself as *superior* when he is object, when he exists in the same mode as the trees and flowers around him; but when he becomes a conscious subject and the world appears merely as being composed of his physical sensations, then the world is lessened, and his "eye is the corpse of light, of color" (99).

As Tournier explained to me in the interview which forms Chapter 8 of this book, and as Robinson's logbook entry implies in this key passage, the theory postulates that the change of a person from object to subject is produced by the world: "The world seeks its own rationality, and in so doing it eliminates this excrement, the subject" (98). Thus when Robinson sees a tree stump move, it *becomes* a he-goat because Robinson's conscious mind cannot believe that stumps move. However, such "contradictions" apparently do not need to produce consciousness. In the shorter version of the story, *Vendredi ou la vie sauvage*, there is a passage in which Vendredi and Robinson think they see a daisy, but the flower flies away. Robinson believes that they simply mistook a butterfly for a daisy, but Vendredi says "A white butterfly . . . is a flying daisy" (109). Some minds, like Vendredi's, may be able to accept contradictions in the world and thus escape being degraded, as it were, into consciousness, or the condition of being subjects.

In a number of ways, *Vendredi* seems to build on Sartre's theories, even if in ways Sartre would reject; it also proposes ideas quite different from Sartre's. I will touch briefly on some cases of agreement first, before going to differences. Both Sartre's idea that time is created by people as a response to Others (*Being* 282-83) and Lévi-Strauss's belief that technologically primitive societies are interested only in seasonal time, not historical time, are reflected in Robinson's attitudes toward recording time. He does not keep a calendar or create a clock until he invents his imaginary society of one; and, more important, when he abandons his imaginary society after the explosion, he also abandons any attempt to record or measure time. His nonacceptance of time is shown most clearly in his belief, expressed when the *Whitebird* arrives, that time has stood still for him. Robinson knows, of course, that he has aged, but he feels that time will have no hold on him unless he returns to civilization (245-46). More important is Sartre's insistence that the world itself is pure "being" and that only people can create "nothingness," or the idea that something is lacking or could be different. Echoing this conception is the obvious self-sufficiency of Speranza, which does not need Robinson's compulsion to civilize, label, and control everything on it (67). Later, however, under Vendredi's guidance, Robinson will free himself of this need. The novel thus suggests that Robinson has accepted the world, or "being," without having to impose his "nothingness" on it.

To Sartre, the Other is typically conceived in terms of struggle for dominance and is considered as creating limits to one's freedom (*Being* 525). Tournier may agree with this view, but Robinson at first needs these limits so badly that he must create imaginary Others. Deleuze claims that Vendredi is not really an Other for Robinson, at first because Robinson thinks of Vendredi only as a slave, and later because Vendredi seems somehow beyond the human (277-78). This is not entirely true, for Robinson changes greatly as a result of what Vendredi teaches him, but Vendredi may not have the psychological power which Sartre typically assigns to the Other.

One passage in which Robinson contemplates Vendredi's eye just before the explosion that will metamorphose their relationship (181) probably derives from Sartre's analysis of the relationship between subject and object and does seem to show that Vendredi at that point does not function as an Other. Sartre says that one cannot be the object of someone's "look" and simultaneously see the eye which is looking; one cannot be subject and object at the same time (*Being* 258). Robinson says much the same thing, but with different emphasis: "the subject and the object cannot exist at the same time because they are the same thing, first integrated into the real world [object], then thrown on the garbage heap [subject]" (100). Robinson sees Vendredi's eye; therefore he does not suffer from Vendredi's "look." It is important, though, that Robinson is transfixed by the eye's beauty and wonders if perhaps the coarse being he takes Vendredi for is only one side of the Indian (181). In contrast to Sartre's negative conception of human relations, Tournier's view allows for wonder and acceptance. After the explosion, Vendredi becomes an Other, capable of looking at Robinson and judging him (225). Vendredi's postexplosion game, in which he dresses and acts like Robinson and Robinson must dress and act like Vendredi (211-13), mimics the changing of object into subject and the reverse. There is no longer a Sartrean relationship based on a struggle to dominate; rather, Robinson and Vendredi respect each other and live harmoniously, and when they disagree or get on each other's nerves, they resolve their differences good-naturedly.

Some of Sartre's ideas appear to be challenged in the novel. Sartre considers sexuality as a response to Others (*Being* 406), whereas *Vendredi* presents sexuality as existing within Robinson. His sexuality has been trained by society into the form it approves, desire for women (133), but his desire does not disappear when there are no Others. Rather, it flows into different channels: first, imagined women, then the tree and the coomb. Later, when Robinson reaches a stage of generalized rather than genitalized sexuality, his desire is evoked by the sun and the heavens (230). Desire, then, is not for Tournier a response to an Other, but a biological and psychological impulse which is usually controlled and channeled by society.

The last major parallel between Sartre's ideas in *Being and Nothingness* and the events of *Vendredi* concerns people's goal in life. Sartre says that "man fundamentally is the desire to be God" (*Being* 566). He means that people want to be the basis for their own existence and that they want to coincide entirely with themselves while remaining conscious beings, a condition Sartre believes is impossible. What Robinson wants is similar to what Sartre says but not the same. For one thing, Sartre does not believe in God, but Robinson does. Therefore Robinson does not want to be the foundation of his own being; rather, he wants to fuse mystically into the being of God, as he does at the end in his "solar coitus" (230). The novel could be read as neutral on the subject of God's existence, but its rewriting of Christianity leads one toward a religious reading, and a number of what would otherwise be unlikely coincidences, such as the rainbow which appears when Robinson prays for a sign from God (31), make it entirely possible to see God's presence in Robinson's world.

Because of Robinson's religious faith, he is able nearly to achieve what Sartre posits as everyone's goal, to coincide entirely with himself, as objects do, while remaining conscious. Sartre believes that to do so is impossible because consciousness is the source of nothingness—that is, desire, possibility, and intentionality, as well as lies—and thus consciousness keeps us from merely being what we are or accepting our present selves and taking responsibility for our being and our actions.

However, at the end of *Vendredi*, Robinson has come close to becoming an "in-itself," while remaining human. He accepts himself; he feels that he has escaped from time; he is unconcerned with the opinion of Others; he has almost no desires or goals. Tournier has said in an interview that his original plan, more "rigorous" than the book's final development, did not include the cabin boy. Instead, Robinson was to be left alone on the island like a "stylite, standing immobile on a column in the sun" (Bougnoux and Clavel 14). This ending would have turned him into a pure "in-itself," but it would virtually have eliminated his humanity. In making Robinson grieve for Vendredi's loss and rejoice in finding Jaan, Tournier has not merely provided the book with a more novelistic ending but has asserted the value of human love, a value about which Sartre was extremely skeptical.

At the end, less rigorous though it may be, Robinson has nearly achieved his philosophical goal, which is to *become* Speranza: he coincides with the island because he accepts it entirely as it is. His doing so means he has found the "other island" that he thought was hiding behind the Speranza which he ordinarily experienced when he was first shipwrecked (94) and which is the actual Speranza ("being"), not the Speranza seen through Robinson's plans and projects ("nothingness"). At one point early in the novel Robinson even uses Sartrean terminology, when he fears that he will be "sucked out by the nothingness which I may have caused to be born around myself" (85). By the end of the novel, however, Robinson has nearly stopped creating nothingness because he has discovered how to accept being; at the same time, he has become a mystic, so he has not abandoned a spiritual dimension.

Although Sartre is the major philosophical influence, the novel does not relate only to Sartre's theories. Tournier also poses the problem of mind and matter in Platonic terms when Robinson writes in his logbook, "I have always preferred matter to form" (81). At the start, Robinson would like to exist in a purely material world, just as he would like to get rid of his head, if he could (88). But his fear of succumbing entirely to matter pushes him dialectically in the opposite direction, wanting the "opaque, impenetrable island, full of hidden fermentations and evil undercurrents" to be "metamorphosed into an abstract and transparent construction" (67). His language indicates that he thinks of the uncultivated island as consisting of brute matter and his civilizing actions as imposing forms on that matter. Later, however, after the explosion, he learns to accept all of himself, including his head of red hair which he used to hate, and to accept the physical world of matter, although he continues to look for meaning in it. He seems to have integrated acceptance of being, or matter, with his human search for meaning, which he believes has been successful.

Putting the Ideas Together

What is this meaning which Robinson believes he has discovered? The new world which Tournier has created could be viewed as either futuristic or regressive, or as both at once. Even on the level of revising Defoe's story,

Vendredi returns to a more primitive level, using some of the elements of the original, historical story which Defoe discarded, notably locating the island in the Pacific off the coast of Chile, rather than near the mouth of the Orinoco, where Defoe put Crusoe's island. In reimagining Robinson Crusoe's story, Tournier has attempted to return to sources in another sense by including events which one supposes would have happened, but which Defoe did not write about. Robinson's sexuality is the most obvious example: surely a man marooned alone on an island would suffer, at least at first, from sexual frustrations. Defoe's Crusoe does not; Tournier's Robinson does.

But in reimagining Robinson's sexuality, and in gradually stripping from Robinson the trappings of his civilization, Tournier returns his protagonist, as we have seen, to very early stages of psychological development. Robinson symbolically returns to the womb and reexperiences the entire process of sexual maturation. But instead of re-creating his previous sexual orientation, he creates first a new adolescent genital sexuality, then a nongenital sexuality of "solar coitus" which involves his entire body in mystic union with the sun. This sexuality is either infantile or beyond adult sexuality. The movement by which Robinson's religion is remade is similar, for he first retraces the events of the Old Testament, then discovers a new religion which could be conceived of as either a kind of paganism or something beyond Christianity as most people understand it, based on mystical love and the Holy Spirit.

The same ambiguity exists in Robinson's retracing of history: after going through the historical processes which have created the modern world (hunting and gathering, primitive agriculture, capitalism), Robinson discovers with Vendredi a new technology and "government" which is either a return to primitive society or a utopian, futuristic life. In his philosophical thinking, Robinson does not appear to retrace the thought of the major historic schools of philosophy, but he does find a vision of the world which first brings him up to Sartre's existentialist view, then lets him find a condition which is either the unconsciousness of primitive tribes or, perhaps, a goal to which the modern world should aspire, a state in which people can accept themselves and almost achieve the happiness of not wanting to change the world. Tournier's expressed goal was for the novel to be "inventive and prospective" rather than "retrospective" (*Vent* 229), but a reader need not believe that Robinson actually points the way to a new future state. Whether he returns symbolically to a distant past or creates a future society, each of the kinds of changes he makes shows that the book is an *antirobinsonnade*, for Robinson does not re-create the England he left but establishes a new kind of existence.

Because the novel does not insist that one accept Robinson's view of himself and his world, the book escapes being a *roman à thèse*: although each of the threads summed up above relates to the others, a fact which makes the several areas treated cohere with each other, one is free to interpret Robinson's development. He may be a holy man or a lunatic, a discoverer of truth or a man driven crazy by solitude. Although the most satisfying reading of the novel is one in which Robinson is conceived as the discoverer of a new way to live with oneself and the world, the persistence of doubt gives the novel that element of ambiguity which is necessary for the success of fiction. Tournier, of course, is well aware that fiction must provide this room for interpretation if it is to succeed.

VENDREDI AS NOVEL

Despite Tournier's care to write a real novel, not a thesis disguised as fiction, *Vendredi* is not entirely satisfying when considered mainly as fiction. Because Tournier's goals were so sweeping, he tried to put more ideas into the story than it could support; because he was forty-two when the book was published, he may also have been trying to make up for lost time. *Vendredi* is the work of a writer not yet entirely at home in the world of fiction: the style is sometimes heavy, the narrator is often too explicit for modern tastes, and Robinson's psychology is not always convincingly developed. At the same time, the book contains a mesmerizingly kaleidoscopic tumble of ideas which cannot fail to keep a reader's attention, though it speaks much more to the mind than to the emotions. One feels that the physical background— descriptions of plants, of weather, of the island's topography—are of secondary interest to Tournier, although he has clearly taken pains to get them right and to include adequate amounts of sensory descriptions. He has said that his models are such writers as Zola, Colette, and Jules Renard who, in his view, "make you smell things and people" (Ezine, "Michel Tournier" 225). But one smells the odor of the study in *Vendredi*, not that of the island; Tournier's research mainly involved reading about primitive societies, and his first-hand study, according to an interview, was limited to inspecting the only mandrake in Paris's Jardin des Plantes (Braudeau 85).

Although to some extent Zola and Colette may have inspired him, another influence is greater. Tournier did not want to write a realistic novel but a "cerebral adventure submerged in a classically novelistic context" (*Vent* 232) by following the model of Paul Valéry and particularly Valéry's *Monsieur Teste*, whose title character is so extraordinary that, in Tournier's view, "his monstrous brain creates an unbridgeable gap between the events and the character," thus providing "an ideal distance for observation" (*Vent* 231). Tournier uses much the same technique in each of his novels, for all of his main characters stand apart from the rest of society due to some attitude or circumstance.

Monsieur Teste makes use of both a narrator who is a friend of Monsieur Teste and selections from Monsieur Teste's diary to tell the story. Somewhat similarly, *Vendredi* uses an omniscient narrator of the old-fashioned sort who explains the meaning of the actions, and Robinson himself, in his logbook entries. These entries are too insightful and explicit to be convincing on a realistic level, but they allow Robinson's psychological and moral growth to be chronicled partly from inside and permit the philosophical theories to seem to develop naturally out of Robinson's circumstances, since it is he and not the omniscient narrator who advances them. Robinson's logbook entries would be more realistic if his style were noticeably different from the narrator's, but one could argue that using the same voice helps to unify the novel.

Like a narrator in a nineteenth-century novel, the omniscient narrator often tells the reader how to interpret events. Sometimes it is hard to tell whether the narrator is simply summing up Robinson's ideas or is explaining personal views, as in the statement that Robinson's "extraordinary situation" in being marooned resembled "a decree of Providence" (26). Elsewhere, the narrator provides what are clearly personal judgments, saying, for example, that Robinson would not be happy living unclothed on his island unless he had a "change of soul" (30) and, later, that a "new man" was being born in Robinson "completely different from the administrator" that he had turned himself into, but that the "worst danger" would be the disappearance of the administrator before the new man was "viable" (125). The narratorial voice is never as explicit as the one that Tournier uses in the briefer version of the story, but it is authoritative and often tells a reader how Tournier wants events to be judged.

The novel's main problem, as a novel, is that it explains both Robinson's and Vendredi's attitudes and feelings too explicitly. Perhaps partly for that reason, they do not quite come to life. For all his occasional despair and exultation, Robinson seems to exist largely in his thoughts, not his feelings, a fact which keeps him from becoming quite real. Vendredi is even more abstract, partly because of the symbolic burden he must bear as savior, partly because he is seen only from the outside, and partly because he seems to have few wishes and desires of his own except to enjoy life in a playful way.

Although Robinson and Vendredi are together on the island for half of the book, there is almost no dialog, and this fact also tends to prevent them from being fully realized as characters. There is more summary than developed scene, more telling than showing. The characters often seem much more motivated by the author's desire to work out the patterns he has set for himself than by their own needs. And as to living those ideas, Robinson can keep on being Robinson only as long as he remains on his island. Unlike Shakespeare's Prospero, he cannot return to civilization a wiser man for what he has learned; like a member of a Stone Age tribe that has been discovered by civilization, he can continue his way of life only by keeping his isolation. This forced isolation undercuts both the novelistic and the intellectual elements of the novel.

If it is looked at from another angle, however, one could say that *Vendredi* is amazingly successful at masking intellectual play as realistic fiction. The book is in no way built around character, Robinson's or Vendredi's, and the plot derives not from Robinson's or Vendredi's attitudes or desires but from *Robinson Crusoe*, the Bible, world technological history, and the other ideas Tournier wanted to explore, particularly philosophical ones. *Vendredi* is Michel Tournier's ontological treatise, his analysis of the nature of the physical world and people's relation to it. With Sartre, he insists on the reality of the physical world, for Robinson must learn to see and accept his island as it is: but, refusing absolute realism, Tournier makes Robinson's mystical experiences function as a valid way of responding to the world: God of some sort, a concept of God related in some ways to the Christian God, remains a possibility. Although, after the book's publication, Tournier felt that "the philosophy stared me in the face from every page" and rewrote the story in the briefer version to make it more novelistic ("Writing" 33), he had come very close to bringing off the trick of disguising his philosophical goals and sugar-coating his revolutionary theories with novelistic techniques.

Despite its faults as a novel, *Vendredi* is a work of genius. I think it is more so than the briefer version, because the full version is not only more complex but much more ambitious, for it aims at nothing less than reforming, by reimagining, all of Western civilization. However, these revisions cause the plot development to be largely mechanical despite the whimsical nature of many of the events. Because Tournier was aware of these defects in *Vendredi*, in his next novel, *Le Roi des aulnes*, he used strategies designed to create a more convincing protagonist and to reconcile the book's intellectual content with a much more concretely developed setting and a more fully realized protagonist.

2

Le Roi des aulnes: The Quest for Meaning

Because he was dissatisfied with the way in which ideas dominated *Vendredi ou les limbes du Pacifique*, Tournier not only reworked that book but in his next novel, *Le Roi des aulnes*, put more emphasis on character and setting, reduced the overt intellectual content, and dealt more deeply with an issue only sketched out at the end of *Vendredi*, a connection between sexual and religious feelings. Tournier had begun *Le Roi des aulnes* before *Vendredi*, but he was unable to reduce it to a manageable length and abandoned it twice, in 1958 and 1962 (*Vent* 193-94). Then, after publication of *Vendredi* and during two years when he was out of work, having been fired by the publisher Plon for striking, Tournier rewrote his material so successfully that *Le Roi des aulnes*, published in 1970, won the most prestigious of French literary prizes, the Prix Goncourt. It was only the fourth novel to win unanimously and the first to do so since 1940 (Robichon 355-69).

In a 1987 interview focusing on the Prix Goncourt and on the Académie Goncourt, to which he was elected in 1972, Tournier said that winning the prize "saved" him because the huge sales which the Goncourt virtually guarantees and the public attention it brought him have since permitted him to live by his writing (Boncenne 62). Even before it won, however, *Le Roi des aulnes* had excellent sales, and it has continued to sell steadily. Like *Vendredi*, this novel has had a stage version: Irène Lambelet wrote a simplified musical version of the story, which was presented in 1983 by three actors and a boys' chorus (Galey, "Oratorio"). But although the novel was hugely successful in France, American and British reviewers tended to greet coolly the 1972 English translation by Barbara Bray (Miller, Prescott, Sheppard, Paul West).

The book's title, which means "The King of the Alders," is a translation of the title of a poem by Goethe, "Der Erlkönig," which is well known in

France and Germany not only as a poem but also as a song with music by Schubert. Goethe's poem is about a sort of ogre who tries to steal a young boy who, at the poem's end, is left dead in his father's arms. Tournier's translation of the poem into French, printed at the end of the novel, emphasizes the poem's sexual undertones, showing the King of the Alders as motivated by a passion Tournier considers "pedophiliac," "amorous and even carnal," but not "pederastic" (*Vent* 119). This figure of the ogre underlies the protagonist of Tournier's novel. The American publisher, no doubt assuming that the King of the Alders would be unfamiliar to Americans, titled the book *The Ogre*, although in England the same translation was called *The Erl-King*.

In part because he was using the myth of the ogre as a springboard, Tournier wanted the book's surface to be as mundane as possible; as he has said, he writes about "monsters with a film of banality that covers them and lets them be accepted" (Joxe 50). The protagonist, Abel Tiffauges, is a rather antisocial Paris garage mechanic who in 1938, at the novel's opening, has just begun a journal in which he explores his childhood and which constitutes the book's first section. He is intelligent in an off-beat way, and though he thinks slowly, he searches unremittingly for hidden meanings behind events. Somewhat like Tournier's Robinson at the end of *Vendredi*, he is not interested in genital sex: at the book's start his mistress has just left him because his sexual attentions are too rapid. He is sexually attracted to children, but he expresses his pedophiliac feelings primarily by photographing children and recording their voices. What he most wants, however, is to carry children on his shoulders, which he calls *phoria*, from a Greek root referring to carrying. When World War II breaks out, Tiffauges, in jail on a false charge of rape, is released to be called up for military service. He serves in the army, becomes a German prisoner of war, and is sent to East Prussia, where he rises to power in a boys' school run by the S.S. At the novel's end he is fleeing Russian troops, sinking into a peat bog while carrying a Jewish refugee boy on his shoulders.

Although Tournier has often said that he is not an autobiographical novelist, he does make use of personal experiences, especially in this novel. He was too young to serve in the war and did not visit Prussia until after the book was published, but this book makes use of his German background: as a child he learned German and spent summers in Germany with his mother (*Vent* 72-74), and he studied at the University of Tübingen in the late 1940s (*Vent* 89-101). He has said that one of his reasons for writing this novel was to say something about Germany (Rambures 165), and part of that message is that, as he says, the French have "every fault that they attribute to the Germans" (Braudeau 89).

Tournier drew also on his experiences at boarding schools (Koster, *Michel Tournier* 153), including the "despotic slavery" he was subjected to by an older boy he had a crush on when he was about seven (*Vent* 24). The novel also reflects another childhood experience, the excitement the teenaged Tournier felt when his restrictive home and school environments were turned topsy-turvy by World War II and the Occupation; he had prayed that war would rescue him from his problems at school, and it did (*Vent* 76). As a child, Tiffauges felt a similar relief when his prayers were answered and a fire saved him from punishment at St. Christopher's Academy; and, later, the experience is repeated when the war frees him from jail and another undeserved punishment. The "ogre" Tiffauges is the character with whom Tournier has been most consistently identified, and though Tournier always denies that he is any of his characters, he admits to some resemblance to Tiffauges: "I'm something of an ogre; I eat children by photographing them" (Braudeau 86). The fact that Tournier was unable to complete the novel which uses these experiences until he had served an apprenticeship writing *Vendredi* suggests that *Le Roi des aulnes* deals with material so highly charged emotionally for him that he could not at first control it. Perhaps that is also why it is the most affecting of Tournier's novels.

This complex novel is perhaps best first approached in terms of its sources so, after briefly considering Tournier's continued use of a mixed angle of vision adapted from *Monsieur Teste*, I will treat main sources of characters and plot: Jean-Paul Sartre, the Nestorian heresy, and the legend of Saint Christopher. Considering Tournier's use of fugal motifs and inversion will prepare us for seeing how the book uses its historical material and how it links sex and religion through the legend of the King of the Alders.

THE NARRATIVE ANGLE OF VISION

As he did in *Vendredi*, Tournier alternates a first-person narration in a journal with omniscient third-person narration. The first third of *Le Roi des aulnes* consists of the punningly named "sinister writings," a journal in which, for the first time in his life, Tiffauges writes with his left, or sinister, hand.

The journal, which Tiffauges believes is inspired by the spirit of Nestor, a boy who protected him at school, pulls one into Tiffauges's odd way of looking at things through his obsessive concentration on whatever concerns him at the moment. This concentration is often amusing because of Tiffauges's seemingly stupid belief, which he takes from Nestor, that "Everything is a sign" (15). William Cloonan treats this attitude as wrongheaded ("Artist" 194-98), but the novel seems to confirm Tiffauges's belief, so the joke is on the reader; as a result, as J. J. White says, although the book seems at first to use symbols like an old-fashioned romantic novel, those symbols go far beyond romantic ones in complexity and meaning.

The journal breaks off when Tiffauges becomes a soldier, when the narration is taken over by a third-person narrator, with Tiffauges as viewpoint character. Still later, after Tiffauges gains some power, he is once more able to keep a journal, and for the last third of the novel the two angles of vision alternate. Tournier is thus once more using the technique he took from Valéry's *Monsieur Teste* and employed in *Vendredi*, playing the protagonist's first-person journal against the account of a third-person narrator. The connection with *Monsieur Teste* actually seems stronger, because Tiffauges's obsessions give him a distance from the events around him reminiscent of the distance between Valéry's character and what he observes. There is, however, one additional fillip—a short section narrated by Stefan Raufeisen, a dedicated member of the S.S., in which he remembers how he became a Nazi (416-21). And whichever narrator is telling the story, there is much more use of sensory detail than in *Vendredi*: odors, tastes, the appearance of the countryside, and other physical sensations are evoked more often.

The Influence of Sartre

Like *Vendredi, Le Roi des aulnes* with its German theme is in part an ambivalent tribute to Jean-Paul Sartre, who had been heavily influenced by the German philosophers Hegel, Husserl, and Heidegger, and who had studied German philosophy in Berlin before World War II. In *Vendredi ou les limbes du Pacifique*, Tournier had appeared to reject Sartre's belief in the necessity of historical dialectic; in *Le Roi des aulnes*, which is much more permeated with the spirit of Sartre, dialectic returns in the development of Tiffauges, who is always changing his attitudes because of some previous failure or partial success.

In addition, Tiffauges reflects in several ways Sartre's ideas about personality. He is the epitome of the searcher, the "for-itself," for he is driven by a quest for knowledge. However, like Robinson in *Vendredi*, he looks for existing meaning in the world rather than creating his own, for he believes that everything is a sign. And like a Sartrean exemplar of bad faith, Tiffauges is a divided person, divided, among other things, between carrying out his quest (which makes him a "for-itself") and accepting values and roles he discovers along the way (so that he often acts like an "in-itself"). He is also divided, as I will show, between his mind and his body.

Sartre's theory of personality also is reflected when Tiffauges forms his conception of himself in response to Others. The most important Other is his childhood friend Nestor, but the influence of Rachel, his former mistress, is incalculable. *Le Roi des aulnes* opens with Tiffauges writing in his journal, "You are an ogre, Rachel used to say to me sometimes. An Ogre?" (13). Tiffauges accepts Rachel's judgment so readily that he increasingly builds his self-image on it, much as in Sartre's theory Jean Genet's being called a thief made Genet become a thief. Similarly, thinking that he may be an ogre leads Tiffauges to act like one: to eat raw meat, drink unpasteurized milk, and indulge in his passion for following, photographing, and recording the voices of children, carrying off their images and their sounds instead of their bodies.

Sartre also served as a model for Nestor, an odd, clever, and mysterious boy who became the protector of the scrawny preadolescent Tiffauges. The book makes explicit the connection between Sartre and Nestor by twice associating Nestor with titles of works by Sartre. *Being and Nothingness* is evoked when Nestor contrasts the "nothingness" of the icy night with human life and says only a cheap bolt separates "being from nothingness" (94). Sartre's *Les Chemins de la liberté* (*The Roads to Freedom*, an unfinished saga in four volumes) is suggested in an incident when two magpies fall into Tiffauges's room just as the radio is playing Rossini's *The Thieving Magpie*, for the coincidence makes Tiffauges feel Nestor's presence as the birds take "the road to freedom" (105). Nestor's physical appearance (he is short and nearsighted), his intellectuality, and his habit of sketching also suggest Sartre. Less obvious but more telling is the fact that the adult Tiffauges, under Nestor's influence, thinks that he has a "viscous" self inside (41): no single word evokes Sartre more than "viscosity." Because viscous things cling and refuse to fit into the categories of liquid or solid, they repelled Sartre and soon came to represent all that he disliked about physical existence. Sartre explored his horror of viscosity most memorably in his first novel, *Nausea* (*La Nausée*,

1938). The fact that Nestor has so many of Sartre's characteristics—his appearance, his habits, some of his words, and his association with viscosity—points clearly to his Sartrean origin.

Memories of Nestor influence the adult Tiffauges much as Sartre's ideas and writings have influenced Tournier himself. Tournier seems to consider Sartre's influence a mixed blessing, for although Sartre is the writer to whom he feels closest, he rejects Sartre's insistence on seeing only "ugliness, stupidity, abjection" in the world (*Vol* 301-02). Nestor, similarly, had a huge influence on Tiffauges, often protecting and helping him, but Nestor was always disquieting, strange, and somehow unhealthy. The parallels are partly caricatural; for example, Sartre's insistence on unpleasant physical details in his novels, stories, and plays is reflected in Nestor's fascination with excrement, which takes the form of choosing only intellectually interesting wastepaper to use in the toilet (39) and of analyzing the architectural structure of his feces (96). But Tiffauges says that eating-digesting-excreting was only Nestor's external concern; his true interest was "deciphering signs" (40). This concern parallels Sartre's lifelong search for understanding existence.

And just as Sartre believed people have a divided nature, Nestor, too, was concerned with dichotomies; particularly, he wanted to unite the soul and the body, brains and fecal matter—what he called alpha and omega. It is natural for *alpha*, the first letter of the Greek alphabet, to represent the head, for *alpha* and the corresponding Hebrew letter *aleph* derive from a Phoenician pictograph representing the head of an ox, and *aleph* is also a Hebrew word which means "ox" and "leader." The association of *omega*, the last letter of the Greek alphabet, with the body, with excrement, and especially with the anus, may be suggested by the shape of the upper-case *omega*. Omega and alpha can be read as other ways of referring to what Sartre called being and nothingness, for omega, excrement, is one way to think of being, or the physical facts of life, whereas alpha, which is the soul, or man's aspirations to spirituality, corresponds to what Sartre meant by nothingness, what people imagine and work toward.

RELIGIOUS HERESY AS A SOURCE OF POWER

Nestor and his preoccupations, including alpha and omega, also have a religious dimension. Because the book of Revelation says that Christ at the

Second Coming will proclaim that he is "Alpha and Omega, the beginning and the ending" (1.8), Christian churches traditionally associate alpha and omega with God, and for the modern French Catholic philosopher Pierre Teilhard de Chardin, omega represented the goal of life: "Christ, here and now, fills for us the place of Omega Point" (100). Tournier must have enjoyed his own scatological joke of using omega to stand for excrement and the anus, especially as he does so without taking away its metaphysical and religious content. He is fond of saying that in fiction "ontology turns itself partly into scatology" (Brochier, "Dix-huit" 11) and points out that in each of his novels there is excrement or garbage, including the pig wallow in *Vendredi* and Nestor's and Tiffauges's interest in defecation in *Le Roi des aulnes* (Brochier, "Dix-huit" 11; Delcourt 25). Tournier's metaphysics and religion are inclusive; his God exists in ordure as well as in beauty.

Christ is often suggested by Tiffauges's reminiscences about St. Christopher's Academy. Sometimes Tiffauges is associated with Christ, as when Nestor saves him from being slapped by a priest beneath a picture of Christ being slapped by a soldier (48), or when Nestor provides Tiffauges with a bicycle for a Palm Sunday outing (51), an act which suggests God's providing the colt and its foal on which Christ rode into Jerusalem on Palm Sunday. Other times it is Nestor who suggests Christ because he is such a mysterious and powerful figure, because of his gnomic preaching to Tiffauges (62), and because of his concern with salvation, but most telling is his death in a fire which damages the school but saves Tiffauges from undeserved punishment. If Nestor does die to save Tiffauges, that is another link with Christ, but it is not clear whether the death is intentional or accidental—another ambiguity. But to Tiffauges, the fire has a religious content, for he had actually prayed that the school would burn down so he would be saved from punishment, and he is certain that the fire was, literally, the answer to his prayers.

On another level, Nestor functions less as Christ than as preacher. Christiane Baroche, a novelist and friend of Tournier's, links Nestor with Bishop Nestorius, who gave his name to a heresy which disturbed the Church in the fifth century ("Matière" 83). (Nestorius shares Nestor's ambiguity, for Nestorius may or may not have been a heretic himself.) Although Catholic doctrine considers Jesus Christ a unified being, God and man joined in "hypostatic union," Nestorian belief considers him two separate persons, Jesus, who died on the cross, and the Word, which is God and which cannot die. The Nestorian heresy thus denies that God was incarnated (A. J. Maclean

327) and can be taken as reducing the importance of Christ in the Trinity, an idea Tournier presented indirectly in *Vendredi* through substituting Jeudi, who represents the Holy Spirit, for the Christ-like Vendredi as Robinson's companion. Additionally, the Nestorian objection to calling the Virgin Mary "Theotokos," or "God-bearer," may have suggested to Tournier the idea of *phoria*, the act of carrying children. In any case, Nestorianism's denial that God and man were united in Christ parallels Nestor's concern with uniting alpha and omega, for Nestorianism asks how God and man can be joined in Christ just as Nestor asks how body and soul (omega and alpha) can be united.

This problem reflects Sartre's concern with the divided self but puts it into religious terms. Just as Robinson's Quaker reliance on the Holy Spirit helped lead to a new religious vision in *Vendredi*, in *Le Roi des aulnes* Nestor's remembered comments on religion combine with the adult Tiffauges's reading the Bible to make Tiffauges question the Catholic Church and look for his own way to salvation, a questioning that reflects Tournier's own belief that Catholicism is "a false Church" preaching the opposite of the New Testament, which Tournier says "despises money," values the flesh, and "inspires a revolutionary attitude" (Hueston 404). As he told me in the interview which appears at the end of this book, he believes that heresy provides creative power, whereas orthodoxy takes away one's freedom.

Perhaps in part because of Nestor's influence, Tiffauges feels divided in several ways. He thinks of himself as being split between head and lower regions (which, following Nestor, he calls alpha and omega), and early in the novel he finds relief from his conflict by sticking his head in the toilet and flushing—what he calls "shampooing-caca" and the "john shampoo" (73). His name also shows his division, for his first name, Abel, is that of the first martyr (killed by his brother Cain), while his last name is associated with the fifteenth-century French rapist-murderer of hundreds of boys, Gilles de Rais, who had a castle near the town of Tiffauges. (Tournier's 1983 novella *Gilles et Jeanne*, which concerns Gilles de Rais, has many of the same themes as *Le Roi des aulnes*, as I show in the chapter on Tournier's short fiction.) Tiffauges's divided self is shown also in a left-right division, for when he begins to keep the journal with his left hand, he remembers things about himself and St. Christopher's Academy that he had buried deep in his unconscious; his writings are "sinister" not only in the etymological sense, being produced by the left hand, but also in the usual sense.

PLOT STRUCTURE: THE LEGEND OF SAINT CHRISTOPHER AND OTHER MYTHS

In *Vendredi*, the beginning novelist relied on the plot of *Robinson Crusoe* to shape the first half of his novel, and in *Le Roi des aulnes*, Tournier again borrowed his plot, this time from many sources. The events of World War II are one, to which I will return, but there are others. Calling himself a "magpie," Tournier admits taking a key scene in *Le Roi des aulnes* from Alain-Fournier's famous novel *Le Grand Meaulnes* and says that *Le Roi des aulnes* is so heavily inspired by Flaubert that it is practically an anthology of his works (Rambures 163). One work that inspired him is Flaubert's "La Légende de Saint Julien l'Hospitalier," which Tournier says derives its force from its allusion to first one, then another of the great classical myths, including the myth of Oedipus (*Vol* 165). Tournier has borrowed something of Flaubert's style in "La Légende de Saint Julien" for *Le Roi des aulnes*, and though he is not literally recounting a saint's life as Flaubert was, he uses the story of Saint Christopher as a major plot source. He also uses Flaubert's technique of alluding to multiple myths, as Michael J. Worton ("Myth-Reference") and Isabelle Contival have shown, and though various allusions to Goethe and parallels with Goethe's *Faust* are important to William Cloonan (*Michel Tournier* 45, "Artist" 191-94) and to Lionel Richard, they also show that he uses other myths as well.

But some myths are more important than others, and the central one is the legend of Saint Christopher, which Nestor once arranged for Tiffauges to read to the other students at St. Christopher's Academy and which is used to foreshadow later events, much as Van Deyssel's prophecies did in *Vendredi*. Saint Christopher, a giant who wanted to serve the most powerful master in the world, first served evil men and the Devil, but when he discovered that Christ is the most powerful master, he began to serve him by carrying travelers across a dangerous ford. Then one night the Christ Child himself came in disguise to be carried across. Christopher had great difficulty carrying the child; but when he succeeded, his staff flowered in token of his being blessed for having served Jesus. This simple story provides the underpinning of this complex novel. Part of the complexity is indicated by the fact that there is more than one Saint Christopher, for after Tiffauges read the legend at school, Nestor drew a sketch showing himself as Saint Christopher (72). It will not, however, be Nestor who acts out the legend, but his disciple Tiffauges, who similarly will serve evil men and the Devil before finding salvation.

Christopher's name means Christ-carrier, and carrying children, or *phoria*, is the novel's main motif, being varied, as Tournier has said, through such stages as *euphoria* and *pedophoria* (Joxe 51). When he carried Tiffauges on his shoulders in a schoolyard game, in the scene derived from *Le Grand Meaulnes*, Nestor discovered that it is "beautiful" to carry a child (78). Later, the large and muscular adult Tiffauges discovers the same pleasure in carrying children. This nongenital sexual experience with its religious overtones is analogous to Robinson's solar coitus at the end of *Vendredi* in similarly combining religion and sex, being religious insofar as the story of Saint Christopher makes one associate any child who is carried with Christ, sexual because of Tiffauges's feelings about *phoria*. Tournier has, in fact, imagined for Tiffauges an entirely new perversion, even as Tiffauges, as Tournier puts it in an essay on the novel, "teems with perversions" that include necrophilia, bestiality, and vampirism (*Vent* 121-22).

The perversions may sound shocking, but a reader should not be overly upset by them, for, as Tournier says, Tiffauges is emotionally a preadolescent (*Vent* 121) with an underdeveloped sexual organ and little interest in normal sex, and he never directly acts out the perversions he flirts with. Like Saint Christopher, Tiffauges wants to serve others, always trying to re-discover a sexual servitude he knew at school, when the bully Pelsenaire awakened Tiffauges's erotic nature by making him lick a bloody wound on Pelsenaire's knee. The use of the story of Saint Christopher makes it structurally inevitable that Tiffauges's search, like Saint Christopher's, will lead through the Devil to the Christ Child.

THE FUGAL MOTIFS

History and myth provide the novel's broad and essentially simple plot outlines, but the specifics come from another structuring technique. Tournier has said that the plot does not come from the characters' motivations but from its own energy (*Vent* 129-30), and that energy is derived not only from the legend of Saint Christopher but also from the repetition of motifs, a patterning noted by Jacques Poirier in his pamphlet on this novel. R. A. York has argued that the last chapter generates each motif, but one could as well think of it as being their culmination.

Le Roi des aulnes repeats and varies motifs much as a piece of music does. Coming from a musical family, Tournier was here inspired by several pieces of music, the main one being Johann Sebastian Bach's *The Art of the Fugue*, especially the last fugues, whose notes spell BACH in German musical notation (*Vent* 128-29; see also Geiringer 344 and Terry 60). As I have shown elsewhere ("Fugal Structure"), Tournier has literally imitated this structure by similarly encoding his name into this novel, so that a succession of eight themes spells his own name: Abel TIFFAUGES, the protagonist; the OGRE that he comes to think he is; the blind elk he discovers in Prussia, the UNHOLD, which resembles him; ROMINTEN, Goering's hunting lodge, where Tiffauges helps the gamekeepers; the military school, or NAPOLA, where he gradually becomes more and more powerful; malignant INVERSION, which is what Tiffauges calls his discovery that what he has loved is actually evil; EPHRAIM, a young Jewish refugee from Auschwitz, whom Tiffauges finds and nurses back to health; and REDEMPTION, which Tiffauges finds at last through his sacrifice of himself as he carries Ephraïm away from the battle raging around the *Napola* at the novel's end in a scene patterned on Saint Christopher's carrying the Christ Child.

More obvious than this hidden and personal sequence are other techniques imitating the way a fugue repeats a pattern of notes many times, usually with variations. Tournier parallels this kind of structure by establishing themes, then varying them. For example, the French army assigns Tiffauges to requisition and look after carrier pigeons. Tiffauges is at once drawn to these "phoric" animals, but he likes most a silvery one, a pair of reddish-feathered twins, and his favorite, a scrawny bird which he finds along the road and nurses back to health. Just before the Germans arrive, his commanding officer roasts the first three birds on a spit, but Tiffauges saves the sickly bird. So, much later, in East Prussia, when Tiffauges recruits for the *Napola* a silver-haired boy and red-headed twins, the reader sees the parallel and is almost prepared for the three boys to be impaled by the invading Russian army on giant decorative swords in the courtyard of the *Napola*, run through like the birds on the spit. Ephraïm, the Jewish refugee Tiffauges finds along the road, corresponds to the sickly bird—like the bird, he is nursed back to health by Tiffauges—and Tiffauges saves him, if perhaps only briefly, from death at the end.

Another theme which is varied like notes in a fugue concerns Communion. Tiffauges resents the fact that the Catholic Church at that time permits communicants to take only the bread and not the wine (207)—the Nestorian rite offers both—but he does commune just before he goes off to serve in the army. Later, he participates in a symbolic but perverse Communion when he eats his three roasted pigeons, figuring that no one is more entitled than he to eat them, and he can thus "nourish his soul in making it commune intimately" with his beloved birds (243). This highly charged act links Christian Communion with ogritude. It also suggests communing with the Holy Spirit rather than Christ, since the dove traditionally symbolizes the Holy Spirit, and so it echoes the emphasis on the Holy Spirit, rather than Christ, which was already present in *Vendredi*.

References to the Seder provide a fugal variant on the Communion motif. The Seder and Communion are related because the Last Supper, at which Jesus instituted Communion, was a Seder he celebrated with his disciples just before his arrest. The Seder specifically commemorates Jehovah's sparing the children of the Israelites in Egypt when His angel killed the first-born of the houses of Egypt and, more generally, celebrates the escape of the Jews from Egyptian captivity. This origin is made explicit by Ephraïm, who equates the Jews' persecution by the Nazis with the Israelites' Egyptian captivity, and the war conditions in East Prussia with the plagues visited upon Egypt (568). The night the Russians attack the *Napola*, Ephraïm celebrates the Seder with Tiffauges, and he even has on his table some wine and a sheep's bone, lamb being the traditional Seder dish. The German boys, like the Egyptians' first-born sons, are killed, but Ephraïm escapes as the Jews did.

The link between the Seder and Communion was actually suggested much earlier. The last night Tiffauges saw Nestor, just two days before Nestor's death, he watched Nestor eat a late-night meal in which a leg of lamb figured prominently (98). This meal suggests the Seder because of its content, but it suggests the Last Supper because of Nestor's connection with Christ and the fact that both died shortly afterwards. To Christians the Paschal lamb and the escape from Egypt prefigure Christ's sacrifice on the cross and humanity's resulting redemption from sin, but in keeping with the novel's pattern of inversion, which I will discuss next, the novel reverses the pattern, and Nestor foreshadows Ephraïm. The novel's many thematic repetitions with variations help to unify the novel and increase its emotional power.

FUGAL INVERSION

The technique of inversion in *Le Roi des aulnes* probably was inspired by two kinds of mirror fugues, both of which Bach wrote. In one kind, notes are written so that they reflect each other vertically, as if one held a mirror above a line of music and looked at both the original and its reflection: this musical inversion helped inspire the idea of moral inversion in the novel. In what he calls "malignant inversion," Tiffauges finds that what he thought was good is actually evil—most notably, he learns from Ephraïm that the things he loves best at the *Napola* are echoes of Auschwitz, such as the hair he has had clipped from the boys and has saved in hopes of having it woven into a garment, and the showers he takes with them, which suggest the hair-clipping of the Jews just before they were gassed and the death chambers made to look like showers. There is also the opposite inversion, "benign inversion," which permits Tiffauges to renounce his desire to dominate the boys and instead to serve Ephraïm. These moral inversions are prefigured earlier when Tiffauges, developing photographs before the war, notices that negatives are an inversion of prints, for what is black in one is white in the other (175). If black can become white, then perhaps evil can change into good.

Tiffauges also notices that negatives can be printed with left and right reversed (176)—an inversion that suggests what happens in the other sort of mirror fugue, where the notes go "backwards" as if read right to left or as if reflected in a mirror held to the side of the page rather than above it. This inversion shows up as movement into the past, as when Nestor's Last Supper prefigures Ephraïm's Seder, and has been suggested from the start, when Tiffauges's discovery of his left-handed self makes him begin the journal in which he explores his past. As Tiffauges says, "it is typical of [his] period that progress should be made by going *backwards*" (106, emphasis in original).

As the story progresses, many events symbolize return to the past: the army's use in World War II of carrier pigeons (which were common in World War I and before); the war prisoners' draining swampland under primitive conditions; Goering's ruling like a medieval baron over his hunting preserve; the technologically primitive life in the *Napola*, which is housed in a castle connected with the early Teutonic knights; and the pre-Christian Germanic society reestablished in the *Napola*, with its sun worship. The apocalyptic final scenes suggest at once the Israelites' flight from Egypt, the Germany of the first century A.D., and the end of the world—a beginning, middle, and end of time, all mixed together. So from the classically simple lines of the legend of Saint Christopher, Tournier has constructed a baroque edifice, the fugue being a prime example of late baroque.

THE PROBLEM OF NAZISM

Unlike the fugal patterns, the historical material which serves as another source has upset many readers. Some, including Saul Friedländer, are disturbed by *Le Roi des aulnes* because it presents the seductions of Nazism, and they think the book implicitly endorses Nazi ideology. On the other hand, the large amount of research with which Tournier supplemented his own childhood experience of Nazi Germany, and which is partially documented by endnotes, has made the book a valuable source of information about Nazi Germany and French attitudes to Germany and the war, as shown by the studies of William Cloonan ("World War II"), Frederick J. Harris, Marie-Agnès Morita-Clément, and Colin Nettelbeck ("Getting the Story Right"). Both the mistaken view that the book endorses Nazism and its value as a source of information result from Tournier's refusal to simplify. He says that he wanted to give a complete picture of Nazi Germany, not just the horrors but the rituals such as parades, to show that the Germans were not "grotesque" but "frightening" (Koster, *Michel Tournier* 154). He did not create the debased appeal of Nazism; rather, he reproduced it to reveal Nazism's emotional power.

Tournier's manner of presenting Nazism derives from his conception of literary realism. He has said that he wants to write in a way which is so minutely realistic—hyperrealistic—that it becomes surreal, like the paintings of Magritte and Dali (*Vent* 114-15). As a result, Hermann Goering, for example, appears in his hunting lodge surrounded by accurate but virtually unbelievable details exposing his instability and egotism. Tiffauges decides that Goering is an ogre, but this judgment about his mythic nature has been prepared for by historical facts: Goering's fascination with deer hunting, his keeping a pet lion, his expertise in reading animals' excrement, his habit of running his hands through a bowl of gems to calm down.

Rather than being idolized, the Nazis are satirized through use of such factual details. For example, Tiffauges learns about the Nazis' racist doctrines after he is assigned to help Blättchen make anthropometric measurements (389-92). This "raceologist" has established his credentials by preserving in formaldehyde 150 heads representing the supposed biological category of *Homo Judaeus Bolchevicus*, or Jewish Bolsheviks (387), but he is so blind to racial characteristics that he thinks that Tiffauges must be German, and probably of noble descent (406-07). Far from looking "typically" German, Tiffauges has dark hair and skin, and he thinks that his ancestors were Gypsies (25), one of the "races" which the Nazis tried to exterminate.

If *Vendredi ou les limbes du Pacifique* concerns itself primarily with ontology, *Le Roi des aulnes* takes as its main philosophical focus questions of ethics, just as Sartre's *Being and Nothingness* bases its discussion of "bad faith" on Sartre's theory of reality. Tournier's ontology, as I have shown, posits the reality of both the physical world and consciousness, and Tiffauges's consciousness, like Robinson's, includes a conviction that God exists and is keenly interested in his fate. If this is the case, the book asks, how should Tiffauges act? The main ethical questions he will face arise in two areas, the personal one of his sexual impulses and the public one of his relation to Nazi institutions, but these questions cannot remain separate once he rises to power in the boys' school in Germany.

Tiffauges always maintains intellectual distance from his captors, for he does not so much believe Nazi ideology as try to understand it intellectually, and his overall concern remains reading signs which will reveal his destiny. He goes along with his captors because, like most people, he does not want to consider fully the implications of his actions; although he knows that the children at the *Napola* are being trained as soldiers and that they will be killed, he usually manages not to think about that fact. Instead, he eagerly recruits— even kidnaps—children from the neighboring farms and villages to help the school keep its full complement of 400 boys, so he can continue to live in the surcharged atmosphere created by the presence of so many male adolescents. Tiffauges must sink to this level if his story is based on Saint Christopher's life, for he too must serve the Devil; at the same time, we must see that he is not himself diabolical, merely human.

The turning point comes when Tiffauges discovers Ephraïm, who has fallen by the wayside from a contingent of prisoners being moved from Auschwitz. When he tells Tiffauges of the death camps, Tiffauges discovers that there is a worse evil hidden underneath the evil he knew. He has thought of Hitler as the great ogre to whom the youth of Germany are being sacrificed (369), but he does not realize the extent of the death-fixation which has taken over Germany until he learns of Auschwitz, the "*Anus Mundi*" (554), the triumph of omega unbalanced by alpha. He then has to admit that what he has done at the *Napola* is like the acts of the butchers running the death camps: Tiffauges's actions "were reflected in the terrible mirror, inverted and made hellishly incandescent" (560)—another image of inversion.

Tournier is exploring one of his major themes, the resemblance between good and evil, Satan's "aping" of "spontaneous and inborn holiness" (Ritzen 6). The surface similarity of good and evil is expressed in part in the resemblance between carrying and carrying off (in French, *porter* and *emporter*). Tiffauges wants to carry young boys and thus, like Saint Christopher, to serve them. The act of carrying a boy may also be playful, as it is when he carries a boy on his shoulders in the Louvre before the war. But as time passes, he more and more often carries boys off, like the ogre in Goethe's poem, stealing them from their parents and the comparative security of their homes and forcing them to be trained as soldiers. One of the major successes of this novel is its combining factual and mythic sources to show how evil can mimic good.

PHORIA: SEX AND RELIGION

Phoria, or carrying, is the morally ambiguous act which unites sex and religion. From his earliest days Tiffauges has wanted to be a beast of burden. Wearing a belt made from a horse's girth and boots suggesting horseshoes (25), the school bully Pelsenaire straddled the half-willing Tiffauges and made him eat grass (29). The ease with which the horsy Pelsenaire turned into a rider suggests inversion, that horse and rider are reversible, as we see when Tiffauges becomes a horseman in East Prussia. Tiffauges's submission to Pelsenaire clearly had sexual roots, for Tiffauges persuaded Pelsenaire to be "tattooed" in India ink with a heart and the words *A toi pour la vie*—"Yours for life" (26). The actual "tattoo" that Tiffauges gave Pelsenaire replaced "A toi" with "A T"—Tiffauges's initials. Pelsenaire was outraged, but Tiffauges had managed to express his love. Tiffauges's ambiguous sexuality—another inversion—is stressed (and probably encouraged) by Nestor, who calls him not Abel but "Mabel" (62), which besides being a woman's name sounds like *ma belle*, or "my beauty." As Phillippe de Monès has pointed out, Tiffauges's quest is in part a search to combine male and female.

However, the ambiguity of the "A T" in the tattoo points to the religious overtones of Tiffauges's quest, for "A T" sounds like *athée*, "atheist." But despite his initials, Tiffauges is not an atheist; he is a questioner who believes he has a destiny to which every event brings him closer. As a child, he was the image of Christ. The adult Tiffauges in Prussia seems to have denied Christianity, love of his fellow human beings, and compassion, but, like Saint Christopher, he can still renounce the Devil and become a carrier of Christ, the destiny for which St. Christopher's Academy has prepared him.

In Prussia, Tiffauges more and more identifies with what he considers the most "phoric" of animals, the horse, and particularly with a gelding which he has beeñ given and which he names Barbe-Bleue. The name means Bluebeard, the name of the ogrelike wife-killer in Perrault's fairy tale who is often associated with Gilles de Rais, but it puns on two other meanings of *barbe*, "gelding" and "North African," for the horse is a gelding with Barbary blood (347-48). The horse is thus non-Nordic and nongenital, like Tiffauges. Tiffauges associates the horse with himself and with anality, or omega, because its power is in its rump and because it defecates "perfectly," and he calls it the "Anal Angel" (353). It is not by chance that he calls it an "angel," for God must be in everything, as Christ is alpha and omega—in excrement as well as in heavenly aspirations.

In contrast, the deer hunted at Rominten represent alpha to Tiffauges, because of their antlers and because their power is in their shoulders. Further, Tiffauges considers a deer a "Phallophoric Angel" (331) because the growth of a deer's antlers is connected with its testicular development, so that the antlers may be thought of as a function—and a symbol—of the genitals. However, Tiffauges does not yet understand the importance of the fact that the relation is inverse, that an overdeveloped antler results from an under-developed or damaged testicle (330-31). Both the gelding and the buck with huge antlers are nongenital. In this they are like the ox (a castrated bull), which inspired the letter *alpha*, and like Tiffauges, with his tiny genitals. All this symbolism suggests that the deer and horse are not the opposites Tiffauges thinks but that spirituality (alpha) derives from anality (omega), or lack of genital orientation.

Tiffauges thinks whenever he carries a helpless child off to the *Napola* that the act is an image of Saint Christopher's carrying the Christ Child, and not just *phoria* but *superphoria* because the horse carries Tiffauges, who carries the child (469); he ignores the fact that he is harming the child, and he is forgetting his earlier identification with the Gypsies, the Jews, and other persecuted groups (433). At the novel's end, however, he learns that when he carries Ephraïm to freedom, in a true act of submission, they unite alpha and omega. With Ephraïm on his shoulders, Tiffauges becomes like the deer; Ephraïm corresponds to the "antlers," and Tiffauges wants to carry Ephraïm precisely because of his own nongenital sexual orientation. But the relation is also religious, for Ephraïm sitting on Tiffauges's shoulders suggests the flowering of Saint Christopher's staff after he carries the Christ Child across the ford.

To carry and to be carried, then, have a variety of meanings which converge in sex and religion. Horse and rider can be reversed through inversion, but it is hardly a matter of indifference as to which one is. Sexually, to carry is to be the submissive partner, and Tiffauges's anal nature implies his tendency toward passive homosexuality, for even with the adolescents, he is never interested in pederasty. The closest he can come to a passive sex act with the children is to carry them. But because carrying children has been linked for Tiffauges with the story of Saint Christopher, to carry a child inevitably has religious meaning for him; any child he carries becomes an image of Christ, and to carry the child properly he must serve that child and do its bidding. Finally, because of the allusion to the Nestorian heresy and because of Nestor's belief that alpha and omega are separate, when Tiffauges finally does serve Ephraïm by carrying him, together they become the image of the Nestorian Christ, soul and body—or boy and man—joined but not completely united.

THE KING OF THE ALDERS: A GERMANIC SAINT CHRISTOPHER

Except for the title (in the French and British editions), the novel's first mention of the King of the Alders comes when a Nazi professor associates him with a body discovered in a peat bog near the prison camp where Tiffauges is first held in East Prussia. The acids in the bog have so tanned the skin and preserved the body, and the man so resembles Tiffauges, who is temporarily missing, that at first the body is even thought to be his, but it is actually about two thousand years old. An autopsy reveals that the man was killed after a "sort of last Communion" (293). The parallel between the man and Christ seems obvious: the man was sacrificed; he ate a ritual meal before his death; he lived in the first century of our era. To the professor, however, the man represents not the Christ of what he calls the "Judaeo-Mediterranean" religion, or Christianity, but a Nordic "Christ" connected with ancient Germanic rites (294), and the professor links this "Christ" with Goethe's King of the Alders. If so, the man would be not a Christ figure but an anti-Christ. Tiffauges is clearly symbolized by the ambiguous peat-bog man, whose bivalent symbolism mirrors Tiffauges's condition at this point of being torn between good and evil; benign inversion has not yet begun to operate.

The emphasis on Goethe's ogre hints at the sexual side of Nazism, which Tournier says was obsessed with youth, its "juvenophilia turn[ing] to pedophilia" (*Vent* 106). This sexual connection is stressed by Tournier's own translation of the poem from German to French, printed in notes at the back of the book, in which the King of the Alders says to the boy, "I love you, your beautiful body tempts me" (584). Tournier defends this translation against the usual "I love you. Your sweet face enchants me" on the grounds of its greater fidelity to the German, which he says could also be rendered "Your beautiful body excites me" (*Vent* 119-20). The sexual implications of the line foreshadow Tiffauges's own later attraction to the boys of the *Napola*, whom he will kidnap, as the King of the Alders kidnaps his victims.

The professor's comments opposing the King of the Alders to Christ fit a pattern in which Germanic rites are consistently opposed to Christian ones— Nazism, for example, has its own saints (414, 434). But although Germanic religious ceremonies are replacing Christian ones, the Christian ones are stronger. For example, the boys celebrate not Christmas but the winter solstice, by burning a Yule log and decorating a tree to celebrate the birth of the "Solar Child" (411), but during the celebration, a gust of wind blows out all the candles and breaks a high window, at which point "A single star [breaks] through . . . the thickening shadows roaring to the East" (413). The Christmas star shines when the candles of the Nazis are extinguished, prefiguring the triumph of Christianity.

Devil worship is usually a perversion of Christian practices, as the Nazi rites are. But the opposite inversion can also take place: Nazi religion can be transformed to true worship of God. The man in the peat bog who is identified with Tiffauges need not be a Germanic anti-Christ: he could be a German Saint Christopher, in which case the head found with him is more important than he is, the head which could be that of a woman or a child, wearing a shepherd's cloak. Because Tiffauges is like the man, the bodiless head suggests both his former mistress, Rachel, and Ephraïm. Rachel and Ephraïm are connected; both are Jewish (Rachel even has the head of a Jewish shepherd-boy [21]), and they are the two people the adult Tiffauges has liked best. In addition, in the Bible, Rachel is the grandmother of Ephraïm. The head from the peat bog, however, suggests Ephraïm the most, not least because it is only a head, for when Tiffauges first finds him, Ephraïm is so lightweight that he seems to have no body (551). Symbolically, Ephraïm is all alpha, just as Tiffauges feels that he himself is all omega, which is why when Ephraïm rides on Tiffauges's shoulders, alpha and omega are joined.

When he carries Ephraïm at the book's end, Tiffauges becomes the King of the Alders transformed into Saint Christopher, sexual predator turned into gentle servant, and Ephraïm then represents Christ. Ephraïm is like Christ partly because he is a child, partly because he is innocent. But his association with the head in the peat bog strengthens the connection, because the head had worn a shepherd's cloak which suggests Christ the Good Shepherd. In keeping with the use of multiple myths, Tiffauges is also identified with Behemoth, the huge animal mentioned in Job which, like the peat-bog man, lives in the swamp (566-67). It is not certain what animal Behemoth is, but its name may come from the Egyptian name for the water ox—and we are back to the letter *alpha*, which has come to represent the soul but which derives from a castrated animal. Like the ox, the nongenital Tiffauges becomes a beast of burden, serving Ephraïm.

Tiffauges's death at the novel's end is triumphant; although he sinks into the marshes, like the peat-bog man, he sees Ephraïm turn into a six-pointed star and rise to heaven (581). In Nestorian terms, Tiffauges is like Christ's human body, which dies, and Ephraïm is like Christ's divine essence, which does not die. In Nestor's terms, omega—Tiffauges—is at once dying and triumphing, for the triumph of omega is to serve alpha and be transformed by that service. In terms of the story of Saint Christopher, Tiffauges is rendering the last and greatest service to the Christ Child.

As the motifs reappear and change in this complex and moving novel, symbols develop which are so powerful that they control the characters. In the words of the aristocratic Kommandeur von Kaltenborn, the Third Reich was produced by symbols so powerful that they took charge of events (476). While showing the appeal of Nazism through a sexual and religious glass, Tournier has successfully used the story of one person to make more comprehensible the hysteria of an entire nation.

NOVELISTIC SUCCESS

The book's success must depend in part on how well it can make the reader care about Abel Tiffauges. Although Tournier has said that he regrets that the book has "only one character who dominates the whole" and that therefore the book is not truly a novel (Daly, "Interview" 412), *Le Roi des aulnes* actually gains in intensity by its focus on this one complex character, who is more fully realized and more interesting than Tournier's Robinson. And whereas *Vendredi* has only two characters (one can hardly count Jeudi, Van Deyssel, or the sailors on the *Whitebird*), *Le Roi des aulnes* has many vivid minor characters—Tiffauges's neighbors in Paris, his commanding officer in the French army, the *Oberforstmeister* who befriends him, and a number of the Nazis, as well as Rachel, Nestor, Pelsenaire, and Ephraïm. Although

Tiffauges is a loner, he has a great need to love someone or something, and he notices keenly the people around himself. Unfortunately, the novel does not make as effective use of suspense as one might expect, considering its wartime setting. This problem is caused mainly by Tiffauges's certainty that destiny awaits him: he never fears for his safety, and he even refuses to escape from the Germans when he has the chance. This fatalism, and Tiffauges's apparent imperviousness to physical suffering, mean that despite the greater use of physical details in this novel, there is an air of intellectuality, of distance, which was also present in *Vendredi*.

On the other hand, because the novel makes greater use of humor than *Vendredi* did, it is more engaging. Tournier is a man of much human warmth and charm, consistently self-depreciating and amused, clearly delighted by his success as a writer, and in *Le Roi des aulnes* he uses his sense of humor with great success. W. D. Redfern has pointed out the great playfulness of the language of *Le Roi des aulnes* and its centrality to Tournier's vision, which is an inclusive rather than exclusive one, and Daniel Bougnoux's discussion of the novel's metaphoric language ("Des Métaphores") also reveals Tournier's wit. Apart from the wordplay, most of the jokes are deadpan humor which Tournier says is partly inspired by Flaubert's Bouvard and Pécuchet (Rambures 163), two characters who had an insatiable appetite for facts but who did not know what to do with those facts or when to stop collecting them. Tournier uses this sort of humor, part of his hyperrealism, when he catalogues in dizzying detail the systems for counting "points" on a deer's antlers, the characteristics of homing pigeons, or the details of the Nazi anthropometry. There is also satiric humor in *Le Roi des aulnes*. Most of it comes early in the book, for example in the portraits of the French army officers and Tiffauges's Paris neighbor Madame Eugénie (especially during a trip to see the execution of the murderer Eugène Weidmann, who is Tiffauges's double), but it also is used later, as in the description of Blättchen.

Most of the humor, however, is what Tournier calls "white humor" and "cosmic comedy," which he defines as humor which arises when one glimpses nothingness through the appearance of things (*Vent* 199). Tournier says that people of religion, science, and politics do not understand white laughter, but his own view of religion does accommodate it, for the nothingness that he glimpses does not exclude God; in fact, it is humor "signed by God" (*Vent* 201). Not to see this humor is Tournier's equivalent of what Sartre calls "seriousness": both errors mean that one takes oneself and the world too seriously, that one does not see the possibility of being wrong about everything.

If God has a sense of humor (and Tournier's God does), then people must be prepared to laugh at what He does. Tournier's humor is always linked with ultimate seriousness; he has said that his motto could be "The more I laugh, the less I'm joking" (Brochier, "Dix-huit" 12).

White humor runs through the entire novel. Examples include the idea that a powerless prisoner of war should become ruler of an S.S. boys' school during World War II; that a modern man should consider himself an ogre and attempt to live according to that idea; that St. Christopher's Academy should burn and World War II should break out just at the right time to save Tiffauges from undeserved punishments, thus convincing him that he has a special destiny; that this strange, immature man should take so seriously everything that happens to him and live his life as if he is cracking a secret code, and apparently be right about it in the long run—the entire conception of the novel is a sort of whimsy gone wild and taken with the utmost apparent seriousness. These scenes do not make one laugh, but they show what may be the humor of God, as Tournier conceives of Him.

Le Roi des aulnes is both more intense (because of its focus on Tiffauges) and broader in scope than *Vendredi ou les limbes du Pacifique*. It is more varied, more specific, more absorbing, and less abstract. Although it is concerned with many of the same ideas, such as nongenital sexuality, a search for a new form of Christianity, and breaking away from society's strictures, it clothes those ideas in physical detail which gives them reality and it develops them thematically through variations which create the ambiguity of real-life events. In addition, the fact that ethics is the focus, rather than ontology, means that the intellectual content, though not less than that of *Vendredi*, is more accessible. In this novel Michel Tournier succeeded in his ambition to create a book which would concern ideas and whose plot would derive from hidden structures, but whose surface would provide the feel of real life.

3

Les Météores: Uniting Heaven and Earth

In 1975, five years after the success of *Le Roi des aulnes*, Michel Tournier published *Les Météores*. It was a best-seller in France for months (Bevernis 198), but its critical reception was mixed. Some critics decried its emphasis on sexuality and its scatology (Kanters, "Creux" 15), and others were bored by its great length (Wolfromm, "Apocalypse" 37), its supposed lack of character development (Freustié 69; Wolfromm, "Apocalypse" 37), and its insistence on ideas (Van Baelen 205), but Claude Bonnefoy felt that the novel proved Tournier a "great novelist," as did the English reviewer Barbara Bray, who had translated *Le Roi des aulnes* into English. Robert Poulet, in an article combining a review of *Les Météores* with a retrospective look at Tournier's career, called Tournier's fiction "antimoral" and "pathological" (93); but, even though he decried Tournier's morality as he understood it, Poulet said that Tournier was the best writer of his generation (101). Poulet's moral outrage was caused in part by his belief that the novel's true subject is "the apotheosis of onanism" (99); in fact, as I will show, *Les Météores* further develops the theme of nongenital sexuality and its connection to religion which Tournier had already treated in *Vendredi* and *Le Roi des aulnes*. The English-language translation of *Les Météores* by Anne Carter, published in 1981 as *Gemini*, was generally well received by American and English critics including William Boyd and Salman Rushdie, though not by the anonymous *New Yorker* reviewer (Rev. of *Gemini*).

It is difficult to know what to make of this occasionally exasperating book, partly because it is so very ambitious. Tournier has often proclaimed it to be his favorite novel, but it seems likely that he considers the book a failure, for after *Les Météores* his writing took a different turn, his subsequent novels being more restrained in tone and much shorter. The five years that he spent on this novel, he has implied, left him feeling that he could have done much better if he had only had strength to continue longer (Braudeau 86), but five years is not, he says, "a human time period," and after so much time "the work grows beyond you" (Ezine, "Michel Tournier" 226). He said that part of the problem was that his original plan, to further develop, through mythology and the theology of the Holy Spirit, the solar cult sketched at the end of *Vendredi*, simply did not work out novelistically (*Vent* 260-61): "I was disillusioned by Joachim de Flore," he told an interviewer (Hueston 404). Nevertheless, to understand the ideas in the novel, one has to grasp the theology of Joachim de Fiore (or Flore) and other ideas Tournier used in this novel.

It is becoming usual for critics to think of *Vendredi*, *Le Roi des aulnes*, and *Les Météores* as forming a trilogy (Cloonan, *Michel Tournier* 55), an idea now reinforced by the publication of the three in a single volume published by Gallimard. The books share a number of thematic concerns, one of which is the role of the Other, here conceived in terms of couples. It is this theme Tournier focuses on in the publisher's note—he is in the habit of writing his own jacket copy (Brenner 107)—when he says "the novel tries to illustrate the great theme of the human couple" and to apply to living beings and objects the "decoding mechanism" of identical twins (he discussed this idea also in the interview with me in Chapter 8 below). Twins had already figured peripherally in *Vendredi*, where Robinson thought of Vendredi as a younger twin, and in *Le Roi des aulnes*, with its twin pigeons and the German twin boys whom the pigeons prefigured. Less obvious but more important is the theme linking spiritual illumination with sexual sublimation. Robinson finds religious and sexual ecstasy in a sun worship connected with the Holy Spirit; in contrast, Tiffauges achieves only a precarious compromise between "omega" and "alpha" when he limits his sexuality to carrying and serving Ephraïm, who represents not the Holy Spirit but the divine nature of Christ. Tiffauges's solution, based on Christ rather than the Holy Spirit, is less satisfactory and less lasting than Robinson's, for it does not unite body and soul—Tiffauges and Ephraïm—so much as let them form a partnership. Another way to see the relation among the books has to do with their different philosophical concerns: *Vendredi* looks at ontology, *Le Roi des aulnes* at ethics, and *Les Météores* at theology, insofar as it concerns primarily not people's relation to the physical world, as *Vendredi* did, not people's relation to humanity, as *Le Roi des aulnes* did, but people's relation to God. This may seem like a strange statement to make about a book concerned with different kinds of couples, but, as I will show, it posits the ultimate couple as a human being and God; all human relations are merely poor imitations of this relationship.

Lynn Carol Bird Jeffress has seen clearly that the quest in *Les Météores* is related to that of *Le Roi des aulnes* and is right to say that the novel is about "the failure of love as the world has known it" (152), for the novel focuses, finally, on failure of human love and a need for mystical acceptance. *Les Météores* specifically contrasts genital sexuality, represented mainly by Alexandre Surin, with the nongenital sexuality and religious illumination Paul Surin believes he achieves at the novel's end. This contrast, as I will show, depends on an explicit contrast between Christ-centered Christianity and a new Christianity centered on the Holy Spirit, which is undoubtedly the new religion Tournier told an interviewer he was attempting to construct for himself (Piatier, "Entretien" 16).

Like *Vendredi* and *Le Roi des aulnes*, *Les Météores* is derived from many literary and historical sources, including Robert Musil's novel *The Man without Qualities*, Jules Verne's *Around the World in Eighty Days*, the Joachimite heresy, and *The Divine Comedy*. The complex patterns set up by these sources relate to the novel's contrast of time and weather and to the theme of the couple, as seen in an anthropological and a religious light. As one would expect, the novel also has political and philosophical implications.

THE STORY LINE AND ANGLE OF VISION

Despite the over 600 pages of text in the "Folio" edition, the basic story of *Les Météores*, like that of all Tournier's novels, is simple. Two main plots alternate in the first two-thirds. One concerns Edouard Surin, his prolific wife Maria-Barbara, and their identical twin sons, Jean and Paul. Edouard divides his life between his Breton home and Paris, where he sees his mistress, Florence; Maria-Barbara devotes her life first to her many children and, later, to the retarded children at St. Brigitte's Asylum across the road. Jean and Paul discover together "oval love" (179), or mutual, simultaneous oral sex, but as a teenager Jean starts to leave the cell of twinship and create an independent life. During the Occupation, Maria-Barbara is arrested for Resistance work and disappears in Buchenwald, and Edouard becomes an emotional wreck and dies shortly after the war. In alternate chapters, the book tells the story of Edouard's brother Alexandre, who runs garbage dumps in six cities and seeks out erotic adventures with young men. His one sentimental attachment, with a young man named Daniel, ends in Daniel's death. Shortly after the war, in Casablanca to inspect one of his dumps, he sees his nephews practicing their "oval love" and, in despair because he will never have a twin to make love with, essentially commits suicide.

The last third of the novel, which many readers find less interesting than the first part, is devoted to Jean, Paul, and a series of people they meet as Paul follows Jean, who is fleeing around the world to escape Paul. The focus is on Paul rather than Jean and the increasing illumination he finds in life as a "single" person. He never catches up with Jean, and in an attempt to escape from East Berlin he is badly hurt and must have much of his left side amputated. Convalescent in Brittany, Paul has a final ecstatic vision of oneness with Jean, God, and the universe. Although every plot element corresponds to an exact organizational vision of the novel, the events seem episodic on first reading and, especially at the end, appear arbitrary if viewed in the light of realism; in addition, the many apparently tangential episodes—each of which nevertheless helps develop the themes—obscure the basically clean line of the underlying story. Interesting as many of the episodes are, they are finally too numerous and too detailed for most readers to see clearly beyond them to the simple main plot.

The book uses many angles of vision. Much of the Surin family story is narrated by what seems to be an omniscient narrator, but occasional comments suggest that Paul is either always or sometimes that narrator; other passages are explicitly ascribed to Jean or Paul. Alexandre narrates wittily the chapters in which he is the principal figure, and because his style is quite different from anyone else's, there is more variety in language here than in Tournier's two earlier novels. The last third, though narrated mainly by Paul, has sections by Jean; Jean's former fiancée, Sophia; Hamida, a woman from Tunis; and Shonïn, a Japanese Zen master. As a result of the variety of narrators, characters are generally seen from both within and without, except for Alexandre, the novel's most interesting figure, who is seen almost entirely through his own eyes.

Although the surface of the novel is realistic, the first page breaks the barrier between fiction and reality by introducing the author into the novel as a character. Michel Tournier is a character in *Les Météores* for a single phrase, when he is said to be reading Aristotle's *Meteorologica* (in French, *Météores*) on the beach on September 25, 1937, the day the novel opens. Tournier's introducing himself into the novel—and reading a book with virtually the same title as the book he is in—suggests the way in which *Les Météores* is *gigogne*, like a series of boxes within boxes, or like the Russian dolls which each have a smaller doll inside.

ROBERT MUSIL AND JULES VERNE

The first page alludes directly to Aristotle, indirectly to the Austrian writer Robert Musil, whose novel *The Man without Qualities* (*Der Mann ohne Eigenschaften*) opens with a meteorological description, like *Les Météores*. Left unfinished at Musil's death in 1942, *The Man without Qualities* is considered a major German literary work. Tournier both acknowledged his debt and played down Musil's influence when he told an interviewer that he had not reread Musil while working on *Les Météores* (Hayman, "Grand Scale" 41), following his usual practice while working on a novel of avoiding related fiction but reading heavily in related nonfiction. (For this novel he read about twins, as well as traveling to Djerba, Iceland, Japan, and Canada to write of Paul's travels.) Tournier must have been attracted to Musil's central theme, the conflict between rationalism and mysticism, for he has said that one theme of *Les Météores* is recovering the lost congruence between the two meanings of the French word *temps*, or "time" and "weather" (*Vent* 272). Joining time and weather implies joining logic (symbolized by inflexible, predictable time) to emotion (uncontrollable weather) as well as joining the two meanings of "heavens," the sacred one and the meteorological one (*Vent* 260).

The first part of *The Man without Qualities* consists largely of a satiric portrait of the upper-middle-class citizens of Vienna in 1913. The protagonist, Ulrich, is called the man without qualities because he is taking a year out from his professional scientific activities to decide what to do with the rest of his life. He is therefore open to new experiences but uncommitted, and his major distinguishing mark is that he cannot take anything personally, including his own feelings. No character in *Les Météores* corresponds exactly to Ulrich, but Alexandre is similarly detached. Other parallels emerge as well. Ulrich is involved with a government-sponsored committee to plan celebrations for the seventieth jubilee of the Emperor of Austria, to take place in 1918, but the reader knows the jubilee will not happen because Austria will be defeated in World War I, just as we know that World War II will disrupt the characters' lives in *Les Météores*. Austria is called in the novel the "kaiserlich und königlich" empire, or "Kakania" for short (32), and this playfully obscene name may have inspired Tournier's naming Alexandre's refuse-collection operation SEDOMU (thus linking garbage and sodomy) and giving Alexandre a rather perverse pride in his profession which makes him name himself the "king and dandy of the garbage dumps" (94). (The name in the English translation, TURDCO, keeps the tone but unfortunately loses the sexual overtones.)

Further, the sections on "Kakania's" ill-fated jubilee campaign, which reveal the intellectual bankruptcy of Vienna just before World War I, are echoed in Tournier's picture of French society from 1937 to 1961.

The second part of Musil's huge novel focuses on mysticism through Ulrich's relationship with his younger sister Agatha, whom he considers a sort of twin. Their relationship is marked by a deep spiritual love and a mystic searching for the "other condition," a nonrational way of living. Although they do not have sexual relations with each other, Ulrich and Agatha are lovers emotionally and spiritually. This part of the book seems to have influenced the story of Tournier's twins, Jean and Paul, who are literally lovers, as well as suggesting the outcome of that relationship, Paul's discovery of a mystical state.

The other main fictional inspiration for *Les Météores* is Jules Verne's *Around the World in Eighty Days* (1873). Jean thinks that he is like Verne's Passepartout because both belong to weather, whereas Paul is like Phileas Fogg, the "living clock" (401). Jean tells his fiancée that Fogg's trip around the world is "an attempt by time to control meteorology" (402), and the same seems true of Paul's trip around the world, but as Tournier told an interviewer, Paul follows Jean "so that his chronology should become meteorology, which happens at the end" (Poirson 50), an idea which suggests merging time and weather rather than one being controlled by the other. Even in Verne's book, when Fogg falls in love with the beautiful Indian widow, Tournier finds the same union of emotion and logic that is symbolized by the union of time and weather (*Vent* 275). I will return to the contrast of time and weather after considering the religious sources and themes of *Les Météores*.

JOACHIM DE FIORE AND THE THIRD TESTAMENT

Tournier says that *Les Météores* began as an attempt to join the Holy Spirit to the weather and create an "aeolian theology" (*Vent* 260), and one cannot understand this book without some understanding of Joachim's theology. As in *Le Roi des aulnes*, a heresy provides the novel's creative basis, for, as Alexandre says, "spiritual delinquents are heretics . . . who disturb the established order to the extent that they are creative" (118). Joachim, a twelfth-century abbot who has been the subject of excellent recent studies by Henri de Lubac, Marjorie Reeves, and Delno C. West and Sandra Zimdars-Swartz, taught that the history of the world consists of three ages. The first one was that of the Old Testament, God the Father, and the patriarchs; the second was that of the New Testament, God the Son, and the priests; the third would be that of the Holy Spirit and monks. Joachim did not teach that there would be a third testament for the Third Age, but many of his followers believed that God would provide a new dispensation and a new testament. After Joachim's death, the popularity of the view that a new age was about to begin was one reason the Church condemned Joachim's doctrine in 1263.

Just as the Nestorian heresy gave Tournier a way in *Le Roi des aulnes* of representing the human division between body and soul and the religious division between man and God, so Joachimism gave him a way to organize the history of individual people as a movement from repression to freedom, from rationality to mysticism, and from human couples to union with God. And both Nestorianism and Joachimism have given him grounds for devaluing Christ and elevating the Holy Spirit. In *Le Roi des aulnes* this elevation is suggested by Tiffauges's "communing" by eating his pigeons (thus communing symbolically with the Holy Spirit) and in the "childish Golgotha" of the three children impaled on the huge swords in the courtyard of the *Napola*, a scene which reflects Tournier's horror of crucifixes. In *Les Météores*, in contrast, the devaluation of Christ is made explicit when the forty-five-year-old Alexandre Surin runs into a childhood friend, Thomas nicknamed Koussek, a Catholic priest serving in the Paris church of Saint-Esprit, which is named for the Holy Spirit. Koussek gives Alexandre an unorthodox theology lesson based on Joachim's ideas, the core of which is that Christ is merely the precursor of the Holy Spirit and that Christ's death on the cross is not necessary for salvation but merely provides a "necessary weight of color, heat, and pain" ("poids de couleur, de chaleur et de douleur" [161]). The church must, he says, "*go beyond*" Christ to the Holy Spirit (154, emphasis in original). His theology requires the Holy Spirit to be at least equal to Christ, but the Catholic Church, Koussek says, subordinates the Holy Spirit by teaching that the Holy Spirit proceeds from both the Father and the Son (155). The doctrine is called *Filioque*, from the Latin word meaning "and from the Son," which was added in the sixth century to the Nicene Creed by Western churches, but Eastern churches reject *Filioque*. Building on the importance of the Holy Spirit, Koussek claims that the Third Testament exists, that it is the Book of Acts (156), and that the Third Age began with the descent of the Holy Spirit at Pentecost.

To illustrate Joachim's doctrine novelistically, Tournier based the plot of *Les Météores* partly on it. The First Age is represented by the seven chapters showing the childhood of the twins Jean and Paul, and the Second Age is shown in the seven chapters concerning Alexandre. The Third Age is shown in the final eight chapters, in which Paul goes around the world.

The First Age, the Age of the Old Testament, which one could consider the world's childhood, is symbolized by the childhood of Jean and Paul, first seen sleeping locked in each other's arms in an Edenic garden, then sharing an apple (13). The Surin world is built around the flesh, especially the twins' identical bodies; the immense fecundity of their mother, Maria-Barbara; and the philanderings of their father, Edouard, the patriarch. Besides several references to the Garden of Eden, the Old Testament is suggested by the way plot events echo other biblical stories. The story of Abraham, Sarah, and Hagar is reflected in the relationships of Edouard, Maria-Barbara, and Edouard's Jewish mistress, Florence; the story of Isaac's twin sons, Esau and Jacob, is also evoked; and many other parallels are developed, as I have shown elsewhere ("Joachim de Fiore" 91-92).

JOACHIM'S SECOND AGE: CATHOLICISM AND SEXUALITY

The Second Age, that of the New Testament and of Christ, is shown in Alexandre's life; and the chapters about Alexandre, like the New Testament in Koussek's eyes, provide "color, heat, and pain." Christianity is discussed primarily in the chapters about Alexandre, and these are the chapters which most attract or repulse readers, in a reflection of the love-hate relation Tournier has with Christianity. Although Alexandre is not a practicing Christian, he thinks almost constantly about Christianity, and his ambivalent attitude to the flesh reflects Tournier's belief that organized Christianity wrongly teaches contempt for the body and sexuality (*Vent* 65). Alexandre shows his ambivalence as he alternates between boasting about his erotic practices and indirectly revealing the self-disgust which underlies them. I will discuss the novel's sexual themes in more detail later, but they must be considered here briefly in regard to Alexandre, to show how they relate to Tournier's view of established Christianity.

The connection between sexuality and Christianity is made through Alexandre's prep school, the Mount Tabor Academy, not only because it was there that Alexandre discovered his homosexuality (43) but because Mount Tabor is traditionally considered the site of the Transfiguration, a miracle in which Jesus' face and garments were shown in glory (Mark 9.2-10, Luke 9.28-36).

The miracle is not usually associated with sexuality, but here it is given sexual undertones when Alexandre links "ecstasies" to the Transfiguration (42). The Transfiguration is sexual for Tournier as well; he called it a "divine striptease" in the interview he gave me which is at the end of this book, and elsewhere he links Christ's transfigured flesh with "the flesh which is loved and celebrated in those whom we love" (*Vent* 65). But despite the "true" Christianity, which accepts the flesh and which could be seen in the students' (homo)sexual life at the Mount Tabor Academy, Alexandre suffered under the repressive weight of the priests' teaching to the extent that he could not truly accept his body and his sexual desires, much as Tournier says that in the church school he attended at Alençon he was oppressed by an "antierotic phobia" on the priests' part (*Vent* 64).

The adult Alexandre, like Tiffauges in *Le Roi des aulnes*, has internalized this divided attitude. In a brilliantly conceived mixture of high camp and philosophical meditation, he specializes in joining what Nestor and Tiffauges called alpha and omega, whether by thinking about garbage and excrement, by handing a shocked woman at a fancy ball a tapeworm to eat (260), by visualizing the Trinity as an erect penis and two testicles (123), or by practicing oral sex. However, this union of body and spirit is always unconvincing. Alexandre avidly pursues sexual experiences, but when he starts to feel love based on pity—a "coprophagous passion" (221)—for young Daniel, he does not know how to act. His lack of love is shown in his slowness in going to rescue Daniel from the rats in the Marseille dump.

Wanting his novels to be filled with humor, Tournier here put much of it into the passages about garbage collecting and processing, one of the "silly sciences" he finds amusing (Poirson 47). Alexandre, the source and butt of much of the novel's humor, is clever and whimsical, and he also recognizes humorous events when fate provides them—when, for example, all the clients in the public bathhouse claim to have a ticket ending in 969, although they actually all have tickets beginning with 696 and have turned them upside down (208). As this episode suggests, much of the humor in the novel is scatological, whether caused by Alexandre's dog Sam sodomizing another dog which is in turn mounting a bitch (225), or by Alexandre's one-night stand with a guardian in the elephant house in the Bois de Vincennes, whose highlight is the elephants' defecation in unison, caused by their sexual excitement (130).

Much of this section's wit relates to excrement because Alexandre lives in an excremental world. He does not identify with waste matter because he manages garbage dumps; he manages garbage dumps because he identifies with waste matter. The fact that the company he runs was founded by his brother Gustave under the name SEDOMU was a major reason he agreed to manage this family business; he was "seduced" by the "inverted" side of the garbage industry (36) and by the idea of "repurgation," Gustave's neologism suggesting both digestive medicine and theology (35). As Anthony Purdy has seen, Alexandre's obsession with waste matter is essentially religious (*"Les Météores"*).

It is a mistake to take Alexandre as the novel's—or Tournier's—spokesman, despite Alexandre's brilliance, for Alexandre represents a false path, and Tournier is quick to say that Alexandre does not speak for him in denouncing the heterosexual world (Ezine, "Michel Tournier" 224). The distance between author and character is also suggested by Alexandre's name, which, as the novel says, evokes Alexander the Great and several Russian czars (251); although Alexandre partly rejects the symbolism, he is as haughty as any ruler and can be violent. Despising equally "Alexander [the Great], Napoleon, and Hitler" (Braudeau 89), Tournier uses this name to suggest Alexandre's self-centeredness and brutality. Alexandre's limitations are clearly shown, and they must be, insofar as the Second Age is imperfect. When Koussek says that only the Second Age "gives homosexuality all its possibilities" (150), he is suggesting a causal relationship between Christianity and homosexuality, and it is not one that flatters either homosexuality or Christianity. Alexandre's death, really a suicide, at the end of this section shows the failure of the Second Age; Tournier told an interviewer that Alexandre has a "beautiful death" because it is associated with his sexuality ("Michel Tournier" 13), but Alexandre dies because he despairs. William Cloonan is right to say that Alexandre believes that "all order is necessarily artificial" (*Michel Tournier* 64), and it is this very rationality, this refusal of faith, which makes Alexandre despair.

JOACHIM'S THIRD AGE: SPIRITUAL FULFILLMENT

The Third Age is shown in the last third of the novel, in the adult experiences of the Surin twins. Koussek claims that the Third Age, the Age of the Holy Spirit, derives from the First Age, the Holy Spirit being the same as the Old Testament *ruah*, the wind which manifested God's spirit (156). In illustration of that idea, the novel's third section derives from the story of the twins (who represent the First Age) rather than that of Alexandre (who represents the Second Age). Paul's spiritual search is represented by his physical search for Jean around the world.

This search represents "going beyond Christ," to use Koussek's words, to find the Holy Spirit. Therefore, though the twins have so far mainly been identified with the age of the Old Testament, Christ must be introduced into their story for Paul to "go beyond" him. This is done through an incident that happened to Jean when, as a child, he went into a carnival ride called the ROTOR, a centrifuge, and while its spinning was plastering the riders against its sides, a Paris garage mechanic—undoubtedly Abel Tiffauges—stood up horizontally against the wall and held Jean in his arms in what Paul, watching from a sort of gallery, thought was a "baptism into the external world" (197). This baptism suggests Jesus' baptism by John the Baptist, and the fact that it is a baptism into the outer world relates both to Christ's ministry to the heathen and to Jean's eventual flight, both of which are centrifugal. Here Jean, like Ephraïm in *Le Roi des aulnes*, is identified with Christ by means of Tiffauges. As Christiane Baroche points out, this event also symbolizes Jean's horizontal nature, as opposed to Paul's need to find a vertical, spiritual dimension ("Michel Tournier ou l'espace" 1180). Like Tiffauges, Jean will be unable to "go beyond" Christianity, though Paul will do so.

The Third Age, Koussek says, begins with Christ's Ascension and the coming of the Holy Spirit. Jean's desertion of Paul at the start of the book's last third suggests the Ascension, and the descent of the Holy Spirit is symbolized by the many birds Paul sees (especially in the chapter called "The Icelandic Pentecost") and by the people he meets. Finally, crossing Canada by train, Paul thinks he sees Jean get off the train, but Paul continues, sensing that it is not his physical twin he is seeking. Paul, the man of the Holy Spirit, is getting ahead of Jean, the man connected with Christ, an act that physically symbolizes "going beyond" Christ. Later, the mystery of the Trinity is evoked in the separation-union of Paul and Jean, who represent the Holy Spirit and Christ, respectively. Trying to escape through a tunnel from East Berlin in 1961, Paul is mutilated so that much of his left side (representing Jean) must be amputated.

Back home in Brittany, Paul thinks that Jean has vanished forever but that, because he and Jean, being identical twins, have only one soul, their "unfolded" soul fills up all the space between them—that is, the whole world. It is in this sense that Tournier can say that the novel's central theme is space, illustrated by the miniature Zen gardens Paul sees in Japan and by the huge Canadian plains ("L'Espace" 51). So the tiny space Jean and Paul once occupied curled together in bed is literally further reduced to the space occupied by Paul's mutilated body but, like a Zen garden, this space expands, in Paul's mind, and his wounds become Japanese gardens (608) that hold the universe. Like his uncle Alexandre, Paul has always looked for order, for reason, for logical coherence, but here he goes beyond logic to acceptance of his condition and mystical union with God. Paul now identifies with the entire Trinity, having been "crucified" in Berlin like Christ (603) and possessing a wing to spread over the sea like the Holy Spirit (623) and the "eye of God" (613) to see the world with. He has discovered, through his incapacitation, the world of contemplation of Joachim's monks of the Third Age: God, rather than Jean, now fulfills him.

The novel's final word, "sublimation," shows the ambiguities of this ending—is Paul simply sublimating to compensate for his injury? Subscribing at least partly to that theory, Colin Davis finds the ending may merely show "self-imposed blindness" on Paul's part ("Identity" 355), and William Cloonan finds Paul's sublimation "akin to madness" (*Michel Tournier* 63), whereas Patricia Mignone (193) and Eric Brogniet (58) seem to find true cosmic enlightenment in Paul's vision. The latter readings are more satisfactory, for they accord with the theme of sexual sublimation in the earlier novels, while sexual sublimation is clearly seen here by Mireille Rosello (184). Another interpretation is that Paul is having a *sublime* experience. This is possible, because for Tournier the sublime "plunges one into an emotion strangely mixing pleasure and terror" (*Vol* 62). Or maybe the meaning is scientific: Paul's weather report, with which the novel ends (and which echoes the book's opening page), is about snow turning directly into vapor, or *subliming*, which symbolizes the derivation of the Third Age from the First Age, without the need to go through the Second Age, just as snow which sublimes does not become liquid before turning into a gas. But one should not choose; Paul has all of these experiences, his exalted spiritual vision depending on physical sublimation.

THE DIVINE COMEDY: ALEXANDRE IN HELL

Tournier used not only Joachim's theory of the Three Ages to organize the plot, but also *The Divine Comedy*, not an arbitrary choice, for Dante was influenced by Joachimism (Gardner 184-98), and Dante puts Joachim into Paradise (12.139-41). The link to Dante has been noted by Jacqueline Piatier, who thought the relation with *The Divine Comedy* was parodistic ("Roman"), and by Christiane Baroche, who calls the novel a "story of Heaven and Hell" (*"Les Météores"* 19) and links Tournier with Dante's Virgil ("Michel Tournier ou l'espace" 1178). The function of the parallel, however, is not parody (although certain passages may be parodistic); rather, it is to reinforce the theme of a spiritual journey from damnation to salvation. Again, the structure is tripartite. In this pattern, Alexandre's seven chapters correspond to the *Inferno*, and the seven interwoven chapters on Jean, Paul, and their family derive from the *Purgatory*. The last eight chapters show the *Paradise*. In each section there are close parallels between events in *The Divine Comedy* and the plot of *Les Météores*.

Alexandre's chapters suggest the connection with Dante most directly, for Alexandre refers to Dante several times; once he calls Dante a ragpicker (212), and he compares making a trip to the Paris incineration plant to reading Dante (150). Appropriately, when Alexandre refers to Dante, it is only in the context of the *Inferno*. In a similar vein, Alexandre calls himself a "condemned man with a stay of execution" (41), and though at one point he denies that the garbage dumps are hell, he calls them a "mirror reflecting the essence of society" (93)—an inverse image of the world, just as Satan's realm is a parody of God's. And just as most readers find the *Inferno* the most interesting part of *The Divine Comedy*, so most readers find Alexandre's sections the most interesting part of *Les Météores*; sinners are more interesting than saints. One must keep in mind, though, that Alexandre's association with the damned— not only with Dante, but with the souls condemned to Hell—shows his original role as Tournier conceived it, as Paul's foil.

Dante's imagined journey through Hell begins with Limbo, and then he progresses downward through the nine circles of Hell, each circle holding people who were more wicked and who are suffering more than the last. Roanne's municipal dump, where Alexandre is surrounded by its "gray matter" (99) and finds books in Latin (92), is a modern version of Limbo, the First Circle, home of the virtuous pagans, mainly Latin authors (Dante 4.121-44). To make the comparison with the *Inferno* clearer, Alexandre is in Roanne to direct the filling of a site called the "Devil's Hole." The name, suggesting both Hell and the anus, provides an image of how Alexandre feels about his homosexuality: for all his boasting of the superiority of homosexuals, he is persuaded that homosexuality is damnable.

Dante's Second Circle contains the lustful; Alexandre's adventures in Roanne show his lust as he chases first Eustache Lafille and then Daniel. The Third Circle of Hell contains gluttons (Dante 6.7-115), and soon we learn that Alexandre has a tapeworm which lets him eat as much as he wants without gaining weight (95-96, 110-11). Misers are in the Fourth Circle, along with spendthrifts (Dante 7.1-96); both groups relate to Alexandre's lodging arrangements at Roanne, where he divides his time between the expensive Terminus Hotel and the shady Grutiers. In the Fifth Circle Dante found the angry (7.109-8.66); Alexandre's corresponding experience is in the Bois de Vincennes where the elephants "strike the walls as if with battering rams" and "make a hellish racket" (130). Shortly after, Alexandre himself becomes angry when he is arrested for attacking a police officer. The next day he needs Koussek's help to get out of jail, just as Dante needs the help of an angel (the only one in the *Inferno*) to reach Lower Hell.

Koussek seems an odd choice to represent an angel, but there is a reason. As adolescents at the Mount Tabor Academy, Koussek and Alexandre belonged to a group of homosexual boys. "Koussek" was actually a nickname, derived from his favoring the *coup sec*, or "dry shot," sexual climax without ejaculation (48), a practice suggesting the twins' "oval love" in that there is no loss of semen. (A "coup" can also refer to a drink of liquor.) At that time, Koussek fantasized that he was Christ's twin, partly because he identified with the apostle Thomas Didymas, who Koussek thought was Christ's twin; and because he associated sex and religion, Koussek wanted to have sexual relations with Christ, which he tried to carry out on a life-size carving of Jesus (48). As an adult, however, Koussek has managed to sublimate his sexual feelings into a belief that all people are his twins (160) and has directed his sexual desires for his "twins" into priestly service to them. As the servant of the Holy Spirit, Koussek is the only person until the novel's end who feels united with God and man, for in serving God through service to his human "twins" he has found a way to combine a mystical marriage to God with practical human activity.

The angel in *The Divine Comedy* helps Dante leave Upper Hell and its sins of incontinence for Lower Hell and the sins of violence, and, similarly, after a rather light-hearted beginning, Alexandre's story now begins to become violent. In Dante's Sixth Circle, heretics stink in burning tombs; in parallel, after Koussek gets him out of jail, Alexandre visits the Paris incineration plant, an "infernal city" (137) which makes him think of Dante's Hell (120) and of society's condemnation of those who disagree with it: for Alexandre, homosexuals are heretics because they are not sexually orthodox (118). Later, in the Seventh Circle, Dante sees the sodomites (15.1-16.124); in the related section of *Les Météores*, Alexandre becomes involved in the violent efforts of the lesbian Fabienne de Ribeauvillé to recover stolen twin Philippine pearl earrings. Images here also reflect the Seventh Circle, where centaurs guard the river of boiling blood, for Alexandre sees Fabienne, mounted on her horse, watch another horse turn the water in a stagnant pond red as it flays itself in a futile attempt to get free of submerged barbed wire (229-30). The pond is a symbol of lesbian sexuality, as the "Devil's Hole" is of male homosexuality.

Tournier does not include male and female homosexuals in his pattern merely because Dante does; rather, they are there presumably because he wants to show that many gay people, including Alexandre and Fabienne in the novel, experience their sexuality as infernal. Fabienne's bloody quest to retrieve the earrings—she cuts off a man's ear to get one of them back—and the violence with which she treats her presumed lover (229) suggest that she is driven by forces she cannot control. As to Alexandre, his sexuality has always been that of a *dragueur*, a pick-up artist; when he begins to care about Daniel, he is as frightened as he is delighted; love is a new experience for him. Fabienne and Alexandre have internalized society's condemnation of their sexual attitudes and of their acts, and Alexandre, at least, has never thought it possible that he could be part of a loving couple. (This is probably also true of Fabienne, or she would not have planned to marry.) As Tournier said in an interview, although Alexandre is "proud to be part of a [homosexual] minority," he is fooling himself because *"homosexuality doesn't exist"* (Sanzio et al. 18, emphasis in original). Tournier goes on to claim that Western society has invented homosexuality as a category; in other societies, people can simply follow their sexual impulses, heterosexual, homosexual, or both, without being labeled. This idea is illustrated in part through the twins, for Jean and Paul, although lovers, never think of themselves as gay, nor does anyone else; although they cannot avoid the stereotyping that comes from being twins, they have avoided sexual labeling.

In the Eighth Circle are panders, seducers, evil counselors, and impersonators, and Alexandre is soon imitating them in his seduction of Daniel, whom he decides to turn into a counterfeit twin of himself. Thinking, however, of the love mixed with pity that he feels for Daniel, Alexandre remembers that Virgil rebuked Dante in the Eighth Circle for feeling pity for the damned (212). A little later, in the Marseille dump, Alexandre experiences hellish terror when the rats invade the boxcar where he is sleeping. Just as

Dante and Virgil seem to be in physical danger in the Eighth Circle, Alexandre is in some peril when he goes outside in his futile attempt to save Daniel from being killed by the rats in the dump. By this time, Alexandre is as frightened of the gulls, which represent the Holy Spirit and the *ruah* (304), as of the rats, which are part of the hell of his garbage dumps: he thinks he is as cut off from God as any soul in Hell.

Alexandre has nearly reached the center of his own hell. Dante's last circle contains traitors; Alexandre's last circle has Hitler, a "brown devil" (341) whom Alexandre sees in Paris at the beginning of the Occupation. Alexandre has thought of himself as the "prince of filth" (341), has implicitly compared himself to Lucifer by calling himself an "angel of light" (297), and has flaunted a dubious elegance reminiscent of folklore about the Devil's foppishness, but when he sees the man who literally treats people like garbage, destroying them in his death camps, he realizes that he is merely human, and he is ready for a sign from the Holy Spirit (342).

After this voyage, Alexandre's death savors of anticlimax, although it has been prepared for by his frequent comments that he hopes to die fighting, sword-cane in hand. He is disillusioned because, having seen his nephews Paul and Jean engaged in their "oval love," he realizes he can never attain that narcissistic ideal, so he searches for an Arab boy at the dangerous Casablanca docks, going to what he knows is almost certain death. In terms of *The Divine Comedy*, Alexandre may now correspond to Cato, the Roman philosopher who committed suicide and whom Dante put in the vestibule of Purgatory. Like Cato, Alexandre has been a rationalist, but that rationality has kept him from being happy or fulfilled. He has lived in hell, symbolically and emotionally, precisely because he has rejected the mysticism which will save Paul from despair at the end.

FROM PURGATORY TO PARADISE

The chapters about Edouard and the childhood of the twins, which correspond to Joachim's First Age, also derive from Dante's *Purgatory*. Just as Dante provides pairs of "checks" and "goads" for each level of the mountain of Purgatory, so Tournier fills these chapters with opposing pairs offering indirect spiritual guidance to Jean and Paul. Edouard, their father, is a check; he is self-centered and self-indulgent. Maria-Barbara, their mother, is a goad; she is an earth mother, loving and giving, as well as a Resistance heroine. The collection of buildings composing the Breton home of Edouard's family also provides checks and goads. The family's textile factory, housed in a desanctified charterhouse, represents a profanation of the sacred and is a check, but, even as a check, it reflects opposing attitudes, for the weaving and knitting mills (Paul's favorite place) represent union, and the factory for remaking old mattresses (Jean's favorite place) represents separation because the mattress-making process begins with carding old mattresses. On the other hand, the asylum for retarded and disturbed children, housed in another part of the former charterhouse, is a goad: the nuns and lay people in St. Brigitte's Asylum devote themselves unselfishly to the children. Significantly, the sister in charge of the asylum is named Béatrice—Tournier has given her the name of Dante's symbol of heavenly love.

Dante shows people being purged of three kinds of wrong love in Purgatory: love which seeks the wrong object, insufficient love, and disproportionate love. Tournier represents love of the wrong object in the story of Franz, who loves man-made, mechanical objects (76, 79); insufficient love in Edouard, who cares only for himself; and disproportionate love in the twins, especially Paul, who puts his relationship with Jean before everything else. At the end of the Purgatory section, Paul is not purged of wrong loves (any more than Dante is when he has finished seeing Purgatory), but he has received a lesson about their nature.

The last eight chapters of *Les Météores*, besides representing Joachim's millennial Third Age, correspond to Dante's *Paradise*, another perfect world. Perfection and bliss are not easy to depict in fiction, and the book's structural commitment to a full-scale development of this theme has made the end seem tedious to some readers, although Tournier has employed travel description to liven up this section. I will briefly sketch in the main correspondences with the *Paradise* and indicate their meaning. In each successive heaven Dante is shown a different kind of love, the lowest kinds first and the greatest last; similarly, Paul discovers ever closer approximations to a state of perfect spiritual bliss. Paul's first stop in his search for the fleeing Jean is Venice, which corresponds to Dante's Heaven of the Moon in that both places are changeable, and Venice is saved from flooding only by the moon's control of the tides (447). He next goes to Djerba, looking for Ralph and Deborah, with whom Jean left Venice. This loving couple's Edenic home, falling apart after Deborah's death, corresponds to the Heaven of Venus, where Dante puts the sensual lovers.

Next comes the Heaven of the Sun, represented by Iceland, land of the midnight sun. Dante meets in the Heaven of the Sun the prudent and those who transcend the physical, and in Iceland Paul meets Selma and Olivier, who transcend the physical by adapting to the long winter nights, and who are so prudent that they have continually put off marriage. In the Heaven of Jupiter Dante rather surprisingly meets two pagans, Trajan and Ripheus; Paul goes to Japan and meets his own "pagan," a Zen master, Shonïn, who teaches him about the power of the mind. In the Heaven of Saturn, Dante finds monks, who are paralleled by Urs Kraus, who has left his girlfriend to go to Vancouver to devote himself to painting as a monk might devote himself to religion.

Dante goes next to the Heaven of the Fixed Stars, and next in *Les Météores* is the vast space of Canada, which Paul finds as electrical and intense as the heavens. The angels in this heaven in *The Divine Comedy* represent knowledge, and it is here that Paul has a new kind of knowledge, the insight that it is not the physical Jean that he is pursuing (568-69, 574). This shift also reflects Dante's change in attitude when he goes from loving the human Beatrice to realizing that she is a symbol of divine revelation. Two spheres are left in Dante, the Primum Mobile and the Empyrean. The first is symbolized in the novel by Berlin, and especially by Frau Kraus's apartment: just as there are no seasons in the Primum Mobile, so in her sealed-up apartment along the Berlin Wall, Frau Kraus transforms August into December to celebrate Christmas (596).

The Empyrean is the final realm, the sphere of bliss where Dante has two final visions of God; Paul finds his equivalent of the Empyrean at home in Brittany, after he has been nearly killed escaping under the Berlin Wall, where he suffers a symbolic death in which he is "crucified" and a rebirth in a slippery tunnel filled with bloodlike "red clay" (603). Dante's first vision is of the blessed souls forming a heavenly rose (30.124-27); Paul's corresponding vision, aided by his binoculars, is of flowers in his own garden (613-14). The binoculars themselves, which have been established as an emblem of the twins and which indicate the power of seeing things from two angles, represent the twins' "superior visionary power" (171), an expression which now takes on a metaphysical meaning. Dante's second vision, of the Trinity (33.115-20), has its counterpart in Paul's conviction that he has become the Trinity and that he fills all space (618-19). Paul's travels may seem random, but they are structured to make a reader think of Dante's journey and see how Paul, like Dante, becomes more and more developed spiritually, until he merges with God. This ending could be ironic, but the association with *The Divine Comedy* suggests that Paul's spiritual and religious quest has succeeded.

TIME, WEATHER, AND SPACE

Structuring the novel's plot around Joachim de Fiore's Three Ages and *The Divine Comedy* committed Tournier to complex and sometimes mechanical patterning, which reflects his long-standing taste for systems more coherent than reality (*Vent* 157). This complexity is partly why both the novel itself (331) and some critical articles (Purdy, *"Les Météores"* 34, 37, and 38 and Baroche, *"Les Météores"* 20) have used diagrams to explain aspects of the book. The contrast between these mechanical systems and the loose way in which real life works echoes what Tournier says is the novel's "profound subject," the reconciliation of time, which is mechanical, and weather, which is unpredictable (*Vent* 272), and which represents the need to reconcile thought with emotion and philosophy with reality as it is experienced. The theme is suggested in part by Jean's discussion of Phileas Fogg and Passepartout in *Around the World in Eighty Days*, Fogg representing time and rationality, and Passepartout representing weather and emotions. As Tournier explains, Paul, who is rational, belongs to the heavens of astronomy, whereas Jean "opens up happily to the unreliable heaven of rain and sun" (*Vent* 275).

These opposites are reconciled in part through "synthesizing" time and space, Tournier says (*Vent* 271). Weather and time both have to do with seasonal change, and space enters the problem because changing spatial relationships—the earth's movement in orbit as it crosses the plane of the ecliptic—determine when each season begins, for the two equinoxes and the two solstices of each year determine the start of each season. The equinoxes occur around March 21 and September 23 and mark the times of the year when day and night are equally long; the solstices occur around June 21 and December 21 and mark the longest and shortest days of the year, respectively. Equinoxes and solstices thus become symbols of Paul's desire to reconcile weather and time (497), which is in itself a symbolic way of reconciling himself with his brother. Most of the key events and dates in the novel are associated with an equinox or a solstice: the book opens on September 25, 1937, in the Edenic Surin garden; Uncle Gustave has died on September 20, 1934 (33); Alexandre sees Hitler on June 23, 1940, "the longest day of the year" (341); Maria-Barbara is arrested at "four-seventeen on March 21, 1943" (358); Jean flees the closed world of twinhood at the spring equinox (419); Paul has a vision of his "unfolded soul" in Iceland in late June, at Pentecost, near (or on) the summer solstice (512); and Paul's final beatific vision comes in "Indian summer" (620), probably at the autumnal equinox.

According to Sophie, his fiancée, Jean was fascinated by seasonal change, wanting to experience winter and summer at their extremes, the summer solstice as far north as possible, for example (398-99). Because he is the emotional twin, Jean is drawn to the "weather" aspect of seasonal change, rather than the "time" one, an attraction shown when as a child Jean raced over the tide flats to the water which had been pulled far from the Breton coast by a syzygy, an alignment of sun and moon (176). In contrast, Paul, the more logical twin, is associated with the time element of seasonal change. When they were children, Jean's clock and his barometer, the reporters of time and weather, were always slightly ahead of Paul's clock and barometer (173-74), a difference symbolizing the fact that, as the novel says, weather is always ahead of seasonal time, in the sense that the weather of each season begins well in advance of the official (time-oriented) start of each season (454). So in their childhood, Jean, the older boy, the one associated with weather, was always a bit ahead of Paul, who is associated with time.

Their relative situations do not change until Paul finally outdistances Jean on the Canadian prairie. Jean, who has significantly called himself "the pre-cursor, the announcer of the good, the wonderful news" (177), and who has been associated, as I have shown, with Christ, must give way to Paul, just as in the Old Testament Esau is overtaken by his twin Jacob and as Jesus, whom Koussek calls the "precursor of the Holy Spirit" (155), must leave so the Holy Spirit can descend. These two parts of a whole—Jean and Paul, Christ and Holy Spirit, weather and time—are united in Paul's final beatific vision, when he thinks that his "unfolded soul" (619), which he believes is also Paul's soul, fills all of space.

THE METEORS: THE THEME OF THE COUPLE

The theme of time versus weather and the theme of Christ versus the Holy Spirit both make part of another theme, the theme of the couple. There are three kinds of human couples in the novel: heterosexual couples, homosexual couples, and the twins, Jean and Paul. Edouard and Maria-Barbara are the main heterosexual couple, and as such they are subject to all the vicissitudes of time and weather: they have children, their feelings for each other change, and they are killed by forces stronger than themselves—despair and illness for Edouard, the Germans for Maria-Barbara. Edouard is unhappy and unfulfilled; Maria-Barbara's life is limited to procreation. Other heterosexual couples include Edouard and Florence, his lover; Edouard and Angelica, another lover; Ralph and Deborah; Ralph and Hamida, his lover; Jean and Sophie; and Jean and Denise Malacanthe, his lover. The fact that many of the men have both wives and lovers underscores the novel's emphasis on the often ephemeral nature of desire.

These heterosexual couples, in Koussek's view, are by nature "low-born." He says that, like Molière's Monsieur Jourdain in *The Bourgeois Gentleman*, who tried to imitate the aristocrats, "the heterosexual wants to lead the free and disinterested life of the homosexual nobles" (146) and have erotic fulfillment without the cares and responsibilities of domesticity. On the other hand, the limitations of Koussek's view are suggested by Paul's vision of Edouard and Maria-Barbara transformed into divinities (620)—a vision Jean also has had (274).

Nevertheless, the sexual life of the novel's heterosexual couples is derisory, representing what Tournier in an interview called the "super-specialized" normal sexual orientation (Poirson 48), as opposed to a sexuality allowing for many kinds of expression, genital and nongenital, so that "pansexualism" could become a way to understanding the world ("Michel Tournier" 13). Koussek's view is differently undercut by Paul's theory of homosexuality, which is that homosexual couples are only poor imitations of true twins. Therefore, Paul compares *homosexuals* to Molière's Monsieur Jourdain, twins in Paul's view being the real aristocrats (387-88). Tournier seems to support Paul's view by saying that incest and homosexuality are merely imitations of twins' sexual relations (*Vent* 254-55), but he also says that "being always confronted by an identical brother" is an impoverishment ("Michel Tournier" 14). Finally, rather than accepting Koussek's idea that the heterosexual couple imitates the homosexual couple, one could just as well consider that homosexual couples imitate heterosexual ones.

In any case, Tournier told an interviewer, "homosexuality in the West is largely the product of heterosexuality" because it derives from "the persecution by heterosexuals" ("Michel Tournier" 14), and Alexandre says something similar (149). Tournier would prefer a society whose attitude would be "don't be anything [but] do what you like" ("Michel Tournier" 14); that is, one that does not classify people into particular sexual categories according to their acts but gives them freedom to do what they wish. If we take Alexandre's relations with Daniel as representing the gay couple in society today—and they are the only male gay couple which lasts any time at all—those relations are not happy ones. As Stephen Smith points out, the novel can be read as a "fundamental rejection of homosexuality" ("Toward a Literature" 343), but a broader view would find instead a rejection of all sexuality as it is generally lived. Alexandre's love is entirely narcissistic, as he himself sees (247), and he seeks in his lover a sort of younger twin (249). This love cannot last. The only hope for him would be to break out of society's mold and achieve the "universal twinship" Koussek tells him about: a belief that everyone is his twin. Koussek, though not a twin, is much like Paul at the end of the book. Just as Koussek's adolescent sexual practice of the "dry shot" suggests the "oval love" of the twins in that there is no loss of semen, so his adult mystical union with the world anticipates Paul's mystical vision.

Like the heterosexual and homosexual couples, the third kind of couple, Jean and Paul, is also condemned to end, but because in Paul's mind he and Jean finally merge, on another level Paul has succeeded in forming with his brother a "sterile and eternal couple" (197), in contrast to ordinary human couples, which face the perils caused by time. He believes that, unlike human couples, mythic couples (such as Romeo and Juliet) are not changed by time (317-18), nor are the mythic heroes who were changed into constellations (197), such as the twins Castor and Pollux, who became the constellation Gemini. In his own mind, Paul like them has transcended time and weather, and for him the two meanings of "meteor" have been united, the one referring to weather, or meteorology, and the one referring to a heavenly body.

To better understand the meaning of the twins' relationship and how they can represent deities and heroes, we must also consider the anthropological meaning of twinship, as seen by Claude Lévi-Strauss, Tournier's former teacher at the Musée de l'Homme. Lévi-Strauss says that in the mythology of the Salish Indians of the American Northwest, twins are associated with atmospheric phenomena, and he implies that this is generally true of myths of coastal peoples. (The Surin house in Brittany is very close to the coast.) The Salish myths, like those of some South American Indians, express an opposition between fog and wind (*Anthropology* 61-62), fog being "interposed between sky and earth, sun and humankind," and wind dispersing fog and so, presumably, letting man and the Divine communicate (*Anthropology* 62). This is the exact opposition Jean and Paul represent, for Jean is the man of weather—of fog and mist—and Paul is, or becomes, impregnated with the wind of the Holy Spirit, which breaks the barriers between man and Heaven, like wind dispersing fog.

Lévi-Strauss also says that twins often function as "intermediaries between the powers above and humanity below" (*Myth* 32) and generally have adventures which "untwin them" (*Myth* 28)—just what happens in *Les*

Météores. One assumes that Tournier hoped to draw on the presumed familiarity of such material suggesting that twins have an "intimate relationship"
with the heavens (*Vent* 242), and, though one might question the relevance to
a French audience of American Indian myths, Lévi-Strauss says that there is
an underlying similarity between Salish mythology and European, especially
French, mythology (*Anthropology* 63). Tournier probably also relied on
readers' knowing the common mythological pattern in which supposed twins
are often the children of two different fathers, one divine and one human (Lévi-
Strauss, *Anthropology* 62), as is true, for example, of Castor and Pollux,
Castor being the son of Tyndareus and Pollux the son of Zeus. Although Jean
and Paul are identical twins and so must have the same father, the common
pattern for mythic twins helps prepare us for Paul to surpass Jean, as if Paul is
the twin with the divine father. Given the choice between "unchangeable
immobility and living impurity, [Jean] choose[s] life" (274), whereas Paul
finds in his amputee's bed the human equivalent of divine, unchanging
existence, as well as a relationship with God which is more fulfilling than any
relationship two humans could have.

   An additional meaning of the end is shown by the Jesus–Holy Spirit contrast running through the novel. Edouard and Maria-Barbara are apotheosized
into a nonsexist God-the-parents (620) of the "mathematical heaven of the
astronomers" (158). Jean/Jesus, the man of seasons who belongs on the "land
of men" (158), has vanished. Paul/the Holy Spirit is between the earth and the
sky of the stars, in the "foggy and unpredictable heaven of meteorology" (158)
where human and divine meet. Not descended from the father "and the son"
(*Filioque*) but from his parents alone, Paul at the novel's end represents the
Holy Spirit, whose function is to "link the heavens of the Father and the earth
of the Son" (158). As in *Vendredi* and *Le Roi des aulnes*, sexual relations, once
sublimated, become religious feelings, but here the connection is made more
emphatically and explicitly.

AN ATTACK ON PLATONISM

   Philosophy remains a thread running through Tournier's fiction, including
this novel. As I showed in the previous chapters, *Vendredi* and *Le Roi des
aulnes* owed much to Hegel and Sartre; *Les Météores* accepts Aristotelianism
and attacks Platonism. Alexandre is a disciple of Plato, who taught that the
material world in which we live is only a copy of an eternal region in which

exist the "forms" or "ideas" which give shape to matter. Alexandre, however, carries Platonic reasoning to a comic extreme: "The idea is more than the thing, and the idea of the idea more than the idea. By virtue of which the imitation is more than the thing imitated" (101). This thinking leads him to prize copies *of copies* more than originals. (Unfortunately for Alexandre, they are hard to find.) Alexandre also sees the Platonic realm of ideas realized in garbage dumps because they are full of packages without contents (103), like forms without matter. Alexandre's fondness for masturbation, as he himself realizes, derives from the same preference, because he can imagine a better lover than he can ever find (88-89).

Tournier is here ridiculing Plato's rejection of the physical. Alexandre's world, despite his search for sexual happiness, is not a fulfilling one because he prizes abstraction too highly. It is the same Platonic rejection of the physical, including the body, which Tournier finds at the root of Catholic sexual repressions, as he said to me in the interview in Chapter 8 below. Not only the victim of Catholicism, Alexandre is a victim of Platonism, which was integrated by the Medieval Scholastics into Catholic theology.

The novel implicitly contrasts Plato's attitude with that of Aristotle, who complained of Plato's theory of ideas that it creates a "dualism between the world of intelligible ideas and the world of sensible things" (Lavine 70) and argued instead that matter and form cannot be separated. Because Aristotle rejected this dualism, he was able to prize physical life and its manifestations, which he wrote about in such works as the *Meteorologica*. The connection between Tournier's *Les Météores* and Aristotle is pointed up on the first page when the "character" Tournier is described as reading Aristotle's book, called in French *Météores*. (If Alexandre remains more a Platonist than an Aristotelian, one should not be too surprised; although Aristotle was the tutor of Alexander the Great, it is generally agreed that he failed to teach his values to his most famous pupil.)

A POLITICAL NOVEL?

Despite Alexandre's morals, which some readers have found shocking, *Les Météores* is not on the surface a revolutionary novel but, as Christa Bevernis has pointed out in her Marxist critique, a bourgeois one (203). There is no social revolt shown, despite a garbage-collectors' strike, and the focus of the novel is on characters' emotional and spiritual problems, not on their few material ones. However, the novel does pose a political issue in the opposition between Jean, who represents left-wing attitudes, and Paul, who represents the extreme right. Tournier makes the political subtext of *Les Météores* explicit in *Le Vent paraclet*, where he identifies Communist attitudes with emphasis on environment, Nazi and other racist attitudes with emphasis on heredity (243-50), and he goes on to say that "Paul would be on the right, Jean on the left" if they were to be situated politically (252) because Paul believes that their destiny is their biology—that being twins has established their nature—whereas Jean believes that he can change himself.

At the novel's end, the amputation of Paul's left side represents the loss of Jean, the "leftist" side of the twin cell, but because in Paul's mind that lost side comes to fill up all of space, left and right are balanced. This corresponds to Tournier's own political philosophy, which he says consists of understanding the role of heredity but acting politically as if it played no role, to give everyone an equal chance (Braudeau 89). In fact, the action of the novel suggests that environment is more important than heredity, for Paul and Jean have radically different attitudes and destinies, despite their identical heredity.

A FINAL EVALUATION: AUDIENCES AND IDEAS

Since Tournier writes to be read, to reach the largest possible audience (Piatier, "Entretien" 16), one must ask whether the book has succeeded on those grounds. Ironically, and unfortunately, *Les Météores* suffers from one of the very problems it is written to combat, too much emphasis on abstractions. Despite its length, and despite the vitalizing presence of Alexandre, it is overall the least specific, the least realized of Tournier's novels. The material was difficult to manage in other ways as well. *Les Météores* contains more characters than *Vendredi* or *Le Roi des aulnes*, which were both essentially one-person novels; Tournier develops Alexandre, Paul, Jean, Sophie, and even Hamida from within and without, and Edouard is treated in great detail by a third-person narrator. A large array of other characters of varying interest adds to the feeling that the book is out of control.

The shifts in narrative point of view, although clearly marked, may be confusing to some readers. On the other hand, and despite the sexual subjects, the language remains classically correct, with hardly a word to bring a blush to anyone's cheek and no explicit sexual description whatever. For 1975, the writing is tame. Despite its many underlying structures, Tournier could claim in an interview that *Les Météores* "follows the plan of the classical novel" (Poirson 47), and casual readers could take it as a conventional family chronicle.

Nevertheless, the book, like *Vendredi* and *Le Roi des aulnes*, attacks society's sexual and religious values and beliefs, in accord with Tournier's desire to act as a gadfly. As he told Jacques Chancel in 1979, he felt that he could accept the Legion of Honor because "all of [his] writings oppose it" (29); that is, he has refused to become conservative, to be bought off by public honors. In his previous novels, Tournier had begun to attack genital sexuality, for Robinson's and Tiffauges's sexual natures are as radical as Paul's, and their sexual sublimation is a main theme of this trilogy, but Robinson's and Tiffauges's radical sexuality had not attracted much notice, nor did Paul's; it was Koussek's boasting about homosexuals and Alexandre's largely failed sexual life that upset people.

But nongenital, sublimated sex was what Tournier wanted to emphasize. As he put it in 1976, he believes that the only way to avoid the evils of birth-control pills and abortion is to invent "new erotic paths, cerebral, not genital but genial"—that is, derived from one's own genius—with each person creating his or her personal new eroticism ("Lewis Carroll" 75). Most readers of *Les Météores* seem to have missed the point. Even as sensitive a reader as Roger Shattuck, who sees the movement toward altruism in Tournier's fiction (218) and calls *Les Météores* and *Le Roi des aulnes* "highly ambitious novels of ideas" (214), does not seem aware of the theme of sexual sublimation and thinks that only Robinson of Tournier's major characters has "a happy love life" (216). This is true on the surface but seems to miss the point.

Similarly, the new religion Tournier was creating, although discussed explicitly by Koussek and illustrated in the action of the novel, has not attracted much attention either, although William Cloonan has recognized that Tournier is developing his own heretical theology, which Cloonan relates to pantheism ("Spiritual" 84-85), and Joseph Garreau says Tournier's religion is a combination of Judaeo-Christian ideas and Graeco-Pagan ones (691). Both views contain truth, but neither acknowledges the strong theological current in Tournier's writing generally and in *Les Météores* specifically, and neither grasps the link, fundamental to Tournier's thinking, between sexuality and Christianity. For him, true Christianity is rooted in people's physical, sexual natures, which find their full flowering in sublimation leading to religious inspiration. This was true for Robinson, who like Paul moved symbolically into an age of the Holy Spirit and found his sexual energies transmuted into divine orgasm, and it was true to a lesser extent for Tiffauges, who could not go beyond Christ but who found partial fulfillment in subservience to (though not union with) Ephraïm-Christ.

If one can judge from the book reviews and the critical articles which have appeared so far, most readers have not discovered these ideas. The length of the book, the complexity of the thought, and the comparatively esoteric nature of some of the sources all added to the difficulties of reading and understanding *Les Météores* and took Tournier far from his ideal of writing clearly and simply so that children could understand him. And even when one does understand these ideas, they do not seem to warrant 600 pages of development: the fiction here simply is not strong enough to carry the ideas. This book marks the end of Tournier's first period as a novelist. He would make a radical change in his approach to fiction with his next novel, but first he would serve an apprenticeship in the essay and the short story.

4

Essays, Sketches, and Commentaries:
Tournier as Autobiographer, Teacher, and Critic

Michel Tournier has called himself a slow worker because he produces a novel only about every five years, but he is much more prolific than this fact would imply, for his writings include autobiography, texts to accompany photographs and drawings, prose sketches, personal essays, and literary and art criticism, as well as short fiction, including fiction for children. Because these short pieces took on added importance in Tournier's literary production between *Les Météores* and *Gaspard, Melchior et Balthazar,* it is appropriate to treat them at this point. I will discuss his nonfiction in this chapter and his short fiction in the next.

When I saw him in the summer of 1987, Tournier told me that he published his first article, an essay advancing a philosophical theory, in 1950 in the last number of a journal called *Espace,* while he was still studying philosophy and planning to be a professional philosopher. Apart from that article, his early publishing experience seems to have been limited to the occasional newspaper article (Merllié, *Michel Tournier* 231) and a large amount of translation from German into French, done to support himself after he left school. However, after he had made a name with *Vendredi ou les limbes du Pacifique* in 1967, he began to publish essays in magazines and newspapers. Some articles are on photography, his hobby; some concern literary theory and history; and still others are autobiographical, in the forms of travel notes, personal anecdotes, or introspection. Instead of "introspection," Tournier might prefer the word "extraspection," for when the newspaper *Le Monde* asked him in 1982 for pages from an "intimate journal," he responded with what he called "extimate pages," saying that not everyone has a talent for introspection ("Extraits" 11). Actually, Tournier *is* undoubtedly introspective, but he writes for his readers, not for himself, and thus "looks outward" in his writing. He does keep personal notebooks, but the contents are, for now, private, except for the bits he sometimes chooses to publish (Merllié, *Michel Tournier* 270).

Tournier's first experience with publishing book-length nonfiction seems to have come when he was the moving force behind *Miroirs: Autoportrait* (1973), a book in which 83 writers described themselves, with each description accompanied by the writer's photograph, taken by the French photographer Edouard Boubat. The last photograph is of Tournier, who compares himself in the accompanying text with both a rather dull office worker and an ogre (Piatier, "Idée" 18).

A more important book is his spiritual autobiography, *Le Vent paraclet* (1977), whose title means "The Wind of the Holy Spirit" but which appeared in English as *The Wind Spirit*, translated by Arthur Goldhammer. In the book, Tournier combines often sketchy autobiography with detailed discussions of *Vendredi ou les limbes du Pacifique, Le Roi des aulnes,* and *Les Météores*, his three novels published as of then. Although the essays are important primarily to students of Tournier's fiction, they have inherent interest, as they discuss France before, during, and after World War II from Tournier's highly personal perspective. In a few places Tournier settled scores with people or institutions he felt had wronged him, such as the university system, but the book is not bitter. Its combination of pain and forgiveness is indicated by the epigraph, which comes from the *Eloges* of the modern French poet Saint-John Perse. The verses, spoken by a child, could be translated as "When you stop combing my hair, I'll stop hating you."

Tournier has published a number of books in which his text accompanies pictures of one kind or another. As part of his research for *Les Météores*, Tournier had traveled across Canada with Edouard Boubat in September and October 1972, and that trip gave rise to a travel account, *Canada: Journal de voyage*, composed of Boubat's photographs and Tournier's day-by-day account of their trip, published in Montreal in 1977; a fuller version, *Journal de voyage au Canada*, was published in Paris in 1984. A voyage to Morocco in 1977 with the American photographer Arthur Tress inspired the short text for *Rêves* (1979), or "Dreams," a book consisting mainly of Tress's surrealistic photographs, many taken in New York in the 1970s. *Des clefs et des serrures* (1979), or "Keys and Locks," is a more ambitious project made up of 40 brief meditations, each with some connection to one or more accompanying photographs by various photographers. A more lighthearted book is *Vues de dos* (1981), or "Back Views," 30 short, often whimsical commentaries inspired by photographs taken by Boubat, each showing the back side of a person or statue, or an unexpected side of a place.

The next year, 1982, saw publication of *Le Vol du vampire: Notes de lecture*, a collection mainly of essays of literary criticism, many of which had appeared first as prefaces. The title, "The Flight of the Vampire," is also the title of the first essay, which compares a novel to a vampire bat, on the grounds that a novel needs to be given life by readers—to suck their blood, to have them participate in the "co-creation" of the work.

Le Vagabond immobile (1984), "The Motionless Wanderer," consists of short, mainly personal reflections and "extimate pages" by Tournier accompanied by pencil sketches by Jean-Max Toubeau, who spent several months drawing Tournier and his friends and surroundings. In 1983, Tournier provided an essay, "L'Image du pouvoir," to introduce *François Mitterrand*, a book of Konrad R. Müller's photographs of the Socialist French president. That essay also appears in *Petites proses* (1986), a collection of short prose pieces, many of which had already appeared elsewhere. The collection is mostly nonfiction but does include a chapter Tournier dropped from his novel *La Goutte d'or*. In 1988 came *Le Tabor et le Sinaï: Essais sur l'art contemporain*, a collection of essays about twentieth-century artists. For Tournier, Mount Tabor and Mount Sinai represent symbols and images, respectively, and in this book named for them, he develops his ideas about written versus visual representation.

The importance of these books lies mainly in the insight they give into Tournier's fiction. As a critic, Tournier writes vigorously but from an idiosyncratic standpoint, a trait more suited to fiction than to criticism; on the other hand, his insights are always thought-provoking. The concerns of the fiction also arise in the nonfiction: Christianity, love, physical life, loneliness, childhood, individuality, how to live. Because in the essays Tournier is openly didactic in a way he tries to avoid being in his fiction, the essays serve as a key to understanding the ideas underlying the fiction.

Besides his published books and essays, Tournier has also discussed his ideas and his books in many newspaper and magazine interviews. His articulateness and his experience (he once was a radio interviewer himself) seem to justify taking his comments in interviews as seriously as his statements in his essays; in fact, the close connection between essays and interviews is shown in the fact that he wrote *Le Vent paraclet* partly to expand on replies to questions he had been asked in interviews. With interviewers, Tournier discusses his work with a combination of humor, personal modesty, and professional self-confidence, but in both interviews and essays he also likes to be deliberately provocative, so everything he says cannot be taken at face value. Nevertheless, his interviews and essays contain many insights into his fiction.

Because little of this material has appeared in English, I will first sum up the most important facts about Tournier's life as presented in his nonfiction and then discuss the main insights this material offers into his fiction.

BIOGRAPHICAL INFORMATION

Tournier has written in some detail about his childhood and youth, mainly in *Le Vent paraclet*. His paternal grandfather was a glassblower in the north of France; his maternal grandfather, a pharmacist in Burgundy. His parents, Alphonse Tournier and Marie-Madeleine, *née* Fournier, met in Paris while pursuing graduate studies in German at the Sorbonne before World War I. After being wounded in the war, Alphonse Tournier created a company to protect the international royalties of artists, such as singers, whose works were mechanically recorded. His business obviously prospered, for the Tournier family lived first near the fashionable Boulevard Haussmann in Paris's ninth *arrondissement* and later in a large house in Saint-Germain-en-Laye, near Paris. By the time of World War II they also had a vacation house in Brittany. Michel Tournier, their first son, was born on December 19, 1924, and he and his two younger brothers and his older sister were raised in an atmosphere of wealth, even luxury; he has remembered being chauffeured to school as a small boy, wearing white gloves and suede shoes (*Vagabond* 51).

However, Tournier's childhood seems to have been far from easy psychologically. He has written of two experiences that stand out for him. The first, when he was four years old, was the removal of his tonsils, which he obviously experienced as rape and which he said had given him "an incurable distrust" of his fellowman (*Vent* 18). The other experience seems to have been even more traumatizing: as an overprotected and fragile boy of six, he was sent for reasons of health from Paris to a Swiss boarding school. His health may have improved, but the price he paid was emotionally devastating; not only was he separated from his protective and beloved mother, but he was subjected by a boy of eleven to a "despotic slavery accompanied by all sorts of torture" (*Vent* 24). This and later school relationships were obviously sexually charged, for 54 years later Tournier wrote that when he was nine he no longer had much to learn about the "joys" and "pains of the heart": "Everything happened for me at the age 'of reason,' and then my psychology became definitively fixed, so that a monstrously precocious maturity gradually developed into an immaturity from which I cannot recover" (*Vagabond* 11).

It is not surprising, then, that the young Tournier was an undisciplined, disruptive student, seldom finishing the school year in the same establishment in which he began it (*Vent* 38), nor that when World War II broke out the fourteen-year-old boy saw in it the answer to his prayers because it disrupted a way of life which he hated (*Vent* 76-77). He says he spent much of 1940-41 on his bicycle, shuttling between the family's vacation house in Brittany and a Neuilly-sur-Seine apartment near Paris, 200 kilometers away, which his parents had moved to when German soldiers were stationed in their home in Saint-Germain-en-Laye. Later, when his mother had gone with the younger children to the Burgundian town of Lusigny-sur-Ouche, where it was easier to find food than in Paris, he constantly foraged through the neighboring countryside for provisions (*Vent* 82). He once barely escaped being deported in a general reprisal against the town of Lusigny for acts by members of the Resistance in the area.

By the time of the Liberation in 1944, at the age of almost twenty, Tournier had become a serious student, though still a rebellious one. The change was due to his discovery in 1941-42 of philosophy, which is taught in the last year of the *lycée* and which Tournier studied at Paris's Lycée Pasteur (*Vol* 379)—until he was dismissed halfway through the school year. Nevertheless, he passed the difficult examination for the *baccalauréat* by studying on his own, under the guidance of Maurice de Gandillac, just as in the previous year he had passed the examination for the lesser *lycée* degree although expelled from school in Neuilly (Merllié, *Michel Tournier* 224). Partly under the influence of the scientist-psychologist-philosopher Gaston Bachelard (*Vent* 152), partly because of the inspiration of his fellow students (including future novelist Roger Nimier and future philosopher Gilles Deleuze), and partly because of his admiration for Jean-Paul Sartre, who was then electrifying the French intellectual scene, Tournier decided to work for an advanced degree in philosophy. In 1946 he sustained a thesis on Plato and received the *diplôme*, which is roughly equivalent to a master's degree, having previously earned two *licences*, or bachelor's degrees, one in letters and one in law.

Rather than continue directly at the Sorbonne, however, in 1946 Tournier went to study philosophy at the University of Tübingen, one of the few German universities which had escaped war damage. What was intended as a brief visit lasted four years. The huge influence of German philosophy on twentieth-century philosophy in general, and notably on Sartre's thinking, accounts for Tournier's desire to study in Germany, a desire no doubt augmented by his having spent summers in Germany with his mother when he was a child and his having learned German at home when he was very young.

A third, decisive event happened to Tournier in 1949 on his return to France, as intellectually devastating as the tonsillectomy and the boarding school had been emotionally devastating: he failed the *agrégation*, a test for a teaching certificate equivalent in its rigor to a doctoral examination. The failure was all the more shocking because he thought he was "clearly the best" philosopher of his generation (*Vent* 163)—or, as he put it with characteristic self-mockery in an interview, "the Popeye of philosophy" (Braudeau 83). Although he presented himself as a candidate again the following year, he had not prepared for the test and again failed (Merllié, *Michel Tournier* 229). In his words, he "slammed . . . the door" on his plan to become a teacher of philosophy (*Vent* 163) and supported himself through translating German novels and doing other work for the Paris publishing house of Plon.

So began a time for emotional and intellectual regrouping as Tournier sought a new career which would let him communicate his ideas with the world. He worked in radio, mostly as a publicist, from 1949 to 1958, and he was responsible for establishing a television show about photography, called "Chambre Noire," or "Darkroom," which ran from 1961 to 1965 (Merllié, *Michel Tournier* 232-33). From 1958 to 1968, he headed Plon's translating department (Braudeau 84). Despite having what someone else might consider a successful career, Tournier thought of himself as a failure: "I wasn't unhappy, but things weren't going well. To be a failure is fine when you're young, but the older you get, the harder it is to stand it" (Sanzio et al. 10). He published his first novel, *Vendredi ou les limbes du Pacifique*, in 1967, 17 years after leaving school. He was then forty-two years old. The next year he went on strike in sympathy with other workers, and although he was fired, his severance pay allowed him to devote himself full-time to writing *Le Roi des aulnes* (Braudeau 84). The financial success of that novel and his appointment to the reading committee of Gallimard, France's premier publishing house (and the publisher of all of Tournier's novels) allowed him to devote himself full-time to his own writing (Braudeau 84), which has been highly successful with the public. His five novels have all been best-sellers in France, and according to Gallimard, all of them have also been published in English, Spanish, German,

Japanese, Portuguese, Swedish, and Dutch. In all, he has been translated into at least 27 languages, including Arabic, Basque, Bulgarian, Danish, Finnish, Hebrew, Norwegian, Polish, Romanian, Serbo-Croatian, Slovak, and Czech. Since 1968 Tournier has been a highly visible member of the French literary community, although he does not live in Paris but some 20 miles away in the hamlet of Choisel, where in 1957 his family bought a former rectory as a weekend house (Merllié, *Michel Tournier* 232). He has since made it his permanent residence, adapting it to his needs by converting the one-room dormered top floor to a combination bedroom, photographer's studio, and writing room. Although at first he commuted regularly to Paris from this home, he told me when I saw him in 1987 that now he avoids going in to the city except for business and literary activities.

Despite this comparative isolation—which is due at least partly to his commitment to his work—he keeps up with French intellectual trends and is keenly interested in reaching a large audience not only through his writing but through radio, television, and personal appearances. His activities as a member of the Académie Goncourt, to which he was elected in 1972, also keep him involved in literary life in France. Tournier's personal and emotional life seems to have become primarily channeled into his fiction, and he discusses this side of his life in general though candid terms. He has written, presumably about himself, that the "polymorphous perverse in the novelist goes no further than the initial impulse," finding its end in "fabulous [or fabulating] over-compensation" (*Vent* 123); and, more directly, he said in an interview, "the wreckage of my sexuality lets me recreate a world, by means of which I can write novels" (Braudeau 89). Casting an oblique light on this point is his surprising reflection that on the "rather rare" occasions when someone loved him, it was mainly or entirely for "physical reasons," although he thinks that any distinction he has is "in the brains department" (*Vagabond* 59).

Tournier is neither a hermit nor a misanthropist. He has made his home a haven for the neighbors' children, who drop in after school to raid the refrigerator; and after the death of the parents of a young boy he knew, he raised the child himself (Braudeau 87-88). Tournier also makes frequent visits to schools to talk with classes which have read his books. His adult friends include professional photographers, and Tournier himself is a technically accomplished photographer, although he considers that he lacks the talent of a creative photographer and confines his own work largely to portraits of friends and to nudes. He helped to establish and is a frequent participant in the annual Rencontres Photographiques, held in August in the south of France, at Arles.

POLITICAL VIEWS

Compared to other French writers, Tournier seems rather unpolitical, mainly because he does not adhere to any single party line and because he is more interested in general principles than specific programs. He has been unfairly accused of having Fascist tendencies, partly because some readers thought that *Le Roi des aulnes* was inadequately anti-Nazi. Then, too, in *Le Vent paraclet*, Tournier engaged in some debunking of the myth that most French people supported or were in the Resistance, and he protested against the condemnation of French writers who collaborated during World War II, particularly Robert Brasillach, who was executed for collaboration (*Vent* 79-80 and 87-88). Tournier's stated grounds for the latter attitude were that any French writer, even a "mediocre writer and major traitor" like Brasillach (*Vent* 88) is more French than any nonwriter could be. This deliberate provocation of both left and right produced the furor that might be expected. Tournier responded to the protests by saying that he identified *being* French with *writing* French and that the Senegalese president, Léopold Senghor, was in his view more French than most white French citizens because Senghor had passed the *agrégation* in French grammar and was a fine poet (*Vent* 308). Because Tournier attacks racism even as he defends writers whose anti-Semitism during the Occupation led to their condemnation, he has made himself the target of both left-wing and right-wing groups.

Although they resist easy classification, Tournier's politics appear to be mainly liberal, running toward advocating better material conditions for ordinary citizens (Tournier, "Extraits" 11); opposing racism, which he defines as liking or disliking someone on the basis of appearance (Tournier, "Extraits" 13); and trying to puncture the balloons of the complacent. It is entirely in character that he contributed the introductory essay to *François Mitterrand*, which celebrates France's Socialist president, and that he never once mentions Mitterrand in the essay. Tournier's politics in the broadest sense call for a complete change in society. He says that it is because he was raised in a privileged environment that he can be a revolutionary, as opposed to someone who was born poor and who thus can only be a rebel, or a "bad revolutionary" (*Vagabond* 51). What Tournier seems to mean, and what his entire body of work supports, is that he does not accept the social, monetary, and racial inequalities in French society—or in modern Western society in general—and that his attitude is the result of thought, not an emotional reaction to child-hood deprivation. Further, he implies that he is working for change by means of his art, by giving people a new vision of life, rather than through directly political means. He has, however, written political articles on occasion.

The same refusal to accept an established political position is shown in Tournier's claim that one must "think heredity and act environment," which means to understand and excuse people's acts on the grounds of heredity but attempt to influence the future by changing society (Braudeau 89), the first being in his view a right-wing and the second a left-wing attitude (*Vol* 145). Another mixture of left and right shows up in some of his comments on sex: his condemnation of birth control and abortion has a conservative sound until he goes on to condemn what he calls the "bone-heap" of heterosexuality (Hueston 405) and to praise nongenital sexuality (Tournier, "Lewis Carroll" 75).

The result of these positions and of Tournier's refusal to fit into the stereotypes of the literary world—to be either solely a popular or solely an intellectual author—is that he is at once accepted and rejected by the institutions of French society. He is one of the most visible members of the highly influential Académie Goncourt, whose main activity is honoring one "best" novel each year, and he is an *officier* of the Legion of Honor. When he was first made a *chevalier* of the Legion of Honor in 1977, political passions caused a famous episode in which some people waited for him in the street and "decorated" him with tomato juice, apparently (according to Tournier) because they considered that his accepting the red ribbon was a sign that he was becoming a conformist. In response, Tournier claims that he accepts official honors in order to work from within to change society (Poirson 50). Perhaps the tomato juice episode has become mythologized, because Jane Kramer recently wrote that Tournier had been attacked because of the Goncourt jury's 1977 choice (91).

This sort of confusion may reflect the difficulty many have in relating Tournier's writing to his politics—or separating the two, as the case may be. Political attitudes are particularly influential with French critics, as indicated by the fact that although his books sell well and many reviewers take them seriously, there has been surprisingly little scholarly work done on them in France until quite recently; it is in Canada and the United States, where he is much less successful in the market, that critics most appreciate his work. In France, as Roger Shattuck put it, Tournier has been "quietly shut out" at the "higher cultural levels" (206) because his works appeal to a broad audience and do not seem adequately avant-garde, and because his politics are not easily understood. One sign that this situation may be changing, however, is that in August 1990 the *colloques* held annually at Cerisy-la-Salle, literary discussions tending to focus on avant-garde writers, included a week of discussion on images and signs in Tournier's works.

CHRISTIANITY AND SEXUALITY

Tournier's situation in regard to religion is as complex as is his political position. He claims to be a Christian and always to have wanted to be a Christian writer (Montrémy), but he does not accept either Catholicism or any other organized form of religion. His main complaint in his "love-hate relationship with religion" (*Vagabond* 33) is with what he believes to be Catholicism's insistence on pain and suffering and concomitant refusal to accept the joys of the flesh, especially sexual joys. Tournier's insistence that the Transfiguration is more important than the Crucifixion stems from his belief that Christ rehabilitated the flesh (*Vagabond* 109; see also the interview in Chapter 8 below). He also criticizes the Church because it does not promote a revolutionary attitude and attack bourgeois society (Hueston 404).

Tournier has devoted much time to studying Christianity, and he says that he considers the Gospels the most important books ever written. He has made much use, he says, of the 20-volume Bible with commentary which once belonged to his great-uncle, a priest (Desarzens), and many of his prose meditations are on biblical events. Nevertheless, Tournier's relations with Christianity remain strained, as he searches for a way to reconcile his own feelings and attitudes with what is generally considered Christian.

One particularly thorny issue in this context is sexuality. Tournier is completely opposed to the idea that sex should be engaged in uniquely for the purpose of offspring; in fact, he would entirely divorce sexuality from procreation if he could do so. He considers eroticism "innocent" if conception is not possible, as in the case of homosexual relations ("Michel Tournier" 14), and he claims that eroticism does not hurt anybody, not even children (Escoffier-Lambiotte). But his conception of sexuality is an extremely broad one, not in the least limited to conventional sexuality—in fact, he says that if the sign of a perversion is a need to repeat certain acts according to a fixed formula, then "normal" sexual relations are simply "everyone's perversion" (*Vent* 121).

His promotion of "genial" ("Lewis Carroll" 75) or "general" (Poirson 49) sexuality, rather than "genital" sexuality, is closely related to his condemnation of what he sees as society's refusal to provide children with enough physical contact. He claims that once children are considered too old to sleep with their parents, they are denied all human physical contact until they are teenagers (Poirson 48-49). Thus they are fitted into a mold which makes the majority of them believe that they are heterosexuals, whereas left to their own devices they would find many different kinds of sensual expression, homosexual and heterosexual, genital and nongenital. A logical correlative of this view is his attraction to the androgynous figure. This attitude is shown, for example, in his celebrating the "incomparable beauty of the girl-boy and the boy-girl" (*Vagabond* 45). Similarly, man-as-mother has a great appeal to Tournier, shown in his placing Philippe de Monès's essay "Abel Tiffauges et la vocation maternelle de l'homme" in postface to the "Folio" reprint of *Le Roi des aulnes.*

Tournier's opening his house to the neighbor children and his having raised one child himself reflect his own maternal, nourishing tendencies. They are literally nourishing, for he enjoys feeding children, but he goes further than that. In one brief sketch, he fantasizes about a truck he saw in India which carried rice mush from village to village to feed children: "I dreamed . . . of being the tank truck itself and, like a huge sow with a hundred flowing teats, giving my belly to feed the starving little Indians" (*Clefs* 36). Elsewhere, he explains that the action of his short story "La Mère Noël" "reflects the frustration of the *pater nutritor* who cannot become *almus pater*. Fellatio can't compensate for this weakness despite the obvious affinity between sperm and milk" (*Vagabond* 79). He is apparently charmed to learn of tribes where men nurse the babies, having eaten the placenta in order to do so (*Vagabond* 61).

The sex act is thus linked for him with deep emotional needs and is necessarily secondary to mutual trust and accommodation: "To live as a couple it's more important to sleep well together than to be good at sleeping together" (*Vagabond* 29). Traveling in Canada, he meditates on the fact that continence is provoking in him not sexual climax but "floods of tenderness toward a certain face or body" of an unknown seen in a crowd (*Canada* 50). Sublimation turns up elsewhere, too; for example, he is keenly aware of the relationship between taking someone's picture and "taking" that person sexually (*Clefs*

131), just as he is of sexual overtones in contacts with food, animals, and other physical objects (Poirson 49).

The Novel and the Message

Tournier's condemnation of heterosexual society, his desire to see people adopt less rigid sexual roles, and his interest in nongenital sexuality all find expression in one way or another in his fiction, although without the bald statements Tournier uses in essays and interviews. He knows that a piece of fiction is gravely harmed if it is too obviously didactic: "A novel can certainly have a thesis, but it is important that the reader, not the writer, put it there" (*Vol* 14). Still, this statement, like similar comments in the interview included in this book, is a bit misleading; Tournier freely claims that he writes because he has something to say, but he recognizes that fiction must be somewhat ambiguous if it is to succeed in moving an audience. Tournier can be candid about his desire to teach, saying in an interview, "My only literary problem is pedagogical, how to make clear and pleasant the subtle and difficult things I have to say" (Rambures 165) and "I want to be an edifying writer!" (Ezine, "Michel Tournier" 224). But because he knows that readers of novels are not looking for sermons or theses, he strives to subordinate his ideas to the demands of fiction. He also realizes, even welcomes, the fact that his readers may find meanings in his novels that he did not know he was putting there but which are indiscutably present.

Tournier is clearly excited by the ability of fiction to influence people, and he chose the novel as his major literary form because it would give him the widest possible audience (Piatier, "Entretien"). He calls fiction an art which can influence the future by changing how people see themselves (*Vol* 13). This is true largely, he believes, of the sort of literature which enters the general human consciousness as myth and which thus lets us see ourselves as Tristan or Isolde, Don Juan or Romeo, so that our acts may seem justified. It follows that Tournier believes myths to be antisocial; they do not seek to promote people's integration into society but arm them against society's demands (*Vol* 31-32). The novelist's power is great, for he or she can renew old myths or change their interpretation and thus reshape society, but only as long as the myth remains alive; that is, only if its meaning is kept from becoming fixed as an allegory's meaning is (*Vol* 390).

NEW WINE IN OLD BOTTLES

The other side of the coin to Tournier's concern with communicating ideas through his fiction is his seeming lack of interest in experimenting with form. In this regard, he has compared himself to Richard Strauss, who was not a musical innovator but whose work was easily accepted, in contrast with Strauss's contemporary Schoenberg, an innovator whose work has had difficulty finding an audience (Ezine, "Michel Tournier" 225). Like Strauss, Tournier wants to reach a broad audience, not alienate it by writing in the fashion of the "new novelists" and "new new novelists," who may eliminate plot, character, and setting, to say nothing of capitalization or punctuation, in their effort to stretch the definition of the novel. In contrast, Tournier says that when he started to write fiction he took as models such Realist and Naturalist authors as Zola, Jules Renard, and Colette, who record "the smell of people and things" (Ezine, "Michel Tournier" 225). Tournier's language is also conservative—grammatically correct, clear, and proper. In the fiction, slang appears only in dialogue, and then seldom. No matter how shocked some readers may be by what a character does or thinks, they will never find explicitly described sex and almost never an obscenity. This reticence, too, is part of the Realist-Naturalist tradition into which Tournier fits himself.

For all his interest in the physical world and desire to represent that world in his fiction, though, Tournier is not truly the Naturalist or Realist he often claims to be. His fiction may have affinities with those schools, but one can tell that the ideas are more important than the plot or the characters. Tournier has essentially said the same thing when he has explained that he began writing fiction as another way to practice philosophy (Rambures 165) or when he described his fiction as "storytelling with as conventional an appearance as possible, covering a hidden metaphysical underpinning which is invisible but which exercises an active influence" (*Clefs* 193).

In the fiction I have discussed so far, I have shown that hidden structures are the true mainsprings of Tournier's plots and the key to his meanings. The fact that this use of hidden structures reflects Tournier's view of the world is indicated not only by the references in the novels to codes, not only by the secret, underlying structures he builds those novels on, but also by his dwelling in his essays on the idea of breaking a code or looking for a key to a cipher. Speaking of codes and ciphers comes almost automatically to Tournier; to take just two examples, he says that Ernst Jünger used a painting by the *douanier* Rousseau as a deciphering grid (*Vol* 392) and that the painter Enrique Marin's use of grillwork implies a decoding grid and suggests that for Marin "the image is only a secret language" (*Tabor* 124). A related, though less pervasive, image is that of locks and keys; for Tournier, "the whole world is only a pile of keys and a collection of locks" (*Clefs* 8), including the people in it.

Tournier seems to think of the world as a complex cryptogram or lock and of works of fiction as simpler coded messages or puzzles because any fiction proceeds from a single sensibility which has organized the material so that it relates to a central idea or attitude. It is this inner coherence that Tournier is undoubtedly alluding to when he says that a novelist should "*create* through his power a world different from the external one, having just enough resemblance to the external world to . . . force it to resemble the fiction" (*Canada* 31, emphasis in original). One must note that it is difference from the world, rather than resemblance to it, that he stresses, despite his professed admiration for such writers as Colette and Zola; in what he thinks of as the key respects, Tournier does not want his art to imitate life, even though it has a surface resemblance to reality, but to change life. As a student, Tournier was fascinated by the fact that philosophy created systems that were more coherent than the real world—and therefore, to his mind, superior to it (*Vent* 159), and he still feels that coherence guarantees that something is real (Poirson 50).

As I have shown in previous chapters, Tournier provides coherence in his novels through meticulous plot constructions which bring out the underlying ideas; as he says, he constructs rather than writes his books, so that "the most nauseating or violent passages in my novels are always strictly deduced from the rest" (Ezine, "Michel Tournier" 227). Each novel's plot derives from at least one rational structure of some kind, and it also tends toward symmetry. *Vendredi ou les limbes du Pacifique* and *Le Roi des aulnes*, as Tournier says, are "made up of two different parts separated in the middle by a crisis" (Rambures 166). *Les Météores* is constructed around a more complex pattern, but it is clearly constructed and did not just grow, as might be true of a purely Realistic novel.

Tournier's attitude toward decoding not only sheds light on his plot structures but also helps explain one of his philosophical theories. This theory, which he first developed in his early article in *Espace* and which serves as a foundation for *Vendredi*, holds that the world is full of contradictions; to resolve them, the world creates conscious beings whose perception of the world eliminates contradictions, apparently because they do not or cannot see them. (Tournier's fuller explanation of this theory is in the interview in Chapter 8 below.) On the literal level, this idea seems to make no sense, for it claims that people are the result of the world's desire to rid itself of contradiction. But if one takes this theory symbolically, it does make sense. According to this reading, although the world is full of contradictions, each person has a coherent way of seeing the world, one that leaves out many things which then cease to be true for that person. We see and we acknowledge only what fits our world view, unlock only what our keys will open. As a novelist, Tournier wants to give us different keys so that we will unlock more doors.

THE USE OF HUMOR

To change how we see the world, Tournier wants his novels, like a jackhammer, to "make a hole in reality to reveal what is hidden below" (Rambures 165). The resulting effect is what he calls "white humor," which is both "comic" and "cosmic." White laughter comes when one "has just glimpsed the nothingness between the loosened stitches of things" and realizes that "nothing matters" (*Vent* 199). It is different from what he calls "pink humor," which is caused by ordinary social events, and black humor, which has a morbid edge. He calls white humor "God's laugh" because it comes when we see through the surface we believe in to the nothingness it hides (*Vent* 198). This is why he says that a "good" reader of *Vendredi* "should be (at least from time to time) shaken with laughter" (Gorin). He sees white laughter as both subversive and celebratory. It is subversive because it undermines our usual view of life, but at the same time it celebrates the hidden nature of the world (*Vent* 204).

Tournier creates white humor in part by insisting on trivial details to the point that reality itself becomes hallucinatory, a technique he compares to that of Surrealist painters such as Magritte and Dali, in contrast to Surrealist writers, in whom he finds no humor (*Canada* 58). He points out that he has used this technique of representing reality in such great detail that it becomes unreal in the complex lore and nomenclature of hunting in *Le Roi des aulnes* and the "science" of garbage in *Les Météores* (Poirson 47).

The humor Tournier favors is often a sort of intellectual clowning. As a child, Tournier played over and over a record of a monologue by the famous Swiss clown Grock (*Vent* 34-38), whose specialty was to play the "red clown," the butt of all jokes and inevitable victim of disaster. Traditionally, the red clown has for his foil the "white clown," an elegant figure who is the instigator of humor. According to Tournier, the red clown's art consists in a "servitude" which is both "positive" and "negative"; he must use every technique at his disposal, but he cannot avoid being ugly or ridiculous (*Vent* 36). Tournier takes this contrast between the red and the white clowns to symbolize not only two different kinds of humor but two different attitudes to life, the one consisting of drawing attention to oneself through self-accusation or pride (often the two sides of a single coin), the other based on staying uninvolved and becoming a "sarcastic witness" of one's time (*Clefs* 75). Tournier obviously prefers the red clown, and the rebellious boy who was class clown in elementary school (*Vent* 38) can be seen in the major fictional characters, who play the red clown by narrating their own stories, displaying their weaknesses and shames, and suffering disasters and misfortunes. This is true for Robinson, Tiffauges, Alexandre, and Paul in the early novels, and it is almost as true of Taor and Idriss in the later fiction, for although they are not narrators, they have no hesitation exposing themselves to the mockery of others.

There is something of the red clown, too, in Tournier's rather strange conception of the relationship between himself and his novels: "As the servant of my novel, I think of myself also as its waste matter. I feel that the novel goes along on its own, and I'm the result of its 'going'" (Ezine, "Michel Tournier" 226)—a scatological self-image that helps account for his having at one point considered taking as a pen name his maternal grandmother's maiden name of Anus (Merllié, *Michel Tournier* 217). Tournier is like Grock: hidden behind the words on the page as Grock was hidden in makeup and costume, Tournier is at once implicated in his characters' stupidities, mistakes, and buffooneries, and above them as their creator.

FICTION AND REAL LIFE

Despite the psychological relationship with his main characters I have just touched on, the large part assigned to ideas in Tournier's fiction allows him to write novels which are not directly based on the external facts of his own life. In fact, he usually creates a gulf between himself and his characters to prevent readers from identifying him with any of them, situating them in a different time period from his own and giving them different physical, educational, and social qualities from his. And he has never written a novel about an artist of any sort. This strategy has been successful except for Alexandre in *Les Météores*, whose antisocial vigor brought him startlingly to life for many readers and caused them to take him for Tournier's spokesman. So many readers have done this that Tournier has varied between saying that he is "a mixture of Alexandre, Abel Tiffauges, and many other characters" (Bougnoux and Clavel 16) and "I'm not any of the characters in my novels" (Ezine, "Michel Tournier" 224). Both statements are true: the major characters are not Tournier, but they are all necessarily created out of some part of his personality, as shown in part by the fact that he tends to begin writing by imagining himself in his characters' situations (Ezine, "Michel Tournier" 224). As Tournier says, a novelist has to use his or her personal life as the source of fiction (*Vol* 302) and "the writer makes the crowd admire what is most intense, most intimate, and perhaps most shameful in his or her own life" (*Vol* 164).

Tournier's resistance to writing literally autobiographical fiction relates to his preference for the *conte*. In "Barbe-Bleue ou le secret du conte," he compares the *conte,* or tale—such as a fairy tale or a legend—to a "translucent medium" in which a message or moral cannot be clearly seen but only glimpsed (*Vol* 37). Tournier contrasts the *conte* with the *fable,* such as the fables of La Fontaine, which have clearly stated morals, and also with the *nouvelle.* The word *nouvelle* can mean a rather long short story or novella, but it can also mean a news item, and so a *nouvelle,* by implication, is based on real life. For Tournier, *fables* have a "crystalline transparency" and *nouvelles* a "brutal opacity," both of which remove almost all interest in the story, whereas the "translucency" of the *conte* "touches and enriches us, without enlightening us" (*Vol* 37).

These comments will be useful in the next chapter, when I will consider Tournier's short fiction, but they also help in understanding his novels, which he has called "an interweaving of tales" (Brochier, "Dix-huit" 12). In fact, that description of the novels becomes more and more true, for each succeeding novel seems more easily to break up into nearly self-contained sections, and Tournier actually published separately certain chapters of *Gaspard, Melchior et Balthazar* and *La Goutte d'or.* Not only do the novels have parts which can be free-standing, but their plots as a whole have the constructed quality of a tale rather than the sprawling one of current events, and the characters are carefully conceived to play off against each other. Tournier thus avoids the "opacity" of a newspaper story. Occasionally, however, in his short fiction he errs in the other direction and provides readers with some toned-down version of a fable's moral, creating a "crystalline clarity" which threatens to undermine the reader's ability to be a "co-creator" in the fiction.

TOURNIER AS CRITIC

Generally, novelists make poor literary critics and critics make poor novelists, for the novelist must have a view of the world which he or she holds strongly and clearly enough to make it come to life for readers, but a critic, on the other hand, must be flexible enough to accept the world view which the writer is presenting and to see it clearly before analyzing and evaluating it. Tournier insists, however, that the reader must do at least half the work of making a book come to life. There is much to be said for this view, for certainly no two readers will find just the same meaning in any novel, at least not if the novel has the necessary texture and ambiguity to be interesting. Furthermore, twentieth-century literary theory, especially in France, has tended to emphasize the reader's role in fiction under the guidance of such theorists as Sartre, Maurice Blanchot, and Roland Barthes.

So, when Tournier has written prefaces, mostly for reprints of novels, adding to the "multiple molehills raised here and there by literary critics" (*Vol* 52), it is not surprising that he has reserved his warmest comments for novels in which he finds both minute realism and a metaphysical system, as he does in Pearl Buck's *The Mother* (*Vol* 252-60) and Günther Grass's *The Tin Drum* (*Vol* 320-28), or in books where good-natured humor plays a major role, such as in *La Vie devant soi* by Romain Gary writing as Emile Ajar (*Vol* 329-44) or *Un Garçon en l'air* by Didier Martin (*Vol* 373-76). Realism combined with metaphysical systems and humor are qualities Tournier strives for in his own fiction and values in that of others.

Another quality that attracts his interest and admiration has more to do with the author than the book. It is salvation through writing, as in the case of Alphonse Boudard, a convict who by writing of his prison and hospital experiences saved himself from prison and hospital (*Vol* 319). But Tournier sees salvation through writing also in the lives of Herman Hesse (*Vol* 272), Thomas Mann (*Vol* 284), and, above all, André Gide (*Vol* 229). He argues that each was able to escape from an oppressive, puritanical, middle-class society mainly through writing. In Gide's case, which he considers in the greatest detail, Tournier is clearly fascinated with what he believes to be Gide's ability to remake himself through personal effort.

In fact, somewhat surprisingly, Tournier as critic is often less interested in interpreting a book than simply explaining something of the circumstances of its creation or the life of its author. The most interesting and revealing of the essays in which he does that is a preface to a collection of several of Sartre's major works, which he said was difficult for him to write because it felt as if he were writing about himself (Brochier, "Qu'est-ce que" 85). In that essay, "Jean-Paul Sartre, romancier cryptométaphysicien," he offers the theory that although Sartre was the most influential thinker of the twentieth century, he could never be a great writer because he was not an innovator in his use of language (*Vol* 303) and because he was too much a member of established society to have the "marginality" necessary to use his own life as a source of fiction as did Proust, Gide, and Céline (*Vol* 309). If we apply those same rules to Tournier—and he seems to invite us to do so—we must say that he, too, is no innovator in language, but that his marginality (unhappy childhood, failure at the *agrégation*, perceived failures in human relations) has given him a distance from which to criticize society and a personal capital on which to draw.

INITIATION, NOT EDUCATION

As I have shown, Tournier believes that literature should not simply reflect its time but show society how to change—not to predict but to help create the future, to give people models to emulate. As a novelist, he wants to help to shape that future, so it seems reasonable that he should take children as one of his major audiences, not merely because he likes children but because they are malleable. One of his complaints against children's education is that it provides children with information but does not initiate them—that is, it does not stimulate their feelings and imaginations and make them feel a part of the world, as he believes religious and classical education did before the French Revolution ("Point de vue").

In all his fiction, as I have said, Tournier seeks to shape his readers' perceptions of the world, to break through the "real" we see around us to a deeper truth, a nothingness which makes us pose metaphysical questions and makes us laugh with a "white laugh." But especially in his fiction for young people, he creates models of one sort or another to awaken feelings and to show how to live. In doing so, he says that he wants to avoid both the negative attitudes of the Ancien Régime, which saw the child as a monster of depravity, and the sentimentality of the nineteenth century, which he identifies especially with Victor Hugo and which made the child into an innocent angel. Tournier believes that children are simply people, but people who need to be initiated into society, not separated from it because they are either too wicked or too pure to live in it. By initiation he does not mean that they should be brainwashed into accepting everything in society—far from it—but that they should be made to feel themselves a part of a community, loved and appreciated, awakened in their feelings and judgments.

A more biographical approach is to say that Tournier's fiction can be thought of as a long, encoded letter written to comfort and reassure the unhappy child he once was, much as Abel Tiffauges seeks to find and comfort his younger self through the boys in the *Napola*. This view is implied in the way Tournier opens *Le Vent paraclet*. He tells an anecdote about his grandfather as a child which ends with the image he proposes as frontispiece for his book, a "crying child hidden by the book which he is carrying" (*Vent* 11). There is self-mockery here, a little clowning, and an emotional truth which it hides; the unhappy little boy who was Michel Tournier may be hidden in or by his books, but we are aware of his tears.

One must feel, though, that this unhappy child, the unruly adolescent, and the rebellious and proud young man have become both more radical and more relaxed with time as they developed into the mature adult. As Tournier puts it, after he "tossed overboard family and ideology" and lost his "fear of solitude, independence, and the risks caused by creation" (*Vagabond* 41), he discovered, perhaps to his surprise, that his works became less and less aggressive (Ezine, "Michel Tournier" 224). This happened undoubtedly because by freeing himself from the fears and constraints that were suffocating him, he also freed himself from the pain they caused. In *Vendredi* he tried to remake virtually everything in Western society; *Le Roi des aulnes* concluded in apocalypse; by *Les Météores*, despite the provocativeness of some of the sections, he looked for a way in which one could live, however marginally, in France in the 1950s.

Wisdom is a key word for Tournier. He believes that, with time, people can become wise, but that acquiring wisdom depends on keeping a child's ability to learn and change (*Vent* 290). True wisdom, which is revolutionary, involves both creation and its necessary condition—at least for a writer—of solitude (*Vent* 293). One must also learn to appreciate the beauty of the world and of other people (*Vent* 297-98). With the passage of time, he has learned that happiness comes from "devoting oneself without reserve to someone or something" ("Extraits" 13). The something to which he has devoted himself is his writing, by means of which he devotes himself to his readers.

This commitment, along with Tournier's typical self-mocking humor, is shown in the last passage of *Des clefs et des serrures* (also the last piece in *Petites proses*), where Tournier writes his obituary. He imagines whimsically that his tomb will be in his own garden, surmounted by a recumbent carved likeness of himself, "face masked by an open book" and carried by statues representing six schoolboys (193). This is the red clown mocking himself, but with good humor. And he does more than accept life; he celebrates it in the epitaph he proposes for himself at the end of the obituary: "I loved you, you repaid me a hundredfold. Thank you, life!" (195).

5

The Short Fiction

Tournier's short fiction is worth studying both in itself and as a key to understanding the difference between his three novels published by 1975— *Vendredi ou les limbes du Pacifique, Le Roi des aulnes,* and *Les Météores*—and his two subsequent ones, *Gaspard, Melchior et Balthazar* (1980) and *La Goutte d'or* (1985). The first three use complex language and aim at a highly literate audience; the last two employ a much simpler style and are readily accessible to the average reader. The first three include sections which have shocked readers; the last two are more good-humored and comparatively nonprovocative. The first three have plots which, though simple in outline, bristle with interesting but often tangential incidents; the plots of the last two are much more straightforwardly developed.

These changes seem to have resulted, at least in part, from Tournier's concentration in the late 1970s on short fiction aimed mainly at a juvenile audience, for whom clarity and brevity are essential. If that were the only reason to consider his short fiction, it would be enough. But the fiction is worthwhile in itself; Tournier puts the same care and energy into his writing for children that he does into his novels. This dedication to a young audience is, paradoxically, the reason that he does not like to have his work divided into "adult" and "juvenile" fiction, for those categories seem to imply that children's literature is lesser than adult literature. But Tournier claims that the opposite is true. He says that when his writing is at its very best, it is so clear that it can be understood by adults and children alike; when it is not so well written, only adults can read it ("Writing" 33-34; Bouloumié, "Tournier" 21). He also regrets the modern idea that fiction read by children should not treat sexuality, money, or power, saying that in the "great tales" those are the main themes (Joxe 53), and he does include those subjects in his short fiction, though more indirectly than in the novels. As a result, his children's fiction is unconventional by today's standards. It is, however, in the tradition of the authors whose children's fiction he admires, including Charles Perrault, Rudyard Kipling, and Selma Lagerlöff (Bouloumié, "Tournier" 21), who also treat elemental themes.

Children now compose Tournier's major French audience, partly because his fiction is taught in many schools in France and other French-speaking countries, and he cultivates this audience by visiting school classes and corresponding with classes by tape cassette (Tournier, "Writer" 180). He often has said that, if he had become a teacher as he originally planned, he would have wanted to teach philosophy not when the curriculum calls for it, in the last year of the *lycée*, but to eleven-year-olds, a desire reflected in the fact that his books read by children of that age are "disguised philosophical treatises" (Joxe 51). Interestingly, just as his "juvenile" fiction is read in elementary schools, his "adult" fiction seems to be used regularly in *lycée* classes. The novelist Patrick Grainville, for example, has written of teaching *Vendredi, Le Roi des aulnes*, and *Les Météores* in the last year of the *lycée*.

In keeping with his goal of using fiction to teach philosophy, Tournier tries through his juvenile fiction to reach the most malleable of audiences. His belief that children are deeply influenced by the fiction they read derives from his study of anthropology, which has made him keenly aware of the initiatory function of the myths and legends which children learn in many societies; he is certain that "myth is childish at its base, metaphysical at its summit" (Brochier, "Dix-huit" 11). He wants, however, through his fiction to initiate children into society not as it is but as he thinks it should be. As Joseph McMahon says, Tournier's children's fiction does show more overt "commitment" to the values of society than do his adult works ("Michel Tournier's Texts" 166), but Tournier wants not merely to help children integrate themselves into society but also to make them question some aspects of it. This is not an abstract idea; Tournier writes for children because he likes them, and he wants his fiction to be useful to them in their struggles to understand themselves and the world.

REWRITING *VENDREDI*

Tournier's first piece of fiction accessible to children, *Vendredi ou la vie sauvage* ("Friday, or Primitive Life"), was a revision of his first published novel, *Vendredi ou les limbes du Pacifique*. He says that he rewrote the book because the original version was too intellectual and not rooted firmly in physical life. Despite the success of *Vendredi ou les limbes du Pacifique* and *Le Roi des aulnes*, Tournier had a difficult time finding a publisher for this new book ("Writing" 33), but it was ultimately brought out in 1971 by his regular publishing house, Gallimard, which has since published it in a variety of formats. In the United States, Knopf put it out as *Friday and Robinson: Life on Speranza Island*.

The book was not successful in the United States despite favorable reviews (Heins, Showers), but *Vendredi ou la vie sauvage* has enjoyed enormous popularity in France. Not only is it read in class by many schoolchildren, but since 1983 it has been available in a package including two cassette tapes on which Tournier reads the text—apparently the first in Gallimard's series of book-cassette packages for children. The story's popularity with young people can also be gauged by the fact that in 1973 it was made by Antoine Vitez into a stage play (Dumur) and in 1982 it was produced in a six-hour version for French television, starring Michael York, which was the basis for a special edition of the book illustrated by photographs from the show. *Vendredi ou la vie sauvage* was also the first braille book published by the French Institut National des Jeunes Aveugles, and on Christmas Eve 1982 Tournier distributed the first copies to 130 students at the Institut (Tournier, "Préface" 11).

Although the rewritten *Vendredi* is less than half the length of the original novel, almost none of the events of the original have been removed, the notable exception being Robinson's and Vendredi's sexual relations with the island. What have been omitted are all but one of Robinson's logbook entries, Robinson's philosophical speculation, and many of the religious references. Use of a somewhat intrusive omniscient narrator reduces ambiguity but enhances clarity, and leaving out most of the philosophical reflections in the original makes the story more action-centered. A few incidents which do not appear in the long version, such as Vendredi's teaching Araucanian sign language to Robinson, should appeal to children, especially as Tournier made them up while telling the original story to children (Tournier, "Les Enfants" 56). And here and there Tournier has softened the original. For example, in both versions, Robinson first sees Vendredi when the latter is running away from Indians trying to kill him, and in both versions Vendredi escapes because Robinson kills one of his pursuers. But whereas in the long version Robinson is actually trying to shoot Vendredi, in the "Junior" version he is aiming at one of the pursuers.

The clarity of the rewritten book has been admired by Michael J. Worton

("Ecrire" and "Michel Tournier") and Jean-Michel Maulpoix ("Des Limbes" 37), but I miss the ambiguity of the original. The narrator sometimes sounds like a teacher, as when he explains that when Robinson decided not to eat any of the wheat from his first harvest he "followed a new tendency, *avarice*, which was going to do him a great deal of harm" (34), and he sounds like a parent when he explains that although Vendredi chewed maggots before feeding them to a sick vulture, meat or hard-boiled egg will do very well instead (76). Oddly, the revision is less amusing than the original, whose humor depends largely on the incongruity between Robinson's actions and his surroundings and on a deadpan style of narration.

The story's themes remain unchanged. The revision, like the original, implies that Western civilization needs to be saved by "primitive" responses to the world, just as Robinson needs to be saved by Vendredi from pointless activity. The theme of return to the womb is developed clearly, with the grotto described as "so soft, so warm, so white that [Robinson] couldn't help thinking of his mother" (55). The book's action also still retraces the story of the Bible, with Robinson associated with the Old Testament, Vendredi with the New, and the *Whitebird* with the Holy Spirit. The ram Andoar's role as both scapegoat and Christ is stressed when Vendredi says that Andoar "died saving me" (125). And as in the original book, after Vendredi leaves on the *Whitebird*, Robinson finds a millennial happiness on the island with the ship's cabin boy, who is at once an avatar of the Holy Spirit and a playmate to whom he can teach the games which Vendredi has taught him. However, although Tournier claims that the longer book is just a "rough draft" for the shorter version (Joxe 53), the latter has not generally been admired by critics (Worton, "Michel Tournier" 24). It is, in fact, much weaker than the longer book—a not entirely successful attempt at producing the clarity and simplicity he was striving for.

TOURNIER'S SHORT STORIES: AN OVERVIEW

I find Tournier's short stories more appealing than *Vendredi ou la vie sauvage* because they are less explicit. His first collection, published in 1978, *Le Coq de bruyère* (translated into English as *The Fetishist*, 1983), includes thirteen stories and a one-act play. Several of those stories have been published individually in illustrated editions for children, including "Amandine ou les deux jardins," "La Fugue du petit Poucet," "Que ma joie demeure," and "L'Aire du Muguet." (Another of the stories, "Le Nain rouge," was published separately as an illustrated piece of mild erotica.) The stories which appeal most to children, "Amandine ou les deux jardins," "La Fugue du petit Poucet," "La Fin de Robinson Crusoé," "La Mère Noël," and "Que ma joie demeure," were reprinted in 1984 in *Sept contes* ("Seven Tales") in Gallimard's "junior" series along with two other stories by Tournier, *Pierrot ou les secrets de la nuit* and *Barbedor*, both of which have also appeared individually as illustrated children's books. Like *Vendredi ou la vie sauvage*, *Sept contes* is available in book-cassette combination, with Tournier reading the stories, and "La Fugue du petit Poucet" is read by Raymond Gérome on a cassette which includes another children's story by Daniel Boulanger. In all of these short fictions, it is even more obvious than in the novels that Tournier is not inspired by real events; these are true *contes*, tales which begin from ideas, rather than *nouvelles*, or stories inspired by true events. The stories are rigorously constructed, with characterization subordinated everywhere to plot, and plot subordinated to theme, earning Salim Jay's praise of Tournier as a prince of tale-tellers ("Plumes" 145).

Because of their thematic connection, I will discuss together the thirteen stories and one play in *Le Coq de bruyère*. The most obvious structural device is length: each story is, roughly speaking, longer than the previous one, an increase in length which signals a gradual increase in complexity and sophistication. There is also chronological progression, for the first stories are set in the distant past and the later ones are clearly fixed in contemporary times. But there is a more important thematic unifying device, suggested by the number of the pieces, fourteen, and the stories' focus on moral choices. It seems clear that the first seven stories—the stories which children can most appreciate—each illustrate one of the seven cardinal virtues, and the next six stories and the play each illustrate one of the seven deadly sins. Taken as a whole, the book makes a comment on morality in our time.

LE COQ DE BRUYERE: THE VIRTUES

The seven cardinal virtues are generally considered to be composed of the three "theological virtues" of faith, hope, and charity, listed by Paul in the First Epistle to the Corinthians (13.13), and the four "moral virtues" of prudence, justice, temperance, and fortitude. The classification of the moral virtues results from the synthesis of ancient Greek ideas and Christian doctrine by the Scholastics, particularly Thomas Aquinas.

Faith, the "substance of things hoped for, the evidence of things not seen" (Heb. 11.1), is illustrated in the first story, "La Famille Adam," which narrates the Creation up to Cain's murder of Abel and—an event added by Tournier—Cain's eventual reconciliation with God. Many of the events are whimsical, including the account of an Adam with both male and female genitals, whom Jehovah splits into male and female halves so he will produce children. This concept owes less to the biblical account of Eve's creation from Adam's rib than to a playful theory which Plato puts into the mouth of Aristophanes in *The Symposium*. (Although Plato presumably subscribed to the theory which Socrates develops later in *The Symposium*, in which physical love is less important than mental love, Aristophanes' robustly physical view of sex has had great appeal to many people, obviously including Tournier.) According to the idea ascribed to Aristophanes, man originally existed in three forms—all male, all female, and androgynous—but Zeus cut man apart to reduce his strength. Ever since, people have been trying through sexual relations—whether homophile, lesbian, or heterosexual—to rediscover their original wholeness (Plato, *Symposium* 30-32). In Tournier's story Jehovah is jealous of Cain's ability to cultivate fields and build houses and so to create his own "Eden II" (16). But even when God drives Cain away in punishment for the murder of Abel, Cain illustrates faith by believing Jehovah will return. And He finally does, tired of wandering around in the smelly Ark of the Covenant with the nomads.

Hope, which relies "on the readiness of [God's] almighty power to come to our assistance" (Ramirez Dulanto 140), is shown in its negative side, despair, in "La Fin de Robinson Crusoé," a tale of lost paradise. Crusoe returns to England but is unable to forget his island. He finally goes searching for it, in vain, realizing only at the story's end that he has seen it without recognizing it, for it has changed just as he has (24). Hope must look toward the future; Crusoe despairs because he wants, impossibly, to recover the past.

Although charity is traditionally listed third in the theological virtues, it is considered the most important, for, as Paul says, "though I have all faith, so that I could remove mountains, and have not charity, I am nothing" (1 Cor. 13.2). Charity means loving both God and neighbor; and reconciling the love of God with the love of man is the main theme of "La Mère Noël" ("Mother Christmas"). The Breton town of Pouldreuzic is divided between the devout Christians, who attend mass on Christmas Eve, and those in the anticlerical group, who support the schoolteacher's dressing up as Father Christmas, or Santa Claus, and giving toys to the children on Christmas Eve. A new teacher seems to belong to both camps, for although she is divorced, she attends mass, and when Christmas comes, she continues the tradition of dressing as Santa Claus but lends her baby to represent Jesus in the church's "living crèche" (30). The climax shows that one can combine love of God with love of man: when the baby cannot be quieted at the mass, its mother, still dressed as Father Christmas, strides into church and, pushing aside her long white beard, nurses her child.

This vision of a man-woman nursing a baby is central to Tournier's thinking, what he calls a "fundamental fantasy" about man's nourishing function (Coulaud), and he says that she is the character in all his work to whom he feels closest (Braudeau 87). He even posed as "Mother Christmas" for a drawing on a band going around the cover of *Le Coq de bruyère* (Braudeau 88). Adam's androgynous original condition (according to "La Famille Adam") seems to be recovered, for if Father Christmas turns out to be *Mother* Christmas, then sexual division is not absolute. The tale also implies that one can serve both God and man, for the teacher gives presents to the children and also supports the church's crèche, just as in nursing her own baby she is also, symbolically, serving the Christ Child, whom her baby represents. The appeal of this story is suggested by the fact that it has been offered as a model text for class use (Kirpalani).

The next four stories, illustrating the four moral virtues, are less innocent and less childlike, although they too can be read and understood by children. "Amandine ou les deux jardins" illustrates prudence, the "perfected ability to make right decisions" (Pieper 6), the virtue by means of which knowledge is brought "to bear on an individual course of action" (Gilby 927). Amandine is a ten-year-old girl, and the two gardens of the title are the too-well-tended one of her parents and another, secret one behind the wall of her parents' garden. As Tournier has explained in an interview reprinted in *Le Coq de bruyère*, the story is about initiation into the secret, sexual adult world symbolized by the hidden garden (337). This story also touches on androgyny by contrasting the rigid sexual separation in Amandine's parents' house with the sexual ambiguity of nature. This ambiguity is presented humorously at first, when Amandine cannot tell whether her cat is male or female because it is named Claude, but it emerges more seriously at the end when Amandine's expression is compared to that on a statue of the male god Eros (46). Amandine's passage to adulthood is symbolized, rather too obviously, by the onset of her first menstrual period at the end of the story, and less obviously by her realizing that Claude's kitten is pregnant. At the end, the reader sees that

Amandine is prepared to be prudent, in the theological sense—she can bring knowledge to bear on her actions.

The second moral virtue, justice, "the strong and firm will to give to each his due," is also "the mediator in the personal order of love" (Häring 69). Justice should, therefore, be subordinated to love. "La Fugue du petit Poucet" ("Little Poucet's Flight") contrasts repressive justice with forgiving love. The story is a whimsical variation on Perrault's "Le Petit Poucet," generally translated as "Tom Thumb," which is about a woodcutter's boy who tricks an ogre into killing his own seven daughters and steals the ogre's seven-league boots. Perrault's details are all updated by Tournier—the woodcutter in "La Fugue du petit Poucet" is responsible for removing trees in Paris to make room for more cars, the ogre is replaced by a hippie named Logre, and the seven-league boots turn into Logre's knee-high buckskin boots (57).

Little Poucet runs away from home on December 23 and finds himself in the forest south of Paris, close to Tournier's village of Choisel, where he discovers Logre and his seven little daughters. Logre incarnates an androgynous ideal, a man as "handsome as a woman" (57) with his long hair, heavy jewelry, and fringed clothes, and his pacifist philosophy and vegetarian diet give little Poucet an insight into love he does not see at home. On that night of the winter solstice, Logre tells a story of the fall of man showing Yahweh, the Old Testament's God of justice, as narrow and vindictive; but Logre teaches that man can live in harmony with himself and nature if, like a tree, he remains firmly linked with earth. False justice appears to triumph when police the next morning arrest Logre for "corrupting minors" (64), but Logre, looking like Christ in his long tunic, his hair "parted in the middle, fall[ing] freely on his shoulders" (63), shows love by giving Poucet his beautiful boots to wear "in memory of me" (63), a phrase echoing Christ's words at the Last Supper. At the story's end, on Christmas Eve little Poucet is wearing the "dream boots," which change him in imagination to a huge chestnut tree. The justice of the father has been replaced by Logre's love, just as the birth of Christ signals the end of the justice of the Old Testament and the coming of forgiveness through Christ.

Temperance, the third moral virtue, is illustrated in the cruel story "Tupik," whose title is a phonetic rendering of a little boy's complaint when his father tries to kiss him: "Tu piques!"—"you scratch!" The boy is nicknamed Tupik because he is excessively sensitive to harshness, which he associates with adult males, such as those who use the "comfort station" in the square where he is taken on nice days to play. Because the men's side of the facility is dirty and smelly, Tupik prefers the women's side with its clean towels and sweet-smelling toilet paper. A series of misunderstandings about sexual identity, exacerbated by his nursemaid's threat to cut off his "little faucet" if he doesn't stop wetting his bed (79), results in Tupik's concluding that men can become women if they cut off their genitals. In the story's hair-raising conclusion, he does just that. True temperance is not hatred of the body; it is "selfless self-preservation" shown in "chastity, continence, humility, gentleness, mildness" (Pieper 150-55). But Tupik's world makes him hate his sexual identity. The story implies that Christianity is more than a little responsible for this attitude, for it is partly because of a painting of the Last Judgment (71) that Tupik associates the men's side of the toilet facility with Hell and the women's side with Heaven.

The last of the four moral virtues, fortitude, lets one "adhere to a reasonable course of action when faced with . . . grave peril" and includes a "willingness to endure suffering" (Kane). This virtue is exhibited by the protagonist of the funny and sad "Que ma joie demeure," named for the Bach cantata known in English as *Jesus, Joy of Man's Desiring* (which also gave its name to a well-known novel by Jean Giono). Raphaël Bidoche, whose name could be roughly rendered as "Raphael Crumb," is a talented pianist forced to earn his living by betraying his talent: he becomes a wildly successful musical parodist. He does not so much enjoy success as suffer it, for it pains him to betray his art. Nevertheless, his fortitude lets him live with his destiny. He is finally rewarded on Christmas Eve, when his piano, instead of exploding as planned while he is performing in a circus, works perfectly so that he can play *Que ma joie demeure*, and let the crowd "commune" (98) with each other and, presumably, with God. A miracle takes place at the end: the Archangel Raphael, Bidoche's namesake, emerges from under the piano lid. Bidoche, though beset by a corrupt world, remains innocent through fortitude.

LE COQ DE BRUYERE: THE VICES

The last seven fictions in *Le Coq de bruyère*, only one of which is likely to interest a child, reveal the seven deadly sins as Tournier sees them. The first three sins in the traditional listing are considered to be "cold"—anger, envy, and pride. Lucien Gagneron, protagonist of "Le Nain rouge" ("The Red Dwarf"), is angry because he is so short. His anger leads him eventually to murder his mistress, then to humiliate and sodomize her husband, whom he has framed for the murder. He vents his anger also in his circus act, in which he externalizes his hatred for normal life and ordinary-sized people. The story would be unrelievedly cruel, but Lucien is at least partly redeemed by his closeness to children. At the end, he treats a whole tentful of children on Christmas Eve to a private performance, where the children's applause "washed him of his bitterness, made him innocent" (121). The story implies that even someone eaten up by anger can be saved, and its title reminds us that a red dwarf is a kind of star, maybe even a Christmas star.

"Tristan Vox" illustrates the pointlessness of envy, "culpable sadness or displeasure at the spiritual or temporal good of another" (Herbst) resulting from "the belief that one cannot acquire" that which one wants (Lyman 185). Tristan Vox is the romantic performing name of a radio announcer, whose real name is the prosaic Félix Robinet ("Felix Faucet"). Robinet is balding and middle-aged, but his audience imagines him as young, handsome, and romantic. The surprise is that the listeners most caught by this false belief are Robinet's wife and secretary, who desire what they cannot have, for they are jealous of a Tristan Vox they know to be imaginary. The story begins light-heartedly, but it ends with the secretary's suicide and the wife's continuing obsession with Tristan Vox, who is now played by another announcer.

Pride, which springs from self-love and which may result in using other people "solely toward the achievement of [one's] own private ends" (Parmisano 766), is shown by the title character in "Les Suaires de Véronique" ("Veronica's Winding-Sheets"). For the sake of photographic experiments, Véronique destroys her model, Hector. She controls his life, ruins his skin, and seems, finally, to have destroyed Hector himself by making "dermographic" reproductions (171) of him on light-sensitive linen in which she has wrapped his naked, solution-dipped body (169). The tiger's tooth she takes from Hector symbolizes her pride, or *morgue*, which has resulted in a photographic exhibit that suggests a "morgue" (171). Véronique is clearly a negative counterpart to Saint Veronica, on whose handkerchief was supposedly imprinted the countenance of Christ. The story's complexity is shown in the fact that an entire number of the journal *Incidences* was composed of six essays analyzing it (Bourbonnais et al.).

Neither cold nor warm is the fourth sin, *acedia* or sloth, "a disgust with the spiritual because of the physical effort involved" (Voll 83). Sloth is illustrated by Mélanie Blanchard, the heroine of the bizarre "La Jeune Fille et la mort," named for Schubert's quartet *Death and the Maiden*. She suffers from a perpetual "crisis of boredom" (179) and can stay interested in life only through sensations and ideas suggesting death. She finally decides to kill herself to end the "nausea of existence" (198), but before she can do so, she dies of a crisis of laughter brought on by a "divine surprise" (199), the delivery of a functional scale-model guillotine. Mélanie is actually joyful when she dies on September 29, the feast of the Archangels Michael, Raphael, and Gabriel. Like Raphaël Bidoche, she may have had an angel watching over her, for her sudden death saves her from suicide.

Three pieces about the "warm" sins end the collection. The title story, "Le Coq de bruyère," illustrates avarice. The Baron Guillaume de Saint-Fursy, called "le coq de bruyère" ("the woodgrouse") because of his womanizing and his bandy legs, is not avaricious for money; his avarice is the sort which takes the form of display and of "mak[ing] objects of all we touch" (Fairlie 149). The baron's life has consisted largely of displaying his prowess in swordsmanship, riding, hunting, and womanizing, and he is ultimately more interested in displaying his conquest of young Mariette than in the girl herself. His wife is avaricious, too, for she wants to display her piety, despite being warned by her priest against self-righteousness. Mariette is simply avaricious for the baron's money. The story is full of twists and turns as the baron and his wife struggle for the upper hand, the aging husband grasping at a last affair and the wife trying to keep both her husband and her belief that she is a good Christian, but the baroness seems finally to win when the baron has a stroke and becomes partially paralyzed. His body is fixed in a position which seems to mock his earlier gestures when he falsely claimed that he had found "perfect happiness" with Mariette (257), although he may have found happiness in being stripped of everything.

Gluttony is the subject of the next story, "L'Aire du Muguet" ("The Lily of the Valley Rest Area"), the one story in the second part of the book to be printed separately as a "Junior" book. Gluttony is distinguished by a desire to consume and by haste (Fairlie 168), and haste is the key to the main character, Pierre, a young truck driver. Like a typical glutton, he does not take the time to enjoy his food (273), and he also worships speed (269). Pretty Marinette's charm for him lies mainly in the fact that she is on the far side of the fence separating the rest area from the countryside. Later, his "desire for immediate satisfaction" (282) makes him act irrationally in trying to find her village. Finally Pierre is struck repeatedly as he tries to walk across the toll road, and presumably he is dying as an ambulance carries him away. (In an inside joke, her town is Lusigny-sur-Ouche, where the Tourniers went during World War II because food was easier to find there than in Paris.)

The last sin, lust, excessive love of sexual pleasure leading to "blindness of mind, rashness, thoughtlessness, inconstancy, self-love, and excessive attachment to the material world" (Regan 1081), is illustrated in the one-act, one-character play *Le Fétichiste*, which was produced in Paris in 1974 (*Coq* 340) and 1982 (Rev. of *Le Fétichiste*), Berlin in 1974 (*Coq* 340), England in 1983 (Hayman, "Underwear"), and the United States in 1984 (Dieckman), where Ubu Repertory Theater has published it as the third in its playscripts series. The play's punning subtitle, *Un Acte pour un homme seul,* suggests the masturbatory nature of the fetishism of Martin, whose main interest is women's underclothes. In an interview, Tournier has called fetishism "an absolutely unique kind of perversion" because a fetishist is "hyper-social," having overvalued clothing, which is a creation of civilization, unlike other sexual rebels, who he believes are antisocial (Sanzio et al. 15). The fetishist is, therefore, precisely the opposite of the rebels and "heretics" that Tournier most admires. As to lust itself, if it looks at the body rather than the whole person, it is an aggravated form of lust which looks only at the clothing on that body; or, in Tournier's words, "What is essential [the body] is rejected and only the detail counts—what for so-called normal people is the detail . . ." (Sanzio et al. 17).

Martin, who has temporarily escaped from his keepers at an asylum, explains his lust for women's "frillies" and for men's wallets, especially those carried near the heart; he used to steal men's wallets partly to pay for women's underclothes, but also because of a bisexuality of which he is not fully aware. Martin tells the audience his life story, which is full of burlesque episodes, including his extortion of a garter belt from a woman in the Paris *Métro* at the height of the Christmas rush, but his story is sad, too. As he is taken away by his attendants, he waves a pair of women's panties, saying, "I'm coming back. With my flag. The pirates' black flag. Long live death!" (333). Lust has destroyed Martin's life.

In each of these pieces, Tournier has constructed a plot illustrating the effects of having or not having a virtue, or of succumbing to or resisting a vice. Some of the vices and virtues are presented in an entirely secular context and others are seen from a religious angle, but each story presents a moral issue and shows one way in which a person may deal with it, successfully or not. Plot is crucial. Characterization is generally sketchy, although in some stories, notably "Le Coq de bruyère," it is subtle and penetrating. But no matter how much realistic detail there may be, the stories derive from ideas. Their charm comes largely from whimsical humor, simplicity of language, and plotting which continually surprises with its logical but unexpected developments.

The stories all show remarkable technical virtuosity, wit, and warmth. The narration, especially, shows great skill. The omniscient narrator of "La Famille Adam" is authoritative but amused, but the omniscient narrator of "Le Coq de bruyère" is self-effacing, nearly transparent. The first-person narrator of "Les Suaires de Véronique" could be Tournier himself, but ten-year-old Amandine tells her story in diary form, in an entirely different voice, and the chatty Martin narrates quirkily the story of his life in *Le Fétichiste*. The tone of "La Mère Noël" suggests a legend; "La Fugue du petit Poucet" is whimsical; "Le Coq de bruyère" resembles a tale by Maupassant. In all of the stories, Tournier's wit is much in evidence, although it takes different forms, from wordplay to allusion to unexpected logic-twisting on the parts of characters, and the tone is much more playful than that of the previous novels. The wit is always accompanied by human warmth, even in the most painful of stories, such as "Tupik" and "Le Nain rouge": the events may be cruel, but one always feels Tournier's compassion.

PIERROT OU LES SECRETS DE LA NUIT AND *BARBEDOR*

Two fine later works examine the nature of salvation while remaining adventure stories easily understood by children. In 1979, the year after *Le Coq de bruyère*, Tournier published *Pierrot ou les secrets de la nuit*, which he has often claimed is his best work. This short tale inspired by the familiar song "Au clair de la lune" is now published both in *Sept contes* and by itself in the Gallimard Enfantimages series, although it first came out in a specially designed format intended, Tournier feels, to quarantine it from Gallimard's other children's books because its originality rendered it suspect ("Writing" 34). Tournier calls the book an "adventure-story, with a powerful metaphysical foundation" ("Writing" 34), whose main characters are inspired by the Italian *commedia dell' arte* figures of Harlequin, Pierrot, and Columbine.

Pierrot, a baker in Pouldreuzic (the setting of "La Mère Noël"), loves the laundress Colombine, but she is frightened by the night, which is when he must work. The house painter Arlequin charms her with his cheerful nature and bright colors, and she goes away with him; but when their love fades in winter, Colombine returns to Pouldreuzic with new insight into Pierrot and the night, whose beauty she has at last seen. At the end, Arlequin also arrives, singing

"Au clair de la lune," its words given new meaning by the story's plot, and is warmly welcomed by the other two.

The story's "metaphysical foundation" centers in part on the contrast between sunlight, which bleaches the sheets Colombine washes but fades Arlequin's bright colors, and moonlight, which Pierrot loves and associates with sexuality. The tale also works against sex stereotyping, for Pierrot, as a baker, is feminized by his occupation, while Colombine's resourcefulness, strength, and independence may seem to be masculine qualities. The story, as Margaret R. Higonnet points out, "invokes traditional oppositions and themes" just as Tournier's long fiction does (154). But more important than these oppositions is the religious theme. Just as *Vendredi* rewrote the Old and New Testaments, this story presents the three persons of the Trinity through the three fictional characters. Pierrot, who provides the village with its daily bread, is like God the Father; the vivid, cheerful Arlequin is like Christ, literally bringing color to towns as he paints them, much as Christ, according to Koussek in *Les Météores*, brought "color, heat, and pain" (161) to religion. Colombine, so called because she reminds people of a dove, or *colombe* (*Sept* 9), represents the Holy Spirit, traditionally symbolized by the dove.

The story's conclusion suggests the Last Supper, as Jean-Bernard Vray has pointed out ("L'Habit" 156-58). When Colombine returns to Pouldreuzic, Pierrot sculpts her form in *brioche* dough and bakes it, and after Arlequin joins them, Colombine tears out pieces of the *brioche* and offers them to Pierrot and Arlequin: "taste, eat the good Colombine! Eat me!" (*Sept* 32). This version of the Last Supper unites the Trinity, rather than God and man, but its most important characteristic is that not Christ but the Holy Spirit is the source of Communion and thus, by implication, of salvation. As in *Vendredi* and *Les Météores*, Tournier here insists that salvation comes through the Holy Spirit. Christ and Christianity, like Arlequin, are reduced to interesting but unnecessary steps.

The simpler story *Barbedor*, an Arabian Nights tale embedded in Tournier's novel *Gaspard, Melchior et Balthazar* (1980), also concerns salvation. Like *Pierrot*, it is published separately in the Enfantimages series as well as in the collection *Sept contes*. Barbedor ("Goldbeard") is the nickname of Nabounassar III, a king with a beautiful golden beard but no heirs to the throne. Mysteriously, as soon as white hairs appear in his beard, they vanish during his afternoon nap. He finally has only one beard hair left, but he is lucky enough to see it plucked out and carried off by a white bird. King Barbedor chases the bird and discovers its nest, made entirely of his white hairs, with a single golden egg inside. Then Barbedor realizes that he is no longer a portly king; he has turned back into a little boy. When he returns to his city, carrying the egg, he sees his own funeral—or that of the person he was—and from the egg comes a bird which proclaims the now beardless Barbedor to be King Nabounassar IV.

Tournier is working with the theme of rebirth through the Holy Spirit, which is represented by the white bird that proclaims Barbedor the new king in an echo of the Holy Spirit's appearing in the form of a dove at Christ's baptism when God proclaimed Jesus to be His "beloved Son, in whom I am well pleased" (Matt. 3.17). The elderly Barbedor is symbolically reborn through this bird, as a believer is symbolically reborn through baptism. It is not hard, either, to see that Barbedor, with his full beard, is like God the Father, and the reborn Barbedor, the little boy, is like Christ: the story can be read as an allegory of Christ's birth. Because the story's last lines say that the new king had no successors and began to grow a beautiful golden beard, one must conclude that history will repeat itself: another age, presumably a rule of the Holy Spirit, will succeed Christianity.

GILLES ET JEANNE

Tournier's concern with salvation is also behind *Gilles et Jeanne* (1983), a novella-length *récit*, or narrative, which began as a scenario for a television film which was not made. Unfortunately, this story never succeeds in mastering its complex material, the personal and metaphysical relationship between Joan of Arc (Jeanne) and Gilles de Rais, a marshal of France who fought alongside Joan and who, like her, was burned at the stake for sorcery, although unlike Joan he unquestionably worshiped the Devil. The brevity of the narrative, its frequent chapter divisions, and its simple style suggest that Tournier hoped for an audience of young people—not children, perhaps, but teenagers. However, his inclusion of some of the horrifying details of Gilles's crimes (which even most historical studies did not relate until recently) makes one wonder if young people were really his intended audience. It is only fair to say, though, that he brings out those details after Gilles's crimes are over and presents them only through testimony at the trial.

The *récit* deals with many of the same themes as *Le Roi des aulnes* (Petit, "*Gilles*," and Nettelbeck, "The Return"), including the inversion of good and evil, sexual inversion, destiny, and the voluptuous power of destruction. Like

Tiffauges, Gilles de Rais is obsessional, pursues a pleasure based on the sub-jugation of boys, and seeks metaphysical enlightenment. Tiffauges, however, is not intentionally cruel to the young boys at the *Napola,* whereas Gilles deliberately tortures, sodomizes, and murders hundreds of children, mostly boys; and Tiffauges changes for the better when he comes under the influence of Ephraïm, whereas Gilles does not repent until he is on trial for his life.

Tournier researched the lives of both Joan of Arc and Gilles de Rais, but the book is written, as the publisher's insert says, "in the blanks left by the historical records." Tournier has called this technique a game in which he "respects the letter" of the history he is telling but recounts a totally different story from the familiar one (Bouloumié, "Tournier" 22). He imagines that Gilles became a criminal precisely because of Joan of Arc's influence: Gilles swears to follow her wherever she goes, and, having seen her burned for witchcraft and apparently sent to Hell, he tries to follow her there by raping and torturing boys. Tournier conceives of Gilles as having been attracted to boys from the start (*Gilles* 12) and imagines that Joan's boyish appearance made her into an ideal companion for Gilles, but Gilles's homophilia is not violent until after Joan's death. And even then, the book insists on a close connection between Gilles's sadism and his religious feelings, for Gilles's emotions are most stirred by Herod's Massacre of the Innocents, and he founds and magnificently endows a school in honor of the Holy Innocents, even pos-ing for a painting there of Herod (47).

Gilles's first act after Joan's death is to plunge into debauchery, but later he regains his sense of the sacred under the influence of the Italian Francesco Prelati, or François Prélat. Prélat is imbued with the spirit of the Renaissance, including alchemy, which in the fifteenth century often involved invocations of devils and was condemned by the Church as heretical and blasphemous. Led by Prélat, Gilles not only continues to kidnap, sodomize, torture, and kill children, but also uses their bodies in devil worship. When Gilles is ultimately arrested and tried, Prélat claims that he helped Gilles spiritually by restoring to him the sense of the sacred, "cauterizing the festering wounds" of Gilles with the fires of Hell (135), and says that he expected "benign inversion" to transform Gilles's evil into sanctity as lead is converted to gold (136). Although Prélat is an unscrupulous and cunning adventurer, the story implies that the "benign inversion" worked, for Gilles repents of his crimes and, in addition, Tournier changes some details of Gilles's execution to make it resemble more closely Joan of Arc's. He implies that, if Gilles is judged not by his acts but by his motives and his repentance, he may be a saint. Although such a conclusion is entirely possible from a Christian point of view, from which only God can know one's motives and the condition of one's soul, most readers of *Gilles et Jeanne* have been unable to accept Gilles's possible sainthood both because of the atrocity of his crimes and because of the absence of information about what he is thinking at the end of his life.

Tournier had used many of the ideas in *Gilles et Jeanne* in his previous novels, but their treatment is less satisfactory here than there. Perhaps it is the comparatively sketchy plot development which keeps one from becoming truly involved in the story and interested in the characters, who are outlines rather than developed human beings. The narrative angle of vision also helps keep one at a distance. The third-person narrator takes us freely into the mind of Gilles's confessor, Blanchet, a minor character, but he seldom lets us know what Prélat is thinking. Gilles's thoughts are revealed in the book's early sections, but even before Joan's death he becomes an enigma. And on occasion the narrator merely tells the reader what the people in the countryside see, not what is happening in Gilles's castles. These shifts reveal the book's origin as scenario and its incomplete conversion to *récit*. It is not surprising that *Gilles et Jeanne* was received coolly by many French critics (Boisdeffre, rev. of *Gilles*; Galey, "L'Ange noir"; Hue). One exception is Mireille Rosello, who considers *Gilles et Jeanne* a major novel (16).

THE WISE MEN

In the same year that *Gilles et Jeanne* appeared, 1983, Tournier published *Les Rois mages* ("The Wise Men"), a simpler and briefer version of his 1980 novel *Gaspard, Melchior et Balthazar*. This was his first revision of a novel into shorter form since *Vendredi ou la vie sauvage* and is a somewhat more successful one. In the next chapter I will discuss *Gaspard, Melchior et Balthazar*; here I will concentrate on those elements peculiar to *Les Rois mages* or necessary to understanding its form and focus. The book is composed of three self-contained but complementary tales, the stories of the three Wise Men, as imagined by Tournier: Gaspard, King of Méroé in Africa, who suffers from rejected love and needs to be reconciled to his blackness; Balthazar, King of Nipour in the Middle East, who mourns the loss of his art collection and seeks a new form of art; and Taor, Prince of Mangalore in India, who wants the recipe for pistachio Turkish delight. The adventure of each of the Wise Men is told with wit and whimsy, but Taor's odyssey, which occupies half of the book, is the one on which Tournier appears to have lavished the most care.

As in so much of his short fiction, Tournier uses an omniscient narrator. The several explanatory footnotes scattered throughout unfortunately make it sound at times a little like a textbook, but Tournier avoids preaching or overexplaining much more successfully than in *Vendredi ou la vie sauvage*. He relies more on the reader's judgment here than he did in *Vendredi*, and he usually succeeds in creating the tone of a fable. Tournier makes the most of parallels among the tales—for example, the African king has camels, the Middle Eastern king has horses, and the Indian prince has elephants—and emphasizes exotic elements while introducing occasional anachronisms to bring the story home. Gaspard's concern with skin color and race clearly has meaning for any contemporary reader, and Turkish delight is featured by the many African and Middle Eastern candy shops in Paris.

The theme of *Les Rois mages* is the quest for acceptance and fulfillment. In the first tale, Gaspard falls in love with a white slave, "discovers" his own blackness, and suffers when he finds out that she is deceiving him with the white man she has claimed is her brother. Gaspard's real problem is his rejection of his own blackness, for he thinks that his black skin makes him unlovable. Two amazing—and amusing—discoveries make him able to accept himself again: first, he realizes that the earth from which Jehovah supposedly formed Adam is the same color as his own skin, and, second, he sees that Jesus is black, although Mary and Joseph are white. This miracle—for it does seem to be a miracle—makes Gaspard see black as the color of redeemed flesh. Gaspard recounts the manger scene many years later to his great-grandchildren (39-41), so we also learn that Gaspard becomes an old man at peace with himself.

Balthazar's problem is similar. He has been devastated by the destruction of an art museum to which he had dedicated his life; because his religion, like Judaism, forbids graven images, the priests have incited the public to destroy the supposedly impious art. All of Balthazar's emotional life has been constructed around art: as a young man, he fell in love with a woman in a portrait and married the model, and when she stopped resembling her portrait, he stopped loving her and dedicated himself to collecting art. If the Incarnation redeems the flesh for Gaspard, it redeems art for Balthazar. The art destroyed in the riot was Greek, Egyptian, and Middle Eastern sculpture representing gods and heroes, supermen and superwomen (57), but at the manger Balthazar discovers the possibility of an art showing the inner beauty of ordinary people (76-77). God no longer forbids representation of the human body, because in taking human form God showed that the outward image of an ordinary, sinful person could be joined to an inner resemblance to God (73-76).

The third Wise Man, Taor, arrives in Bethlehem too late to see Jesus. Accompanied by a host of servants and five elephants, he sails up the Red Sea and marches into Judea, losing parts of his train along the way, in his quest for the recipe for Turkish delight. In Bethlehem, he gives a banquet for the hungry children, an act of love and generosity which is a better way of worshiping Jesus than giving him gifts, for serving children is a way of serving God. As Jesus says, "Inasmuch as ye have done *it* unto one of the least of these my brethren, ye have done *it* unto me" (Matt. 25.40). Taor serves others also when, near Sodom, he is moved by pity for the family of a camel driver about to be imprisoned and offers to pay the man's debt. When his treasurer informs him that there is almost no money left, Taor (who has no idea whether the 33 talents owed is a large or a small sum) offers to work off the man's debt himself (136) and is promptly sentenced to 33 years in the salt mines. The horrible conditions in the mines, which may be reminiscent of a descent into a symbolic hell in many fairy tales, are described only briefly, presumably so that they will not be too disturbing. The inhabitants of Sodom, both men and women, are sodomites in the sexual sense, but the explanation given the naive Taor is designed for children: "Everybody does you-know-what [*fait doudou*] from the front. As for the Sodomites, they do you-know-what from behind" (148). This hell becomes Taor's path to Heaven in another benign inversion, for in the mines Taor hears about Christ's teachings, so when he is finally released, he seeks Jesus. He arrives in Jerusalem after the Last Supper is finished, but he eats and drinks some of the leftovers and is carried to Heaven by two angels (158).

Gaspard discovers how to accept his flesh; Balthazar sees that redeemed human flesh can be represented in art; Taor learns how to make his redeemed flesh live forever through the Resurrection. Each Magus has made a greater discovery than the last. Gaspard finds a human happiness; Balthazar discovers immortality through art; Taor achieves literal immortality through the resurrection of the flesh promised by Christianity. I will leave fuller consideration of the implications of the story to my discussion of *Gaspard, Melchior et Balthazar*, but it should be clear that *Les Rois mages* reflects an increasing emphasis on Christian themes and represents a step toward greater limpidity of language and simplicity of organization. As Michael J. Worton says, its stylistic and organizational tactics make it resemble a parable ("Michel Tournier" 253).

SHORT FICTION IN THE NOVELS

Besides writing individual stories, Tournier increasingly encapsulates tales in his longer fiction. He began in *Gaspard, Melchior et Balthazar*, where one chapter became *Barbedor*. *La Goutte d'or*, published in 1985, includes two chapters which are complete in themselves, "Barberousse ou le portrait du roi," published separately in *La Nouvelle Revue Française* in 1984, and "La Reine blonde." Another chapter, "Un Chameau à Paris" ("A Camel in Paris"), although not an entirely freestanding story, was also published in *La Nouvelle Revue Française* in 1985, and yet another chapter appeared that same year in a collection under the title "Il était donc en France" (*Le Deuxième Sud: Marseille ou le présent incertain*). These chapters are reasonably successful at standing alone, for each has a thematic focus and dramatic shape, but I will discuss them in the section on *La Goutte d'or* so I can consider them in context.

"Le Peintre et son modèle," originally intended as a chapter of *La Goutte d'or*, was dropped by Tournier from that book, but he published it separately in the review *Masques* in 1986 (Jay, *Idriss* 101-02) and reprinted it in *Petites proses*. In Chapter 7, I will discuss it in relation to the themes of images in *La Goutte d'or*, but here I will consider it in regard to Tournier's theory of art. A painter, Charles-Frédéric de l'Epéechevalier (*Petites proses* 158), contrasts photography to painting and drawing, explaining that art has abandoned realistic representation to photography and has staked out for itself a new, less representational domain. Then, echoing the theory of art in *Les Rois mages* and *Gaspard, Melchior et Balthazar*, l'Epéechevalier contrasts the art of the Greeks, Egyptians, and Romans, which represents gods and heroes, with Christian art, which represents ordinary people, saying that the latter type of art paradoxically attains a universal impact thanks to its emphasis on the particular because "it is the nature of creation to make the impossible not only real but necessary" (*Petites proses* 161).

Then, after briefly mentioning modern, nonrealistic art, including cubism, fauvism, impressionism, and expressionism, l'Epéechevalier explains that he wants to create a new kind of representational art which will be amusing but not arbitrary (*Petites proses* 163). Two of his drawings provide insight into

Tournier's own work, the first being a floor plan of Notre Dame which shows the affinity between the cathedral and the cloth of a gambling table, revealing, as he explains, the relationship between man's belief in chance and God's plan. The other drawing represents Jean-Paul Sartre as a ghostly face taking form between a beech tree and its shadow, punning on the nearly identical sounds of the French word for "being," *l'être*, a key word in the title of Sartre's *Being and Nothingness*, and the word for "birch," *le hêtre* (*Petites proses* 165).

One can see how l'Epéechevalier's ideas about art relate to Tournier's fiction. The success of films in telling realistic stories is undoubtedly one reason that some writers have turned from realistic fiction to the experimental novel, the nonnarrative novel, the "new novel." Such books may be analogous to the works of impressionism, expressionism, cubism, and abstract art, which were in part reactions to photography's intrusion on the previous domain of art, realistic representation. But Tournier wants to reconquer lost ground by producing art which mirrors the real world but which also carries plural significations, through playfulness and ambiguity.

LE MEDIANOCHE AMOUREUX

Tournier's second collection of short fiction, *Le Médianoche amoureux: Contes et nouvelles*, published in 1989, reflects his continued interest in the contrast between *nouvelles* and *contes*: the first ten stories are realistic, but the second ten resemble myths and legends. The arrangement is thus opposite to that in *Le Coq de bruyère*, which went from tales to realistic fiction. The overall theme of the collection is the function of art (whether literature, painting, or cooking) in people's lives.

The first story, "Les Amants taciturnes," provides a framework: Nadège, an intellectual from an upper-middle-class background, and her husband, Yves, who worked his way up from cabin boy to captain in her father's codfishing fleet, decide to divorce because they have nothing left to say to each other. They invite their friends to a *médianoche*, a "midnight supper," to tell them the news, but the stories the guests tell during the night provide them with so much basis for future conversation that they have no need to divorce: art, in the form of the stories told, has saved their marriage. At the end, Nadège names Yves, who has provided and prepared all the food, the "high priest" of her kitchen (42). The movement of this tale from realism to ritual foreshadows the pattern of the entire book.

The first stories the guests tell are realistic ones of disappointment, vengeance, and loss. "Les Mousserons de la Toussaint" shows the unpredictability of individual destinies and people's inability to recover the past; "Théobald ou le crime parfait" is about a husband's unsuccessful attempt to frame his unfaithful wife for his own murder; "Pyrotechnie ou la commémoration" concerns a long-plotted revenge against a Resistance hero who humiliated a woman for consorting with the Germans; "Blandine ou la visite du père," which had appeared in English in 1984 as "Blandine, or The Father's Visit," shows a working-class father trying to improve his housing situation by cynically using a well-off bachelor's affection for his prepubescent daughter. Unlike almost all of Tournier's previous fiction, each story has a twist of some kind at the end; most are glossy commercial productions. Though well written, they are rather shallow; the characters are types rather than individuals. This lack of depth is deliberate, for it prepares for the seemingly simpler but deeper tales which conclude the book. These fictions are not truly art; they are like realistic photographs or painting which represents the world either as it is or as we would like to think of it. They feed—and feed on—our preconceptions.

The second five fictions, though essentially realistic, are more thought-provoking. In "Aventures africaines," a well-to-do Frenchman with a predilection for young boys finds himself in an ironic situation in North Africa: his hosts' gardener wants him to take his handsome blond grandson under his protection, but the man has already lost his heart to a dark-skinned boy interested only in robbing him. "Lucie ou la femme sans ombre" shows the psychological power a young woman has when she accepts her shadow side and her loss of that power when psychoanalysis removes the shadow. The next three tales seem more like personal, autobiographical essays than fictions. In "Ecrire debout," the narrator, an author, tells prison inmates that a writer must "write standing up," not on his knees (161); taking him literally, they send him a hand-made lectern so he can do just that. "L'Auto fantôme" is about deceptive appearances: returning from a centrally located rest area on a toll road to a parking lot on the wrong side, the narrator thinks his car has vanished, but he has only to cross the road to find it. Finally, "La Pitié dangereuse" shows how a doctor is led by pity to give up his normal life to help a dying patient. These five stories, although mostly about the negative side of life, are less discouraging than the previous ones because stereotypes have given way to real people, and there are no tidy endings to close off interpretation.

The second ten stories, *contes* provoking thought and analysis, begin with "Le Mendiant des étoiles," which serves as hinge between the two parts of the book. The narrator and his friend Karl, European tourists horrified by the starving children they see everywhere in Calcutta, feed them while seeking to avoid being besieged by beggars. On Christmas Eve, however, they accept the risks to which charity can expose them and take a huge basket of food beneath Howrath Bridge, where they have previously found crowds of impoverished people. Amazingly, no one is there, and they have a private *réveillon*, or Christmas Eve supper, seeing at the end only a solitary beggar outlined against the stars, as if begging from God. The story has clear affinities with "La Mère Noël," for both are Christmas stories about feeding the hungry, and, like "La Mère Noël," "Le Mendiant des étoiles" is a key story for interpreting the collection in which it appears, for the realism of its early scenes gives way to the hallucinatory "hell" the travelers first find underneath the bridge and the unreal Christmas Eve scene with which it concludes.

Two more Christmas stories follow. In "Un Bébé sur la paille," when the Mitterrand-like President of the Republic offers to help all French mothers-to-be to have their babies wherever they wish, the first person to accept is an unmarried woman named Mary, who wants her baby, due on Christmas, to be born in a stable. This potential new Christ will apparently usher in a new dispensation, for Mary is expecting a girl, "so much calmer, more reassuring" than a boy (192). The second story, "Le Roi mage Faust," might be material discarded from *Gaspard, Melchior et Balthazar*, for it concerns a Magus whose life has been devoted to truth but who discovers, through seeing the Christ Child, the value of innocence. The fact that Faust's gift to the Baby Jesus is a blank scroll (which Jesus could later write on) implies that language can reveal a path to salvation.

Angus is more complex. Published separately in an illustrated edition in 1988, it is a "revision" of Victor Hugo's famous "L'Aigle du casque," a narrative poem in which Angus, a young Scottish boy, has promised his grandfather to fight the giant Tiphaine. Hugo's Tiphaine kills Angus, but the murder of the innocent is so repugnant that the metal eagle on Tiphaine's helmet comes to life and kills Tiphaine. Unable to accept the sentimentality of Hugo's poem, as he told me when I saw him in 1987, Tournier reimagined this work of Hugo, whom he calls "the greatest French poet" in a note following the story (226).

In Tournier's version, the boy Jacques d'Angus is conceived when Tiphaine rapes Colombelle, the daughter of Lord Angus; Tournier thus provides a reason (missing in Hugo's poem) for Lord Angus to make his grandson vow to kill the giant. The adolescent Jacques wounds Tiphaine mortally in a tournament, but the victory is hollow; his real triumph comes after he learns that he is Tiphaine's son and realizes that he defeated Tiphaine only because the giant was trying not to hurt him. The boy is not angelic, as in Hugo's poem; he is a mixture of good and evil, particularly of pride and humility, but at the end of the story, in accepting his identity as Jacques Tiphaine, he "has become a man" (224). Significantly, it is through written words—a letter Tiphaine writes on his deathbed to Jacques—that Jacques learns his true situation.

The last six stories fall into three pairs. The first is composed of *Pierrot ou les secrets de la nuit*, discussed above, and "La Légende du pain," in which bread again is a means of reconciliation. A rivalry between Pouldreuzic and Plouhinec takes the form of the two towns refusing to eat or drink the same things, so when the son of the Pouldreuzic baker marries the daughter of the Plouhinec baker, they cannot serve at the wedding either the soft *brioche* of Pouldreuzic or the hardtack of Plouhinec. The fiancés therefore invent French bread, which combines crust and a soft center. The new wife, who would like to invent a "vertebrate" bread (225) to complement the "crustacean" bread invented by her husband, finally succeeds by inventing *petit pain au chocolat*. Here creation, in the form of inventing new kinds of breads, is seen as a recombining of familiar elements, which is of course what Tournier does in his own fiction.

The stories of the second pair rely on whimsy. "La Légende de la musique et de la danse," which had appeared in English in 1986 as "The Music of the Spheres: A Biblical Tale," is another story of Eden, in which after they eat the apple Adam and Eve no longer hear the music of the spheres; as a result, they must invent music, which nevertheless does not approach the divine music in beauty. "La Légende des parfums" tells a more positive version of the same story from an olfactory perspective: after their original sin, Adam and Eve are aware only of smells, not scents, but the great French perfume-makers in the twentieth century are gradually re-creating "our paradisiacal past" (258). The artistic creations of music and perfume bring us closer to our prelapsarian past and to God the Creator.

The last two stories are also about Creation. In "La Légende de la peinture," two artists are commissioned to decorate opposing walls of a caliph's hall, while a curtain down the middle keeps each from seeing what the other is doing. The first work revealed is a beautiful garden, but the victory goes to the second artist, who has covered his wall with a mirror: when the courtiers look at it, they see the painted garden with themselves moving in it. The story, illustrating Tournier's belief in the need for co-creation between artist and audience, implies that the greatest art is one which draws the reader into it. At the same time, it valorizes what seems to be—but actually is not—an imitation, for the second artist did not imitate what the first one did but mirrored it. Fiction is often said to hold a mirror up to life; Tournier's fiction more often holds a mirror up to other fiction, as the artist literally does in this story.

Actual imitation is the subject of the last tale, "Les Deux Banquets ou la commémoration," in which two cooks compete to become a caliph's head chef. The first produces a magnificent meal; the second imitates it exactly. The caliph, in choosing the second to be his chef at home (the other will go with him when he travels), explains that the winning chef's second meal is a ritual, a commemoration of the first, for "the sacred exists only through repetition" (268), and so the copy is greater than the original. The story—and the book—end with the same words Nadège spoke to Yves at the end of the first story: "You will be the high priest of my kitchens and the conservator of the culinary and masticatory rites which give a meal its spiritual dimension" (268).

Arranging the stories so that the first ten are realistic, the second ten structured, strengthens the book by giving it a subtext: those in the first group divide Nadège and Yves because they present the venality of ordinary existence unleavened by the power of interpretation; the later stories unite them by showing the possibilities of life and by promoting discussion of the events. Unfortunately, the relation of the first story to the other nineteen is clear only from the publisher's note on the back cover (which says very much the same things Tournier told me in the interview in Chapter 8 below). And although Tournier claimed the *Decameron* as a model, the resemblance is slight, particularly as the narrators are only minimally distinguished (many of them seem to be slightly disguised versions of Tournier), and there is no discussion by the guests of the stories. Nevertheless, the internal resemblances among the stories increase their strength by encouraging a reader to look for patterns of meaning; for example, besides the stories which are obviously paired, one must contrast the two stories subtitled "The Commemoration," one about a long-plotted revenge, the other about the ritual possibilities of food, as well as the first and the last story, which are both about ritual meals.

The slight nature of many of the stories—the weakest, which are in the middle of the book, seem simply to be slightly camouflaged autobiographical narrations—is disappointing, but the concluding tales, with their provocative implications about the nature of art, are equal to any of Tournier's short fiction.

It is difficult to overestimate the effect on Tournier's novels of his work in the *conte* and short fiction generally. Writing for both adults and children in clear prose, in a very limited space, has honed Tournier's language, which tends naturally to a luxuriance which can interfere with clarity. Although this energy was effective in *Vendredi ou les limbes du Pacifique* and *Le Roi des aulnes*, it led to the overwriting of *Les Météores*. In contrast, Tournier's next novel, *Gaspard, Melchior et Balthazar*, shows great restraint, intensity, and clarity, without loss of power. And while humor has always been a major element in Tournier's fiction, the humor in the previous novels was often hidden, or underplayed, or bitter. Beginning with *Gaspard, Melchior et Balthazar*, Tournier was able to incorporate a gentle, relaxed humor into his novels and to create a lighter tone than in the earlier works.

6

Gaspard, Melchior et Balthazar:
In Search of Christ

Gaspard, Melchior et Balthazar (1980), Tournier's first novel to use the control he developed for his short fiction, represents a radical departure in language and structure from his first three novels, which are characterized by inventive exuberance in form and a tendency to embroider stylistically. Although published just five years after *Les Météores*, *Gaspard, Melchior et Balthazar* is strikingly different: it is much shorter; the language is more pristine; the whimsy is more delicate; the characters are more sympathetic. And whereas *Les Météores* evolved from the theology of Dante and Joachim de Fiore, *Gaspard, Melchior et Balthazar* found its first inspiration in a more familiar and simpler source: Matthew's account of the birth of Christ and the visit of the three Wise Men. Not only do the comparative simplicity and good-natured tone of this book derive from the short fiction, but so does its structure, for it is composed of eight semi-independent stories, one of which, "Barbedor," was published simultaneously as an illustrated children's book. Even the novel's subject, the first Christmas, may be partly indebted to the previously published short fiction, for "La Mère Noël," "Que ma joie demeure," "La Fugue du petit Poucet," and "Le Nain rouge" are all Christmas stories. But *Gaspard, Melchior et Balthazar*, besides telling the story of the birth of Christ, also asks how man can be like God.

Despite the importance of Christian issues in Tournier's earlier fiction, there was general surprise in the French literary establishment at the subject of *Gaspard, Melchior et Balthazar*. Even Jacqueline Piatier, usually an insightful reviewer of Tournier's fiction, said that one "expected everything" from Tournier "except that he would present himself as a Christian writer" ("Michel Tournier, romancier" 1). Tournier has said that critics did not receive the book well because those who did not understand Christianity were baffled by it and because the Catholic press resented his use of a Christian subject (d'Ivernois). In fact, the French reviewers generally liked the book (Ezine, "Temps"; Fumaroli; Kovacs; Magnan, "Les Rois"), though some thought it too clever (Garcin; Maulpoix, "L'Or"; Piatier, "Michel Tournier, romancier"; Wolfromm, "Le Rêveur"). Reviewers in English and American literary journals also praised it (Daly, rev. of *Gaspard*; McDowell; Smith, Rev. of *Gaspard*; Sturrock, "We Four"), except for Geoffrey Strickland, who found it lacking "artistic or religious" scruples.

In contrast to the mainly enthusiastic reception the original received, newspaper reviewers of the 1982 translation by Ralph Manheim, *The Four Wise Men*, were generally lukewarm (Baumbach, Gorra, Wordsworth). The difference between the two receptions is perhaps the result of differences between French and English; as Victoria Glendinning says, what is "light and dry" in French may emerge as "laboured and facetious in English," so no translation is likely to capture Tournier's wit. A confirmation of this point is provided by D. E. Flower's account of difficulties his undergraduate students had translating into English "Le Dit de l'âne," the section recounting Christ's birth.

If the critics were not all as enthusiastic as Tournier would have liked, the French public seems to have been, for the novel was a best-seller for months (Smith, rev. of *Gaspard*). This was no accident. Tournier, who writes to be read, must have regretted the comparative failure of *Les Météores*, his "most ambitious" but least popular book (Daly, "Interview" 411), so in choosing the accessible subject matter and whimsical tone of *Gaspard, Melchior et Balthazar*, he was probably trying to reconquer a mainstream audience which he had somewhat alienated with *Les Météores*. He has always worked at promoting his books and told a magazine interviewer that with each new book he is asked to do more radio and television interviews: "I admit that I like it and . . . do it rather well. . . . And then today, a writer has to know how to peddle his wares" (Pudlowski). The novel's timing—it was released just in time for Christmas sales—could not have hurt either. It was perhaps partly a publicity stunt for Tournier to ask the bishop of Versailles for the *imprimatur* for *Gaspard, Melchior et Balthazar*, only to be told that the Catholic Church no longer issues that seal of approval; in a sort of compensation, when Tournier discussed the book on Bernard Pivot's television show "Apostrophes," Pivot brought in several churchmen as panelists (Piatier, "Michel Tournier, romancier" 1).

To avoid alienating a mass audience, in this novel Tournier presents his heterodox theology so indirectly that most Christians will not notice its deviation from standard Catholic doctrine, although the theology is identical to that which Koussek had explicitly argued for in *Les Météores*. Tournier's sources for *Gaspard, Melchior et Balthazar* helped him mix orthodoxy and heterodoxy. Although he began with the account in Matthew of Jesus' birth, supplemented by the European tradition that the number of the Wise Men was three and that one of them was black, Tournier's inspiration failed at some point, so this book, begun as early as 1975 (Ezine, "Michel Tournier" 228), languished until he heard the German novelist Edzard Schaper speak on the radio of a possible fourth Magus who arrived in Bethlehem too late to see the Christ Child (Montrémy). This idea, which Schaper later told Tournier came from a Russian legend (Lapouge 32) and which had formed the basis of Schaper's *Die Legende vom vierten König*, gave Tournier's dormant novel a new direction. Later he discovered the American Henry van Dyke's senti-mental nineteenth-century novel *The Story of the Other Wise Man* (Lapouge 32), another tale of a belated fourth Magus. Thus the "true beginning point" of the novel, the idea of a fourth Wise Man (Montrémy), was a heterodox version of the central Christian story.

Tournier took his historical material mainly from *The Jewish War* and *The Antiquities of the Jews*, both by the first-century Jewish historian Flavius Josephus, but he borrowed his general approach from Flaubert, especially from *Salammbô* and "Hérodias" (Pudlowski); William Cloonan has explored a number of parallels between *Salammbô* and *Gaspard, Melchior et Balthazar* ("Tournier's *Salammbô*"). And just as Flaubert did, Tournier made use of his own travels, going to Israel and Central Africa for background (Lapouge 43). Another important source, not for plot or tone but for theological information, was the 20-volume annotated Bible Tournier inherited from his great-uncle, a priest (Lapouge 37-38). This mixture of sources reflects the novel's balancing between the familiar and the unknown, fantasy and fact, and standard Western Christianity and Tournier's heterodoxy.

THE STRUCTURE OF THE BOOK

Gaspard, Melchior et Balthazar is simple in outline, though not as simple as *Les Rois mages*, its briefer version, which I discussed in the previous chapter. *Gaspard, Melchior et Balthazar* consists of eight connected but semi-independent tales of varying lengths, each advancing an overall narrative. The first three are the parallel stories of the three Wise Men of Christian tradition who go to Bethlehem to adore the Baby Jesus. Next a professional storyteller recounts "Barbedor" at a feast Herod gives for the Magi, after which Herod tells his life story to his guests. In the sixth tale a third-person narrator relates what the ox is thinking at the birth of Jesus; in the seventh tale, the ass gives his version of Christmas Eve. The eighth tale, forming approximately the last third of the book, is the story of Prince Taor, the fourth Wise Man. After discussing the book's use of several narrations, I will treat each of these sections in turn.

Tournier had never before used so many narrators in a novel: *Vendredi ou les limbes du Pacifique* has two; *Le Roi des aulnes* has three; *Les Météores* has six. Using eight narrators gives *Gaspard, Melchior et Balthazar* great variety in style and tone, as well as providing sly humor arising from the contrast between the several first-person narrators' views of the world and the view of a reader. For example, King Gaspard, whose name in French slang means "spendthrift," says that he has ordered a unicorn, a phoenix, and a dragon for his bestiary, paying for them in advance to be more sure of getting them (11). The most distinctive narratorial voice is that of the ass, who has to "control his excessive love of words" (159). As one would expect, the most flexible voice belongs to the third-person narrator of the last chapter.

The novel uses not only several narrators but a mixture of genres. The first three narrations, which are semirealistic, consider love (Gaspard), creation (Balthazar), and power (Melchior), but each of those issues must be reevaluated in light of the mainly true but grotesque story of Herod's life and of the three mythic tales, which treat regeneration ("Barbedor"), the "eternal return" (the ox), and salvation (the ass). Taor's story blends realism with myth, recapitulating each of the previous issues but also treating a new one, the relationship of the body to the soul. The effect of this mixture of genres is extraordinary: one is intrigued by the semirealistic stories of the Wise Men, repulsed by Herod's historical narration, charmed but not persuaded by the myths, and captured by the ultimate blending of realism with fantasy in Taor's tale. Although to a lesser extent than in the previous fiction, Tournier here is continuing to use somewhat baroque development of the simple structure he has begun with.

KING GASPARD OF MEROE

The most engaging of the traditional three Wise Men and the first to tell his story is Gaspard, King of Méroé in upper Egypt. A pagan who prays to

Horus (38), he respects Judaism, beginning his account by altering the words of Solomon's beloved, "I am black but comely" (Song Sol. 1.5), to "I am black, but I am a king" (9). His blackness has troubled him since he fell in love with a Phoenician slave, Biltine, for he fears that his blackness disgusts her. When she betrays him, Gaspard leaves his kingdom to put his disappointed love in perspective. He travels northeast partly to follow a mysterious comet whose yellow tail suggests the woman's golden hair, partly—the official reason for his trip—to visit King Herod. Although full of realistic details of African desert life, Gaspard's story is resolutely anachronistic in tone; he even quotes the twentieth-century French writer Paul Nizan (33). One reason for anachronism is that the theme of racism, which underlies his love story, seems so contemporary in France (as it does also in America) that it is hard not to apply twentieth-century thinking to his situation. In any case, Tournier justifies this approach by pointing out that artists have traditionally painted the Adoration of the Magi as if it took place in their own time; his own approach is more moderate (Lapouge 32).

Gaspard's grief has religious roots, for he has identified Biltine's whiteness with purity (22), a mistake he has aggravated by using incense in their lovemaking, for incense implies worship (28). The religious dimension is made clearer through a mystical experience Gaspard has, after which, because of his blackness, he identifies himself with "Satan weeping before the beauty of the world" (17). His realizing that his grief has a religious dimension makes it more bearable (32), while a visit to the ruins of the temple at Amenophis persuades him not only that the divine is linked to the human—as suggested by the connection between the blond woman and the golden-haired comet—but also that the solution to his disappointed love is in sublimity and grandeur (40). A first turning point comes after Gaspard and his new friend, King Balthazar, like modern-day tourists, visit the field where Yahweh is said to have formed Adam from the earth and Gaspard realizes that an Adam made from the ochre earth would be Gaspard's own color. Although neither king can imagine a black Eve, they agree on the likelihood of a black Adam. As Balthazar says, "Why not?" (47).

The meaning for Gaspard of this discovery is not developed until the last chapter, when Gaspard tells Taor what he saw at Bethlehem, but for clarity I will treat it here. Balthazar has speculated that Adam became white as the result of Original Sin (53-54), and, as Tournier knows, theologians consider Jesus a second Adam or "Adam before the Fall" (Lapouge 39). So if Adam was black, then Jesus too should be black in token of his freedom from

Original Sin (214). And the Baby Jesus whom Gaspard sees in Bethlehem is black, although Mary and Joseph are white. This miracle teaches Gaspard to see those we love through their own eyes (214-15) and not to force them to fit our desires. Gaspard also realizes that he has been seeking a divine love, so when he finds it at Bethlehem, he gives to the Infant what remains of the incense he and Biltine used as part of their sexual practices.

To the book's question of what it means to imitate God, Gaspard's story first says that because we look like God, we should accept our appearance. The point is not that Adam and Jesus were black, but that we should love and accept our bodies, and that in taking on human flesh God was telling us as much. Second, it says that accepting oneself allows one to accept other people; when Gaspard can love his body, he no longer needs to force Biltine to love it. Gaspard's story also shows acceptance of sexual love, for he frees Biltine so she can pursue her own desires, not because he renounces sexual passion. Not only does this attitude reflect Gaspard's cultural values, but it also expresses novelistically Tournier's view that because Christ consistently defended sexuality and the flesh (*Vent* 65), Christianity does not involve renunciation of sensuality.

KING BALTHAZAR OF NIPPUR

King Balthazar's question focuses on the representation of human form in art. Although his kingdom, Nippur, was once part of the Babylonian Empire, its religion seems to be Semitic, for, like Judaism, it forbids graven images. Nevertheless, even though he is a kindly, benevolent monarch, Balthazar has always liked paintings and sculptures more than people; in fact, Tournier has called Balthazar the character closest to himself because his interest in art parallels Tournier's interest in photography (d'Ivernois). Because Balthazar most treasures art's apparent ability to freeze time, his talisman, a block of myrrh used in embalming, symbolizes his desire to make eternal the temporal. Balthazar has become disappointed in art in general, as well as in Greek sculpture in particular, because it represents not people as they are but impossibly beautiful gods and heroes (67); further, his religious scruples have been awakened by the destruction of his museum by a priest-incited mob. (In another anachronism, Balthazar not only has created the world's first art museum but is also the world's first archeologist.) Pondering the story of Creation in Genesis 1.26, Balthazar has decided that if God created man in

His "image" and His "likeness," those two words mean different things: "image" stands for outward resemblance and "likeness" for the "entire being—body and soul" (45), a reading Tournier claims that theologians he consulted were inclined to accept as possible (d'Ivernois).

Balthazar believes that God has forbidden representation of people in art because Original Sin has made them lose their "likeness" to God although they have kept the superficial resemblance, but he thinks the breach would be healed by a savior (46), as happens in Bethlehem through the Incarnation, which causes the "regeneration of the image" (207). Having given Jesus his block of myrrh, Balthazar will return to his kingdom to promote "modern artworks" (208), which will begin by representing the Adoration of the Magi. If Gaspard learns to imitate God by loving unpossessively, Balthazar learns to imitate the Creator through fostering creation. Tournier will treat artistic representation more fully in his next novel, *La Goutte d'or*, but in *Gaspard, Melchior et Balthazar* he already asks whether an artistic representation should be a literal reproduction of the appearance of a person or object. Balthazar thinks that a portrait should resemble the subject's face (71), but Assour, his favorite artist, wants to reveal inner essence, or "eternity drowned in flesh" (95). To an artist, creation is not copying what already exists but revealing what is hidden.

Within Balthazar's story, two incidents reflect Tournier's heterodox theology as developed in *Les Météores*. Years earlier, a man named Maalek taught the adolescent Balthazar about the three stages of the lives of butter-flies—caterpillar, cocoon, and butterfly—and explained that in the cocoon stage the organs of the caterpillar entirely dissolve, complete "simplification" being necessary for a radical transformation (62). Maalek compared this transition to human fear and to a political interregnum, but the context leads one also to relate it to religious history. In this symbolism, the Old Testament parallels the caterpillar stage, the life of Christ represents the cocoon stage, and the world after Christ's death represents the butterfly stage, the three stages reflecting the Three Ages in Joachim de Fiore's theology, so important in *Les Météores*. Seen through this interpretive grid, the Old Testament is associated with physical existence (as it was in *Les Météores*), the Gospels are linked with simplification and change, while the butterfly stage stands for not only freedom but also artistic representation (sanctioned by the Incarnation), because a butterfly which Maalek gave Balthazar had a design on it resembling a portrait. The symbolism may seem to suggest that the Incarnation is neces-sary for man's redemption just as the cocoon stage is necessary for the butterfly to develop, but the "simplification" represented by the cocoon does not have to come from the life of Christ; it could equally be a simplification of people's hearts and minds.

The other story clearly implies that man can resemble and imitate God without the Savior's help. Assour has been trying to reveal in his art the inner beauty of ordinary-looking people. In Jerusalem, he draws an undistinguished-looking woman whose face glows with love so that "the likeness carries and justifies the image, as Balthazar would say" (94). At the intermittently flowing Fountain of the Prophet, where crowds prevented a sick old man from filling his vessel, Assour saw the woman become beautiful through love when she shared her own painfully acquired water with the old man (94). Not only does this woman, even before Jesus' birth, have a likeness to God, but she acts like Christ, for her sharing of water is a human equivalent of a miracle performed by Jesus, who healed a sick man at the pool of Bethesda in Jerusalem because the crowds gathered to be cured by its miraculous water were too dense to allow the man to go in (John 5.1-9). Koussek's claim in *Les Météores* that Christianity is an unnecessary stage in religious history is illustrated by the fact that the woman's "image" coincides with her "likeness" before the redemption of the flesh through the Incarnation and Crucifixion, and her performing a Christlike act before Christ's birth shows that one can act like Christ even without knowing about him.

MELCHIOR, PRINCE OF PALMYRENE

Gaspard is concerned with skin; Balthazar is concerned with the mind; Melchior is concerned with the heart. By rights King of Palmyrène (Palmyra) now that his father has died, Melchior was driven out by his uncle before he could be crowned, so he says of himself, "I am a king, but I am poor" (83). Fleeing for his life, he discovers his political naiveté when Herod reveals to him the immoral, manipulative aspect of rule, teaching Melchior that "violence and fear must be part of earthly rule" (210). As a result, Melchior renounces his ambition to regain his throne. Just as Gaspard discovers at Bethlehem a new kind of love and Balthazar a new kind of art, Melchior discovers a new kind of ruler, the Baby Jesus who unites "strength and weakness" (211). He therefore decides to create a new kind of kingdom, the city of God on earth. To symbolize his renunciation, he gives the Infant his only money, a piece of gold bearing the image of his father, which was to have documented his claim to be the legitimate heir.

Melchior is more deeply moved by seeing Jesus than the two older men are, so his imitation of God is more radical than theirs. Gaspard imitates God in giving freedom to Biltine; Balthazar imitates God by creating, through the artists he patronizes; Melchior will imitate God by founding a religious city. Melchior's life is thus a closer imitation of Jesus' ministry, an imitation prepared for by the fact that his mother was a poor bedouin whom the king married and made queen after she conceived and bore Melchior. His birth reflects, on a human level, Jesus' conception by Mary, a woman of "low estate" (Luke 1.46), before her marriage to Joseph (Matt. 1.18; Luke 1.27).

The Magi have needed Christ's Incarnation to understand how to imitate God, for Gaspard's suspicion that Adam may have been black needs confirmation by a miraculously black Christ; Balthazar's hope that art can be redeemed needs a spectacular first subject, the Adoration of the Magi; and Melchior's disgust with earthly politics needs a corresponding alternative of hope for a city of God on earth. However, exceptional people, like Assour and the woman he sees at the fountain, do not need the Incarnation to learn how to imitate God. As in *Les Météores*, the Incarnation fulfills an imaginative need, not a theological or intellectual one, so those who are especially attuned to others need less inspiration than do ordinary people. But unlike the Incarnation, which may be necessary to inspire ordinary people, Christ's death on the cross is presented as entirely unnecessary; the Magi are reconciled to God and themselves without it. This fact reflects Tournier's insistence that celebration of the flesh should be at the center of Christianity and his belief that Catholicism is wrong to make the crucifix "the center of Catholic worship" (*Vent* 64-65).

BARBEDOR AND HEROD

The next two chapters, "Barbedor" and "Herod the Great," form a striking contrast that can best be brought out by treating them together. "Barbedor" is told at Herod's banquet by Sangali, a tale-teller from the Malabar Coast of India, which is also the home of Prince Taor, the fourth Wise Man. In Sangali's tale, which I have discussed in the chapter on the short fiction, King Nabounassar III, known as Barbedor, is miraculously transformed from an old king with no heirs into his own successor, Nabounassar IV, a child-king whose succession is proclaimed by a supernatural white bird. Although it may be read as a story of psychological rejuvenation, the context requires also that it be seen as an allegory of the birth of Christ: the old king (Jehovah), whose country is stagnating, becomes a new, younger king (Jesus). This new ruler is both the same as and different from the old king, his succession proclaimed by a white bird suggesting the Holy Spirit descending as a dove at Christ's baptism (Matt. 3.16-17). Tournier makes explicit the link between Christ and Nabounassar IV when Herod himself compares the bird to the comet announcing the birth of the new King of the Jews (147). The tale tells Herod to imitate God by allowing his successor peacefully to take his place, but Herod cannot do so. Determined to hold the throne as long as possible, he will soon send soldiers to massacre all the little children of Bethlehem in an attempt to kill the new King of the Jews.

Though it has a Christian meaning, "Barbedor" suggests a nonorthodox theology, for at the end an aging Nabounassar IV resembles more and more Nabounassar III, so that a cycle is suggested in which the birth of Jesus cannot be, as in standard Christian theology, a unique event. This vision at once suggests the many myths of eternal return and implies that Christianity is merely one stage in the development of true religion. Tournier could not develop the latter idea without undercutting the explicit Christianity of the novel, but its suggestion is entirely in keeping with the book's heterodox subtext.

The myth of Barbedor contrasts strikingly to the mainly historically accurate narration of King Herod which follows it and which presents a prosaic picture of Israel and Judea at the time of Jesus' birth. Tournier has said he took this approach from Flaubert, specifically his story "Hérodias," which climaxes with the beheading of John the Baptist (Pudlowski). In that story, Flaubert carefully reconstructs the atmosphere of power politics at the court of Herod Antipas the Tetrarch, much as Tournier creates the terror at the court of King Herod the Great, father of Herod Antipas. As Tournier says, the everyday, "detailed realism" in "Hérodias" with its "prosaic" elements takes on an "incomparable value" because it is carried along by the "irresistible mythic force" of the story of John the Baptist (*Vol* 166). Just as in "Hérodias" a familiar story is told from an unfamiliar angle so that what is normally the foreground becomes the background (*Vol* 166), so in *Gaspard, Melchior et Balthazar* the details of Herod's life are transfigured by the surrounding story of the birth of Christ, while the power and familiarity of that story allow Tournier to indulge in minutely detailed realism.

Herod's tale, based like Flaubert's "Hérodias" largely on the accounts of Flavius Josephus, particularly Books 14 through 17 of *The Antiquities of the Jews*, takes up about a sixth of the book—a good deal more than it needs to, and almost more than the book can sustain. Tournier himself has said he fears that this section may not be well integrated with the rest of the novel (Lapouge 42), but I believe that including the revolting details of the many betrayals at Herod's court is justified by the fact that they counterbalance the lightness and delicacy of the other narratives. Nevertheless, they form a hard lump of bitterness at the book's physical (if not moral) center. The events include the execution of the only woman Herod ever loved, his aristocratic wife Mariamme (called Mariamne by Josephus), who was accused of treason by her own mother; the court intrigues of Herod and Mariamme's sons and their wives, resulting in the sons' execution for treason; the poisoning of Herod's brother Phéroras; the attempted suicide of Phéroras's wife; the machinations of Antipater, Herod's son by his wife Doris, leading to Antipater's execution; a suicide attempt by Herod; and countless other betrayals, diplomatic and personal, all seeming to justify Herod's definition of "reason of state" as "madness of state" (138) because political reasons make people act insanely.

Herod claims that the overriding lesson to be learned from his life is that "power corrupts" (123): a wise ruler must be an evil man. When Herod offers prudent but cruel solutions to the problems of Gaspard, Balthazar, and Melchior, we realize that all three Magi lack the toughness necessary to be real rulers in troubled countries. Herod (whose spies have kept him informed about the troubles of each of the Magi) recommends that Gaspard, so enamored of Biltine's white skin, have it peeled from her body and that Balthazar should assert his power over the priests by burning alive the leaders of the riot which destroyed his art museum (125). As to Melchior, Herod claims he would never have been driven out of Palmyrène if he had followed the "law of power: strike first when there is the slightest suspicion" and killed his uncle before he could usurp the throne (126). Herod, faced with similar problems, has applied the sort of solutions he recommends; this is why, although his kingdom is prosperous, he is hated by everyone at court, including his family, and says, unconsciously echoing Gaspard's and Melchior's statements, "I am a king ... but I am dying, alone and without hope" (122).

The contrast of Herod's real-world power politics to the actions of Gaspard, Balthazar, and Melchior shows that the stories of the three Wise Men, though fairly realistic, belong more to the world of the tale than to the world of experience. Herod's story reflects the intractability of real life, for his narration has the shapelessness of the *nouvelle*, which is based on true events, rather than the *conte*. This difference between the tales of the Magi and a true story is underscored by the fact that Herod is speaking to his guests with the specific goal of winning their sympathy, so he is trying to shape his materials into a coherent form in which he will emerge as the victim of others' intrigues. Herod's manipulation of his listeners through distorting facts and emphasizing his supposed emotional conflicts is all the clearer when one contrasts his version with that of Josephus. For example, Josephus says that the court convicted Mariamne of treason because it saw that Herod wanted her to die, and that her mother accused her only after Mariamne had already been condemned (537 [*Antiquities* XIV.7.4]). Josephus thus makes Herod entirely responsible for her death, whereas Tournier's Herod claims that Mariamme's mother's accusations came before the trial and made the trial inevitable, and he takes no responsibility for Mariamme's conviction (130). Despite Herod's attempt to shape the story to make himself appear a model king, it has all the characteristics of real-life narrations—lack of plausibility, unreliability, shapelessness—unlike the other tales in the book, which are formed, meaningful artistic creations in which the questions posed all find answers, particularly "Barbedor," which immediately precedes it.

This contrast reflects Balthazar's debate with Assour. Just as Assour wants to show the inner essence of his subjects, even if it means changing the surface to do so, Tournier wants to reveal what he believes is the true nature or meaning of life, not merely to reproduce its surface. He comes closest to literal reproduction in Herod's tale because of its basis in Josephus' histories, but he prefers manipulating the surface of reality to a greater extent, as he does in the other chapters, where he gives freer rein to his sense of humor and interest in patterns. Nevertheless, two details apparently of Tournier's own creation enliven the material about Herod and prepare for the last section of *Gaspard, Melchior et Balthazar*, in which food will be a main symbol. The first, recounted by Melchior, is Herod's gleeful explanation that the main dish he is serving his royal guests is roast vulture accompanied by death's-trumpet mushrooms (103-04). The other, which Herod tells, is even more sinister: when his beloved Mariamme was executed, Herod's grief was so great that, to preserve her body, he had it "drowned in an open coffin, filled with transparent honey" and for seven years watched her body dissolve in it (130). Eating vultures and preserving a dead woman in food symbolize Herod's mental sickness, in which death invades life; both actions anticipate the role food will play in the novel's last section; and both are typical of the often grotesque, generally paradoxical symbols Tournier uses to establish a reader's attitudes or feelings.

Two pages recounted by an omniscient third-person narrator end Herod's chapter by returning to the world of the tale—at this point a most reassuring one, after the poisonings, betrayals, and torture of Herod's court. In these two pages, carefully balanced phrases stress the parallels among the Magi's situations: Gaspard, riding his camel, thinks of love; Balthazar, riding his horse, thinks of art; and Melchior, walking, thinks of power. Each king is shocked by Herod's autobiography, each interprets and evaluates Herod's story, and each tries to imagine the future signaled by the white bird of Sangali's tale (150), which they identify with the comet.

THE OX AND THE ASS

That short passage at the end of Herod's chapter makes a transition into the chapter which forms the novel's heart and attempts the most difficult task, recounting the birth of Jesus. The technical problem was enormous: how could anyone retell such familiar material without either destroying its mythic quality through insisting on the ordinary or reducing it to sentimentality through stressing the miraculous? Tournier handles the problem of tone through carefully choosing the angle of vision, carrying Flaubert's technique a step further, for the first half of this chapter is told in third person, from the ox's viewpoint; the second half is narrated by the ass.

Like "Hérodias," the ox's story reconciles the ordinary with the divine by showing the events from an unfamiliar angle, so that our expectations are shifted without being defeated. As one might expect, the ox is neither a talker nor a thinker, but a dreamer. His memory is a racial one, that of all oxen; having been present at the miraculous birth of the Egyptian ox Apis, he is not especially impressed by the birth of the "little god" in the stable, which is only one more divine incarnation in a long chain of them (155). The ox's calm acceptance of the miraculous events introduces them gently, while the unusual angle lets Tournier use our prejudice that animals are more sensitive to the supernatural than we are. Finally, the ox's memories of pagan religion establish a link between paganism and Christianity, helping to universalize the narration as well as to reinforce the heterodox idea, already suggested in "Barbedor," that Christ's birth is only one of many such events, each inaugurating a new religious era.

The ass's story has a radically different tone, for this garrulous first-person narrator has a distinctly human voice, although his ordinary concerns include the harsh treatment asses receive from their owners, the difficulties of plowing when yoked to an ox, and the sore just behind his ear. The ass's name, Kadi Chouïa, means something like the "silly little sage" (157-58), an oxymoron that sums him up. He enjoys explaining the Archangel Gabriel's actions and tells vividly of the birth of Jesus and the visit of the shepherds to the manger.

This chatty style carries the reader through the miraculous events it recounts. Tournier does not risk focusing for long on Joseph, Mary, and Jesus, but quickly passes over them in favor of the Archangel Gabriel and Silas the Samaritan, a vegetarian shepherd who would be considered an unbeliever by the Jews because the inhabitants of Samaria were of racially mixed descent and followed religious practices that differed somewhat from those of the other Jews. Perhaps it is his outsider's point of view that makes Silas ask Gabriel about the meaning not only of the Incarnation but of the animal sacrifices God has demanded for centuries—and, to begin with, he wants to know why God asked Abraham to sacrifice his son Isaac. In the theological discussion which follows, Gabriel uses orthodox Christian interpretation in connecting the aborted sacrifice of Isaac, for whom God substituted a ram at the last minute, with the future death of Christ on the cross (165). Silas, on the other hand, worries about Isaac's fright and the animal sacrifices performed later in Jerusalem, and he asks if God refused Cain's sacrifice of vegetables but accepted Abel's sacrifice of lambs because He is carnivorous. Without answering that question, Gabriel explains that the "Son will soon be offered again as a holocaust by the Father himself" and that from then on "the blood of the Son will flow on altars for man's salvation" (167) so that no animals will ever again have to be offered to God. Gabriel does not, however, discuss whether Christ's death is necessary, nor does he explain why God wants any sacrifice, human or animal. As a result, the orthodox explanation seems incomplete and inadequate.

The discussion ends on a whimsical note when the ass asks whether he has been forgotten; and when Gabriel then assures him that on Palm Sunday the Lord will ride into Jerusalem on an ass's colt, Kadi Chouïa finally feels a part of the "Christmas family" (169). This section walks a narrow line among theological explication, whimsy, and prosaic description. The ass's energy and good humor carry the story through the account of Christ's birth and the theological discussion, which is enlivened through the potential conflict between Silas and the Archangel Gabriel.

TAOR IN "THE AGE OF SUGAR"

The last story, constituting over a third of *Gaspard, Melchior et Balthazar*, is the third-person narration of the fourth Wise Man, Taor, Prince of Mangalore on the Malabar Coast. Here nearly all the previous issues are reconsidered, but from a perspective outside Semitic tradition, so that the stories of the four Magi, although similar in that each recounts a prince or king's search for the Christ Child, are composed of three closely related ones and a fourth, last one which is different in tone, style, and many specifics.

This contrast reflects and probably was suggested by the relationship among the four Gospels. All the Gospels tell the life of Christ, but Matthew, Mark, and Luke, the synoptic Gospels, are very similar, whereas the fourth, John, differs from them in many details, as Tournier knows (Lapouge 33). One important difference is that John appears to be written more for a non-Jewish audience than the other three Gospels are, for it begins not with Jesus' genealogy and birth, as Matthew and Luke do, nor with the preaching of John the Baptist, as Mark does, but with a philosophical account of Creation—"In the beginning was the Word"—which Tournier has called a "metaphysical nativity" (Lapouge 33). Tournier echoes these differences first in the fact that Gaspard, Balthazar, and Melchior all see Jesus at Bethlehem, but Taor does not, and second in Taor's ignorance of Semitic tradition, in contrast to the other Magi, who, although not Jewish, are influenced by Judaism.

In choosing the Malabar Coast of India as the home of the fourth Wise Man, Tournier encourages the reader to associate Taor with Oriental beliefs generally, just as his use of Sangali, Herod's Oriental storyteller from Malabar, reinforces the association of Malabar with a generalized East. Malabar, however, has a particular resonance for Tournier because Malabar was—and, to some extent still is—one of the main strongholds of the Nestorian Church, whose doctrines, alluded to through the character Nestor in *Le Roi des aulnes*, helped to explain that novel's theme, as well as underlying Koussek's theology in *Les Météores*, as I explained in the chapters on those books.

In Malabar, though, most of the Nestorians reunited with Catholicism in 1599 and, after a subsequent breach, returned in 1662 ("Malabar Christians";

for more detail, see Podipara 92-94), but because they belong to the Congregation for the Oriental Church, they do not follow all of the practices of European Catholics (Podipara 95; Von Euw). Tournier had already implied a reconciliation of Nestorianism and Catholicism in *Les Météores* through Koussek, a Catholic priest who seems to be under the jurisdiction of the Oriental Church, for Koussek speaks of becoming a disciple of an Eastern branch of Catholicism which is "close to Orthodox theology" and which will serve one day to unite Catholicism with the Orthodox Church (153). At the same time, Koussek is associated with Nestorianism both by his attack on *Filioque* and by his Paris church itself, Saint-Esprit, which blends modern with Byzantine architecture. Alexandre thinks most Catholic churches are "dedicated more to the cult of death than to praising life" (123), but he finds Koussek's Saint-Esprit cheerful and lively. It does not display the crucifix prominently, and this difference is highly significant, for the crucifix is for Tournier a symbol of death, whereas, he says, "other churches, the Orthodox Church for example, know that Christ is also God triumphant, the Pantocrator rather than a corpse" (Lapouge 40). In choosing Malabar as Taor's origin, then, Tournier is linking Taor with the reconciliation of Nestorianism and Catholicism and may be suggesting that Catholicism can be revived through Nestorian influence. This is not to suggest, of course, that Taor is a Catholic; in a literal sense, he barely becomes a Christian.

Despite his Malabar origin and his differences from the other Wise Men, Taor must travel from ignorance to knowledge just as they do, and he has the longest journey not only physically but spiritually, for he is only twenty years old, and not a very mature twenty. His story is divided into two sections, the first called "The Age of Sugar," in which he moves from a prolonged childhood into adulthood, the second called "The Hell of Salt," telling of his suffering as an adult. Seeing sugar and salt as opposites is particularly French, because the French habitually classify food as either *salé* or *sucré*—literally "salted" or "sugared"—and traditional French cooking does not combine the two flavors; for example, it does not include ham with pineapple or pork with apples. On the other hand, the physical resemblance of sugar and salt and their ordinariness make them effective symbols of related opposites. As early as *Vendredi* Tournier imagined a meal of turtle and blueberries; Robinson, accustomed to keeping such foods separate, disliked it only slightly less than the slices of snake garnished with locusts which Vendredi fed him the next day (210). Just as Robinson had to learn to try different kinds of food, no matter how outlandish they seemed, so Taor will have to learn to accept salt as well as sugar. Sugar, with its natural appeal to children, symbolizes Taor's prolonged childhood in a kingdom where his widowed mother is concerned mainly with keeping power to herself and where Taor is interested mainly in candy, which is why he leaves his kingdom to get the recipe for pistachio Turkish delight, the sort of whimsical incongruity which Tournier has perfected in his books for children. The origin of Taor's quest is not simply whimsical, though, for it demonstrates Tournier's belief that one must embrace sensuality. And food, as Taor discovers, runs through Jesus' ministry, from his first miracle, changing water to wine at the wedding at Cana, to the Last Supper.

Taor, then, sets out on a pleasure trip with five ships, five elephants, numerous cooks, an incredible array of rich foods, and a huge entourage, heading for Judea because his scouts have discovered that prophets in the Judean deserts are eating locusts preserved in wild honey and prophesying the coming of a "Divine Candymaker" who will give people a food so delicious that they will hunger no more (177). During a trip which gradually strips Taor of all his possessions and followers, he has a series of revelations which radically change his quest. This change is hinted at before he leaves Mangalore through the symbols of sugar and salt, for when he tastes the salty locusts preserved in honey, he discovers that "salty sweets are sweeter than sugary sweets" (179), his first suggestion that life cannot, or should not, be all sugar.

Taor's first major discovery comes when his ships stop at the Island of Dioscorides, where the Rabbi Rizza teaches him about the Garden of Eden, telling a "fable" whose "translucency" Taor cannot pierce (189). Yet the idea of fruits conferring wisdom and knowledge suggests to Taor a link between physical and spiritual nourishment as well as showing him their present separation, which can be ended only by divine power (191). The extremely simple meal consisting mainly of bread made of flour, water, and salt which Rizza feeds Taor is important here, too, for it gives Taor his first inkling of the physical and symbolic value of simple food (189). Taor's second awakening is his realization that his supposedly devoted slave, Siri Akbar, may have his own plans and desires. Taor's third awakening comes as the caravan goes by land toward Bethlehem, as a tribe of Baobalis, who believe themselves to be the descendants of the baobab tree, decide that Taor's albino elephant, Yasmina, is an incarnation of their goddess Baobama. Yasmina obviously thinks that their adoration of her is only her due, so Taor must be content with losing her to the adoring Baobalis. Through this farcical episode, Taor is exposed to the idea of the incarnation of a deity.

Taor's education continues when he meets Gaspard, Balthazar, and Melchior. Each of the Wise Men tells Taor of his own quest, but Taor does not see the connection between their interests—love, art, and power—and his concern with food. He does, however, realize that each man's question was answered at Bethlehem, and he expects his own quest to be fulfilled when he also reaches Bethlehem. But several accidents delay him, so he arrives only after the Holy Family have fled to Egypt. Rather than follow at once, Taor shows that he has matured enough to care about other people by giving a banquet for all the starving little children in Bethlehem except the very youngest, who would need adults to care for them. Horribly, the night of the banquet is also the night of the Massacre of the Innocents, so while Taor is feeding the children older than two, soldiers are carrying out Herod's orders to kill all the male children under two.

This juxtaposition of banquet and bloody massacre is a turning point for Taor, who discovers wickedness and begins to feel that he has a destiny. Even before the massacre, he thinks that in Judea everything has hidden meanings, including himself (223), and that finding out his own meaning will lead to abandoning his past and accepting whatever the future brings. When he learns of the massacre, he feels that there is a "hidden connection" between the feast and the killing, that the events are only a sort of "awkward rehearsal" for another event which would blend "friendly meal and bloody death" (227)— in short, though he does not yet know it, the Last Supper and the Crucifixion. This connection is not just due to the temporal proximity of the Last Supper and the Crucifixion; rather, theologians have argued that the Last Supper and Communion "both were integrally related to the one immolation on Calvary" ("Eucharist" 476) and that they are "a means through which the efficacy and power of the death and resurrection of Jesus (the unique eschatological event) is applied to successive generations" (Wallace 244). It is this theological connection that Taor anticipates.

TAOR IN "THE HELL OF SALT"

The shock of the massacre moves Taor from his childhood "Age of Sugar" to adulthood, where he will discover in the mines of Sodom "The Hell of Salt," in the words of the title of the second half of his chapter. Unlike sugar, salt is corrosive, but it is both a preservative and an element essential to life, which is presumably why Jesus in the Sermon on the Mount called his followers the "salt of the earth" (Matt. 5.13). As a symbol of adulthood, salt also represents knowledge and experience of evil, which may cause pain but which are necessary for maturity. Taor tasted salt first when he ate the locusts preserved in honey, next when he had a "baptism" by being drenched in the waters of the Red Sea (184). His third encounter with it begins in a place which Siri calls Satan's Kingdom because the land is so low-lying and menacing (227), where Taor experiments with floating in the salt- and mineral-clogged waters of the Dead Sea. There he experiences his first miracle: the palms of his hands bleed with the stigmata. The corrosive water is capable of opening new wounds, but Taor has no recent scars; rather, he bleeds as if obeying a "mysterious order" (229). This little miracle foreshadows Taor's subsequent imitation of Christ.

That imitation, which began in a sense with Taor's leaving his comfortable principality for a risk-laden journey, starts in earnest at the south end of the Dead Sea, in the city of Sodom. Although destroyed by God for its wickedness (Gen. 19.23-25) and now lying in ruins as if annihilated by an atomic bomb, with silhouettes of men, women, and animals imprinted on the walls and pavements (232), Sodom remains an underground city and major exporter of salt. There, after freeing his few remaining followers, Taor finds his destiny when he gives up his freedom to save a young father who is about to be sentenced to the salt mines for debt. The 33 years that he must work correspond to Jesus' life on earth.

Like Herod's tale, the salt mine section reveals a sort of hell. Herod's court is a hell of intrigue and suspicion; Sodom is a hell of artificiality and impersonality. The section is both about living in the salt mines (this part based on historical research) and about living in an imaginary civilization in which sodomy is the norm, for the inhabitants of Sodom, who administer the mines, are all sodomites, men and women. Tournier has said that these pages were difficult to write because he wanted neither to defend nor to condemn the Sodomites, and because he wanted the society to be "great" because "after all, it is Hell" (Lapouge 43). Taor is interested in food, not sex, but he carefully observes the Sodomites, whom even God's wrath could not entirely destroy. In their thinness, dryness, and lack of tenderness (239), as well as in their intelligence and cruel wit (252), they are reminiscent of the homosexual Alexandre in *Les Météores*; like him and Koussek, they have elaborate theories about their superiority and that of their sexual practices, which preserve women's virginity and prevent unwanted conception (255). Not surprisingly, Taor is especially interested in their food, which is so assimilable that their intestines remain empty and sperm can move from the sphincter throughout the body, after first going *up* the digestive tract (254-55)—a special kind of inversion.

This fantastic and imaginative treatment of a civilization which literally exists underground is a symbolic representation of "underground" homosexual society today. The "pity and repulsion" Taor feels (254) strike the dominant note of the entire passage, which describes people who do not love themselves or each other and whose goddess is Lot's wife, a symbol of unwillingness to change because God turned her into a pillar of salt when she looked back on the destruction of Sodom. The Sodomites call her the "Dead Mother," in a play on words, for that name, "la Mère Morte," sounds just like "la mer Morte," or the Dead Sea. Salt is necessary to life, but too much salt kills it, just as the abundance of salt in the Dead Sea kills all animal life in it. The whole culture of Sodom celebrates a kind of deadness; Taor correctly sees the Sodomites as "prisoners of an unshakable attitude of denigration and corrosion" (252). This denigration, however, read in the context of Tournier's entire *œuvre*, does not derive from their sodomy itself but rather from two other causes. First is their rejection by other Jews, which makes them secretive and defensive about their beliefs and practices; their conception of themselves as a persecuted minority, like Alexandre Surin's view of himself, is a product of society just as, in Tournier's view, society has created homosexuality by labeling it and classifying its practitioners, rather than simply letting people follow their sexual impulses (Sanzio et al. 18). Second is their inability to sublimate sexual feelings, for sublimation of sexuality is the source of fulfillment for Tournier's protagonists, whatever their sexual orientation.

Forced to learn to sublimate his desire for sweets, Taor manages to accept everything that happens as part of his destiny. That destiny begins to make sense when he befriends a fisherman, Démas, who has heard Jesus preach and knows of some of his miracles. Naturally, Taor is most interested in anything concerning food, and much of the charm of this section comes from its insistence on the importance of food and drink in the life of Christ. Taor listens eagerly to Démas's account of Jesus changing water to wine at the wedding at Cana, feeding the five thousand with five loaves and two fishes, causing the miraculous catch of fish, and telling the parable of the rich man's banquet. Taor likes especially his saying that he is the "living bread" (John 6.51) and that man must eat his flesh and drink his blood to be saved (260). Taor realizes at once that Jesus is predicting his own death and connects that death with the Massacre of the Innocents, thinking that "feasting and human sacrifice had not taken place together at Bethlehem by accident: they were the two faces of the same sacrament" (260). Taor also feels, suddenly, that his years in the salt mines are justified, for the banquet he gave at Bethlehem was merely a present of the merchandise of his caravan, but his sacrifice for the children of the bankrupt man was a "gift of his flesh and his life" (260).

At the start of Taor's story, he wanted the recipe for pistachio Turkish delight, but it is now salt-free water that he most longs for. That is why he is deeply moved when Démas tells him that Jesus said that he is the living water which will quench thirst forever. "No one knew better than Taor that this was not a metaphor" (261). How can this be? Literally, it *has* to be a metaphor. But Taor, remembering Rizza telling of the fruits of the Garden of Eden which fed both the body and the soul, longs not only for such divine food but for a condition in which body and soul are one, the condition (although he does not think of it in these terms) in which man possesses both God's image and His likeness. Finally, Démas tells of the Sermon on the Mount, where Jesus says, "Blessed *are* they which do hunger and thirst after righteousness: for they shall be filled" (Matt. 5.6). Démas, however, mentions only thirst, so Taor feels that the verse is directly addressed to him because of his unremitting thirst, and a miracle happens: a salt-free tear rolls from Taor's eye into his mouth, letting him taste his first drop of pure water since his incarceration.

Without knowing it, Taor has become a saint, and Tournier has moved the narration back into the realm of the miraculous, where it was when the ass told of the birth of Christ. Released after 33 years, Taor searches for Jesus, sustained by invisible angels in his journey first to Bethany and then to Jerusalem, where Jesus is celebrating Passover with his Disciples. It is what the Christian Church will call Maundy Thursday, the day Jesus instituted the Last Supper, the day before the Crucifixion. Taor arrives at the house of Joseph of Arimathea after Jesus and the Disciples have left for Gethsemane, but when Taor is let into the upper room where they have eaten the Passover meal, he finds the remains of the unleavened bread and the wine. Suddenly hungry, Taor takes some of each, so that the "perpetual latecomer . . . received the Eucharist the first" (265)—first after, of course, the Disciples. In the book's final sentence, he is immediately carried off to Heaven by the two angels that have been following him since Sodom. One cannot be sure, but perhaps not just his soul but his body also ascends to Heaven, soul and body finally fully united (Petit, "Salvation" 63-64).

This ending is not easy to bring off, as Tournier runs the risk of being accused of sentimentality and bad taste here more than anywhere else in the novel. I think he does escape sentimentality, partly through using a fairly bare narrative style in the last pages, seasoned with such realistic details as he can include without compromising narrative directness. The most sentimental thing he could have done would have been to introduce Jesus at the end without making him convincing; as Tournier candidly told an interviewer, he did not have the ability to include Jesus as a character (Daly, "Interview" 408). (In Henry van Dyke's *The Story of the Other Wise Man*, the presence of Jesus even in the distance at the book's climax adds to the sentimentality.) Also, since Taor shares with most of Tournier's protagonists the gift of refusing to pity himself, a reader is unlikely to feel pushed into sympathizing with him.

Taste is harder to judge. Any attempt to present elements from the life of Christ in a religious framework is likely to seem in bad taste to someone. But Tournier has prepared for the angels and the miracle at the end through the presence of Gabriel at Bethlehem, in a context where one expects an angel, and through his use of the miraculous in that narration and, to a lesser extent, in Taor's own life. The novel also prepares for the miraculous ending by having the events of Taor's story echo successively each of the previous narrations. Taor's safe world of teenaged gluttony resembles Gaspard's harmonious kingdom and his lust for Biltine; Taor's learning of the Garden of Eden from Rizza reflects Balthazar's concern with the creation of Adam, just as Rizza's desire to unite spirit and flesh reflects Balthazar's concern with the Incarnation; Taor's discovery of Siri's political ambitions parallels Melchior's lesson in politics; Yasmina's "incarnation" as Baobama is as whimsical as Sangali's story of Barbedor's reincarnation; the Massacre of the Innocents, taking place at the same time as Taor's banquet for the older children, has the same combination of violence and food as Herod's tale narrated at his banquet, while Taor's life in the salt mines reflects the historical realities of the time and place just as Herod's life does; Démas's accounts of Christ's ministry, told as they are by someone only moderately impressed by them, echo the ox's blasé account of Jesus' birth; and Taor's communing and ascension to Heaven have the same miraculous quality as the ass's narration of Christ's birth.

Besides the preparation provided by the parallel events I have just listed, Taor's taking the Eucharist at Jerusalem has been prepared for by the many references to food throughout the novel. Gaspard, who makes a number of observations about food and finds too bland a meal of beans spiced with onion and cumin (38), sleeps with Biltine for the first time after a revoltingly sumptuous banquet including ewes' tails and zucchini stuffed with puppy brains (24). Balthazar is not especially interested in food, but because his name is slang for a banquet, Tournier apparently first imagined him as a big eater (Ezine, "Michel Tournier" 228). Barbedor generally eats heavy lunches, but they presumably could not match in outlandishness the foods Herod serves, not only the previously mentioned roast vulture with death's-trumpet mushrooms, but also camels' tongues and peacocks' brains (102). Most of these foods, which reflect the banquets Flaubert describes in *Salammbô* and "Hérodias," are repulsive to a modern reader and are described unappetizingly: "The jaws closed, sharp teeth sank in, Adam's apples rose under the effort of swallowing" (102).

In the first part of the novel, the richness of most of the food is repulsive, but in Taor's section, foods are too sweet rather than too rich, such as the banquet he gives the little children at Bethlehem, which includes pineapple fritters, litchi-nut soufflés, and a huge "pièce montée" (reminiscent of the "pièce montée" at the wedding in Flaubert's *Madame Bovary*) reproducing the palace of Mangalore in nougat, marzipan, caramel, and candied fruits (222). Food leads Taor to his salvation, but he must renounce the childishly sweet concoctions he has loved before he can learn to appreciate simple, wholesome food, such as bread and wine, these foods foreshadowed not only by the simple bread Rizza gives him and by his diet of salt fish in the mines, but by his learning of Christ's miracles involving bread, wine, and fish. Throughout, characters have found meaning in their foods, and the contrast between bread and wine and the too-rich, too-sweet, and too-odd foods of the banquets reinforces the difference between self-indulgence and simple enjoyment of the physical pleasure of eating.

Not only does the end bring together the key symbols in the novel; it also provides the final answer to the question of how one can imitate God. As the only person to sacrifice his life for someone else, Taor has unknowingly imitated Christ's Incarnation and ministry, and his ascension to Heaven confirms his saintliness. Ironically, he gives his life before he knows anything of Christ, but this irony is the point, for it reinforces the subtext that one does not need to know anything of Christ to be saved. What Taor learns from Démas of Jesus' teachings merely confirms or explains to him his actions; it does not influence them. Like the woman at the well whom Assour sketched, Taor has not lost his inner likeness to God, although he has had to discover his destiny through a difficult journey; and though his life is a rough parallel to Jesus' life, he sacrifices himself and later communes in Jerusalem instinctively, not because self-sacrifice or Communion are commanded or offered as models.

It is difficult to judge to what extent Taor's salvation stretches Catholic theology, for the Catholic Church holds that those "who, without fault of their own," do not know about Christ and who "follow the dictates of their conscience" are members of the Church and so can be saved (Eminyan, "Necessity" 997). This definition seems to apply to Taor, for though he is not exactly ignorant of Christ, he does not know much of Christ's teachings or deeds except insofar as they concern food, and he does follow his conscience. Taor may thus be one of the "invisible members of the Catholic Church," those who are "vitally united to Christ" through grace (Eminyan, "Extra Ecclesiam"). Also, because Tournier called Taor's drenching in the Red Sea a "baptism," he seems to want to make Taor at least symbolically a member of the Church. Nevertheless, the same theology that motivated *Les Météores* is illustrated here: Christ's death is not necessary for salvation. Because Taor is carried to Heaven by the angels on the night before the Crucifixion, he is not saved by Christ's death, not justified by his Resurrection, because those events have not yet happened.

The book's popular success in France was due no doubt in part to its seeming orthodoxy, the same cause of its lesser success with reviewers, who took it as a pious tale. In fact, as I have shown, it fits clearly into the sequence of stories using revisionist Christian theology which Tournier has been constructing since *Vendredi*, the major difference being that Tournier here has created a less controversial surface so his story can reach a large audience. Rather than considering what to most readers would be abstruse philosophical questions, it asks the more familiar question "What does it mean to imitate Christ?" Although the book seems to be simpler than the earlier novels, it is not; it is merely written in a more accessible style, with fewer details, less embroidering, and less use of deliberately provocative words and ideas. There is a consequent gain in novelistic emphasis, for analysis and explanation have been replaced by action. The major loss in this book, compared with the previous novels, is in characterization, for the main characters are all fairly uncomplicated, unlike Robinson, Tiffauges, and Alexandre, who each had a developed intellect and a strong propensity to explore and justify their negative sides. Although plot has always been the key to Tournier's fiction, the reduction in importance of characterization in *Gaspard, Melchior et Balthazar* throws plot into even stronger relief than in the previous novels and reveals more clearly than before, even rather starkly, how Tournier shows his ideas through plot action. In his fifth novel, *La Goutte d'or*, he will carry this process even further.

7

La Goutte d'or: Images and Signs

At the end of 1985, five years after *Gaspard, Melchior et Balthazar*, Michel Tournier published *La Goutte d'or*. Although in 1978 he had thought that it would be his next book (Brochier, "Dix-huit" 13; Braudeau 82), he interrupted work on it to complete *Gaspard, Melchior et Balthazar*, and perhaps because of this overlapping composition, the two books have a stylistic resemblance, both using simple, accessible language, *La Goutte d'or* being even more pared down than *Gaspard, Melchior et Balthazar*. On the surface, the two books are different, for *La Goutte d'or* tells the story of an Algerian teenager who emigrates to Paris looking for work, and his misadventures give rise to a largely satiric treatment of modern France, but the book's theme, the relationship between signs and images, is one Tournier had already begun to treat in the story of Balthazar.

Critical reception of *La Goutte d'or* was mixed. By 1985 Tournier was one of the best-known writers in France, not only for his novels but also for his other activities, particularly his membership in the Académie Goncourt, his essays in newspapers and magazines, his literary criticism, and his fiction marketed for children. Therefore, publication of this novel was an event. Interest in the book had no doubt also been whetted by previous publication of parts of it: in 1984 *La Nouvelle Revue Française* had published the embedded *conte* "Barberousse ou le portrait du roi," and in 1985 it printed several other pages under the title "Un Chameau à Paris" ("A Camel in Paris"), while, also in 1985, a special number of the *Cahiers Pierre-Baptiste* had published the section of the novel set in Marseille, under the title "Il était donc en France" ("So He Was in France").

Other publications helped draw attention to *La Goutte d'or*. The January 1986 *Magazine Littéraire* devoted to Tournier a "dossier" section illustrated by a selection of his favorite photographs and consisting of several brief critical essays, a review of *La Goutte d'or*, and an interview of Tournier by schoolchildren. Also, the first two books published in France about Tournier appeared in 1986, Serge Koster's *Michel Tournier*, containing Koster's rather impressionistic reflections about Tournier's previous fiction accompanied by 32 pages of photographs, and Salim Jay's *Idriss, Michel Tournier et les autres*, 24 alphabetically arranged meditations on French and North African culture, all inspired by characters and events in *La Goutte d'or*.

This publicity presumably contributed to the book's commercial success; its first run was an unusually large 80,000 copies (Jay, *Idriss* 101), and it headed the French best-seller list for four weeks. It is also the only one of Tournier's full-length novels to be available on tape cassette, read in its entirety by François Chaumette with an introductory "presentation" by Tournier. Despite this apparent consecration of the novel, its reviews ranged from the enthusiastic (Boisdeffre, rev. of *La Goutte*) through the merely favorable (Montalbetti; Piatier, "Michel Tournier et le voyage") and the non-committal (Dey; Merllié, rev. of *La Goutte*; Pancrazi) to the frankly hostile (Rinaldi, "Connaissez-vous"). Like the French original, the English translation by Barbara Wright, published in 1987 under the title *The Golden Droplet*, was also both condemned (Kakutani, Sieburth) and praised (Allen, Buzbee). Some of this mixed reaction was no doubt due to a misunderstanding of the theme of *La Goutte d'or*, which is visual art's relation to and difference from literature, expressed through a contrast between Moslem culture, which in theory forbids representation of people and animals, and popular French culture characterized by advertisements, television, shop windows, and other visual displays.

I will consider some philosophical and historical background before going on to the basic structure of *La Goutte d'or* and showing how the theme of image versus sign is treated throughout the novel.

THE PHILOSOPHICAL QUESTION

Because of his interest in photography, both as a skilled amateur and as a friend and admirer of professional photographers, Tournier has long been interested in the relationship between pictures and words. Recently he turned his attention to contemporary artists, writing short articles on 21 of them; these essays, along with several related meditations on art, were published in 1988 as *Le Tabor et le Sinaï: Essais sur l'art contemporain*. Tournier makes explicit the connection between *La Goutte d'or* and *Le Tabor et le Sinaï* by moving, in the latter book's introductory essay, from a discussion of the role of images in *La Goutte d'or* to the question of what it means for a work of art to be a representation (9-12).

To most writers, an image probably refers only to a mental picture or other mental sensory impression created by words, but Tournier approaches images through philosophy, which concerns itself with both physical and mental images and which almost always focuses on whether an image is a true representation. In *The Republic*, Plato holds that all artistic representations are at two removes from reality, for they are merely imperfect reproductions of the appearance of physical objects, while an object is only a "shadowy thing as compared with reality," that is, with the world of ideas (326). This idea is echoed in Pascal's *pensée* 134, "How useless is painting, which attracts admiration by the resemblance of things, the originals of which we do not admire!" (38), a statement which the teenaged Tournier thought ridiculous (*Vent* 158) and which he continues to condemn as an adult (*Tabor* 129). He has two reasons for objecting to Plato's and Pascal's criticisms: first, both rest on the belief that physical existence is unreal or ugly, and, second, both assume that the function of art is to represent the world. In contrast, Tournier celebrates physical existence and maintains that art should resemble not its "exterior model" but "its author, as a legitimate child naturally resembles its father" (*Tabor* 12).

Artistic representation, though, has been treated less by philosophy than mental images have been. As one would expect, Tournier's thinking has been influenced by Jean-Paul Sartre, who considered mental images in two of his earliest works, *Imagination: A Psychological Critique* (*L'Imagination*, 1936) and *The Psychology of Imagination* (*L'Imaginaire: Psychologie Phénoménologique de l'imagination*, 1940). In *Imagination* Sartre surveys nineteenth-century philosophical and psychological theories of images in order to show their methodological or conceptual failures. Unlike those theories, Sartre denies that a mental image is an emanation passively received by the mind and, indeed, says it is not any kind of thing; rather, he insists that it is action: "an image . . . is surely thought. We *form* images, we *construct* schemata" (*Imagination* 105, emphasis in original). In *The Psychology of Imagination*, Sartre says that, rather than a copy of something external, an image is "a consciousness" (4), an act performed by the mind. To think this way is to free an image from the need to represent while still admitting resemblance, and to stress the creative function of images.

Sartre incorporates artistic images into his theory by holding that a painting of an absent person makes that person present in the same way that a mental image does (*Psychology* 32). Sartre also says that the painter creates a "real" object (paint on canvas) through which he creates something "unreal," which is what one sees through the painting, such as Charles VIII (*Psychology* 274-75); the novelist makes "an unreal object"—the story itself—"by means of verbal analogues," which are the real words on paper, or the real marks which represent those words (*Psychology* 277). "Unreal" is not pejorative; it is the equivalent of "nothingness" in his *Being and Nothingness* and refers to the ability to imagine what does not exist.

The importance of Sartre's thinking to *La Goutte d'or* is suggested by a chapter Tournier dropped from the novel but published elsewhere, "Le Peintre et son modèle," in which an artist explains his own theories and illustrates them in part by two portraits of Sartre (*Petites proses* 164-66): Sartre was on Tournier's mind during the novel's composition. Sartre's influence is also shown in the fact that Tournier follows Sartre's classification, in *The Psychology of Imagination*, of words as signs (28), images as symbols (138). To Sartre, the written sign directing the traveler to the appropriate office in the railway station has meaning by virtue of "custom" and "habit," so it is arbitrary (28-29), whereas an image is based on resemblance and involves "imaginative comprehension" (144). But though Tournier also explicitly treats words as signs, images as symbols, he shows, in the working-out of the novel's action, that they are less distinct from each other than this division implies.

Unlike his previous fictions, *La Goutte d'or* is not concerned overtly with Christianity, but Tournier's thinking reflects Balthazar's idea in *Gaspard, Melchior et Balthazar* that images are sanctioned by the Incarnation. In *Le Tabor et le Sinaï*, Tournier symbolizes Hebrew and Moslem condemnation of images by Mount Sinai, Christian acceptance of images by Mount Tabor (10-11). On Sinai, God hid His face in smoke and gave Moses signs in the form of written tablets containing the law; when Moses descended from Sinai to find the Israelites worshiping the image of the golden calf, he broke the tablets, Tournier says, "because the sign and the image are not compatible" (10). The lesson of Mount Sinai, then, is that images, whether God's face or a man-made idol, are so powerful that one must protect oneself from them. Mount Tabor gives the contrary lesson, Tournier says, for there, when Jesus appeared transfigured to Peter, James, and John, it was a "triumph of the image over the sign" in which the positive value of the image is affirmed (11). Both events show the power of the image, but at Mount Sinai the Israelites were not able to withstand the power, whereas on Mount Tabor the Disciples, perhaps because Jewish practices had established the power of the sign through making writing central to the culture, were ready to be shown a powerful image, Jesus in his glory. This reading of events, though ignoring the statement in Exodus that Moses and 70 elders of Israel "saw God" (Exod. 25.9-11), provides a deciphering grid for *La Goutte d'or*, for it implies that signs, and particularly words, can be intermediaries when one confronts powerful images.

THE NOVEL'S HISTORICAL BACKGROUND

False ideas which Algerians have about the French, which French have of the Algerians, and which each group has of itself are all explored in *La Goutte d'or*. Tournier says that the novel had its genesis more than 20 years earlier, when he was recording interviews about the Sahara for radio and was struck by the fact that Saharan natives had almost nothing to say about their region, whereas French people who had lived there could not stop discussing it (Tournier, Présentation). He concluded that the French image of the Sahara was based almost entirely on false images, in contrast to the austere vision of the natives of the region, who nevertheless also did not see their world clearly.

La Goutte d'or also needs to be read in the context of the complex relationship between the French and the Algerians. A French possession since 1847, Algeria became independent only after a fiercely fought and divisive war lasting from 1954 to 1962, and both before and after independence many Algerians emigrated to France, an arrangement which benefited not only France, which imported cheap labor, but also Algeria, which lessened its unemployment problem and gained economic benefits from the money the workers sent home. French workers, however, often resented the competition. To further complicate the situation, many Algerian workers established families in France, creating a generation of French-born Arabs and Berbers who could choose French citizenship on turning eighteen. This situation brought out a latent French racism, exacerbated by cultural differences between the French and the North Africans, the vast majority of whom are Moslems. The differences in ways of looking at the world and the hard feelings caused by the war of independence are both, Tournier believes, responsible for the "misunderstanding" between the French and the workers from the Maghreb (Rollin 43).

As he did for his other novels, Tournier relied on research to get the details right. He had visited North Africa for pleasure as early as 1970 (Boncenne 62), but in order to write *La Goutte d'or* he crossed the Sahara several times (Hayman, "Grand Scale" 41; Rollin 41), spent a morning in a slaughterhouse (Rollin 43), visited immigrant workers' housing in Paris (Braudeau 85), and spent ten minutes using a jackhammer (Braudeau 82; Rollin 43). Such incidents as the emigrants' watching television ads on the ferry taking them to France also come from his own experience (Rollin 42). He did other research, too, reading anthropological literature and consulting experts, especially the calligrapher Hassan Massoudy, as he explains in his postscript to the novel. Tournier even claims that, except for the novel's two embedded *contes*, he did not make anything up (Rollin 42)—an obvious exaggeration, but the statement underlines his concern with accuracy, especially because North African readers, or readers of North African ancestry, would not necessarily accept a Frenchman's attempt to write about Algerians.

Despite the research, this novel is neither a political tract nor a sociological or anthropological study. In fact, because he has his protagonist, Idriss, arrive in France during what appear to be the student-worker strikes of May 1968, which brought about profound changes in French politics and education, Tournier may be emphasizing the possibility for change in French society. One also notes that, although the mistreatment of the immigrant workers is explained at some length by Idriss's cousin Achour in Paris, Idriss encounters little conscious racism. Instead, he runs across a more subtle and pervasive prejudice: everyone sees Idriss through cultural preconceptions, and although many of them are positive, all of them are limiting.

TECHNIQUE AND STRUCTURE

Like *Gilles et Jeanne*, *La Goutte d'or* started as a screenplay, but unlike *Gilles et Jeanne*, it successfully transformed itself into prose fiction. Idriss, who is only fifteen years old at the start of the novel, is the least reflective of Tournier's major characters, so action predominates over analysis. This tendency is enhanced by the angle of vision; like the last third of *Gaspard, Melchior et Balthazar*, *La Goutte d'or* has a limited third-person narrator who occasionally offers explanatory or interpretive comment, while Idriss himself never speaks directly to the reader. Because the style of *La Goutte d'or* is somewhat simpler than that of *Gaspard, Melchior et Balthazar*, Tournier could say that although it is not written for children, a ten-year-old would be able to read it, and he hoped children would read it secretly, despite parental censorship (Bouloumié, "Tournier" 21).

The novel includes two tales, "Barberousse" and "La Reine blonde," which provide thematic keys to the novel, much as "Barbedor" did in *Gaspard*. Tournier's growing interest in tales also shows in the episodic nature of *La Goutte d'or*, which is made up of a series of short narratives recounting various scenes from Idriss's life but capable, many of them, of standing alone as short stories. It is through these episodes that the novel raises its issues, successive points of view being presented by other characters in a series of episodes, almost all of which end with a vivid event. The semi-independence of the chapters may reflect the book's origin as a scenario, as may the fact that each scene ends with a little moment of revelation, a rather Joycean epiphany, but this slight discontinuity of narration also emphasizes the fact that the narration is deliberately artful, displaying virtuosity in creating suspense, providing climax, and looking for resolution. In this it resembles traditional tales, so much a part of Moslem culture. It also derives from philosophical narratives such as Voltaire's *Candide*, in which another innocent journeys through various societies which are explored and exposed, and Montesquieu's *Persian Letters*, in which Parisians are satirized by being described by visitors from Persia much as modern Paris life is satirized by being seen through Idriss's eyes. Tournier aims, however, for a more Realistic and even Naturalistic style than those narratives use; his desire to create a physically realized world in his fiction may be why he has pointed out that his main Paris setting is the one Zola used in *L'Assommoir*, a novel employing huge amounts of detail to show the life of the Paris underclass in the middle of the last century (*Golden Droplet* 204).

Myth, too, has contributed to the story, which is partly based on Hans Christian Andersen's "The Snow Queen," as Richard Sieburth has noted. This story, which Tournier greatly admires (*Vent* 52), tells of a boy, Kai, whose vision of the world is deformed when slivers of a distorting mirror made by the Devil get into his eyes and heart, making all good things look bad, and who is later carried off by the Snow Queen to her ice palace in the far north. The splinters' distorting power corresponds to the false images Idriss will see of himself and others, and the Snow Queen is like the various blond women who both exploit and are indifferent to Idriss. In Andersen's tale, Kai is rescued by his playmate Gerda, but in *La Goutte d'or*, Idriss must save himself, thus incorporating Gerda's role as well as Kai's, and he also has her power, which comes from her innocence ("her power . . . is in her heart, for she is a sweet and innocent child" [Andersen 88]). Idriss's journey resembles Gerda's, for both go on a long voyage north and both are aided (and sometimes hindered) by a succession of others, each of whom has a story to tell or attitude to express. Finally, when Gerda rescues Kai, pieces of ice in the snow palace form the word *eternity*, freeing Kai, and when Idriss finally saves himself, he too will do so through written words. In "The Snow Queen," Gerda is really a part of Kai's psyche, since no one can be rescued psychologically by anyone else, although others can serve as guides, so Tournier's combining their functions into a single character only makes explicit what Andersen implied. Basing the novel in part on this well-known children's tale helps prepare the reader for Idriss's trials and his final triumph over them.

PORTRAIT OF AN OASIS

In the first half of *La Goutte d'or*, set in Algeria, Tournier describes many North African customs and beliefs, particularly those of the inhabitants of Idriss's native oasis of Tabelbala, for the reader must understand Idriss's culture in order to understand his later reactions to Paris. Tabelbala is a coherent, organized society in which many beliefs, often animistic rather than Moslem, give the oasis dwellers a badly needed sense of security, living as they do on the bare edge of subsistence. In oasis life, every problem has at least a theoretical solution, and there are only two likely futures for a teenager like Idriss: to stay at the oasis and marry or to emigrate to France looking for work.

Idriss wants to leave, in part because he is responding to some of the cultural changes of the 1960s, for he has seen (though not heard) a radio, and he knows by hearsay about television and movies. The novel opens with the event which will trigger Idriss's emigration: a Frenchwoman in a jeep takes his picture and promises to send it to him. The woman, with her bleached platinum hair and brief clothing, represents to Idriss everything desirable about Western civilization, but he is disturbed by the fact that she takes his image away in her camera. To him, as to the other inhabitants of Tabelbala, that image is part of himself, so it seems natural to them that he should later go to Paris to find the woman and recover that image. Idriss will progress to a deeper understanding of images, but at the start he thinks of his image as not only real but literally coming from himself.

The novel's first chapter includes another key event, the death of Idriss's friend Ibrahim, a one-eyed Chaamba nomad. Ibrahim butchers a camel which has fallen into a well, and when he has finished, he dances in triumph on the worm-eaten wood of the wellhead. Ibrahim has just been calling Idriss a "round-tail" or ninny, and, pointing his penis at Idriss, he boasts that he has a "pointed tail" (24). What follows is startling: covered with the camel's blood, a bloodclot in his empty eye socket, Ibrahim is dancing like a devil when he suddenly disappears into the earth as the wellhead collapses. Ibrahim is in some ways a mentor for Idriss but, as Nestor was for Abel Tiffauges in *Le Roi des aulnes*, he is an ambiguous one, subterranean and bloody as well as intelligent and bold; his having only one eye suggests that his vision of the world is limited, while the unusual sharpness of his eyesight implies that a monocular view of the world has its advantages because it can be less confusing than a binocular one (13).

The theme of images, introduced by the photograph of Idriss, is expanded by a contrast between images and abstract signs that owes something to Sartre. Although their Moslem beliefs should forbid all representation of people and animals, Idriss has been permitted to carve camels to play with, and now that he is too old for such play, he continues to make them for his little brothers (26). However, Tabelbala is much more used to various established abstract signs than to such images, including hairstyles that show who is married or who was symbolically "sold" to the blacks in infancy to prevent death (29). Clearly, these symbols have meaning only when a person has learned the symbol system of the culture; Idriss will discover only slowly that the same is true for images.

The nature of symbols is explored as Idriss watches a black woman dancer, Zett Zobeida. She wears many traditionally symbolic ornaments, such as crescents, stars, hands of Fatima, and gazelle hooves, commonplaces in the symbol system of Idriss's culture, seemingly "abstract forms" acting as "signs, not images" (89), despite being based on natural objects, but around her neck she has one very different jewel: the golden drop of the novel's title. This jewel is called a "pure sign" which "means nothing but itself," and it is silent, unlike her other amulets, which tinkle against each other (35). Because the drop of gold is not part of a symbol system Idriss knows, it seems to mean "nothing but itself" (35). That is why Zett Zobeida and her jewel are called the "emanation of a world without images," which is the "antithesis and perhaps the antidote" for the woman in the jeep (35): the abstract symbol which is the golden drop and the mute speech of her undulating belly, called a "mouth without lips" (35), refer indirectly to writing, which will ultimately save Idriss from the confusing world of images he will find in France, whereas the blond Frenchwoman with her camera seems to Idriss to be all image, no meaning, because he does not realize what she represents. Idriss does not understand the contrast between the two women, nor does he understand the song with which Zett Zobeida accompanies her dance and which says—punningly, in French—that the "cricket's wing is a piece of writing" and the "dragonfly's wing is a document" (34) and that both teach life's secret and reveal death's tricks. Only later will he begin to understand.

BARBEROUSSE: THE TRUTH OF THE IMAGE

Before Idriss has had a chance to absorb the message about signs, he listens to a professional storyteller recount a tale about images, the story of the Barbary Coast pirate Kheir ed Dîn, known as Barberousse (Barbarossa). At its original publication in slightly different form in the *Nouvelle Revue Française*, Tournier dedicated the story to "Aly et Kerstin ben Salem," presumably the real-life inspirations of "their imaginary ancestors," the two artists in this tale, Ahmed ben Salem (Achour in the earlier version) and Kerstine ("Barberousse" 1). Barberousse suffers because his red hair is interpreted by everyone as a sign that he was conceived shamefully, during his mother's menstrual period (41), so he hides his hair beneath a turban and his beard in a cloth sheath. When Barberousse becomes King of Tunis and must have an official portrait, Ahmed, the portraitist, tells him that he always paints the truth of his high-born subjects in such a way that everything about them looks noble, even their warts; at the same time, he accentuates their facial characteristics (43-44). In other words, for Ahmed the truth of an image lies not in its fidelity to appearance but in its revealing inner qualities through a heightened rendering of appearance. Ahmed's ideas relate to a contrast Baudelaire made between portraits which are like history and portraits which are like novels. According to Tournier, Baudelaire said that historical portraiture's method is to "render faithfully . . . the shape and form of the model, which does not exclude idealization," and to exaggerate strong characteristics while de-emphasizing the insignificant (*Tabor* 105). This is Ahmed's style, in which the successive sittings allow the artist to see beyond the concerns of the moment into the lasting truth of the sitter's personality (44).

The second kind of portrait, what Baudelaire calls "novelistic" portraiture, also appears in the story. Ahmed sketches Kheir ed Dîn from memory, working in black and white at the former pirate's orders, creating a portrait that is already moderately symbolic, for Barberousse seems to incarnate brute force (48). But Ahmed is not satisfied, although Barberousse is. Fearing that producing a regal portrait of Barberousse is beyond his power, Ahmed asks Kerstine, a blond Scandinavian artist, to use his sketch as the basis for a woollen tapestry. Her work represents Barberousse in a highly symbolic way, for it can be interpreted either as a portrait of the king or as a depiction of an autumnal European forest with foxes and squirrels, all in reddish colors, the very colors Barberousse has hated because they reminded him of his red hair. This portrait corresponds to the second kind of portraiture, the "novelistic" sort, "more ambitious" than the other kind because it requires more imagination (*Tabor* 105-06). Barberousse obviously brings that imagination to the portrait, for, when he sees Kerstine's image of himself—an image which, being of wool, can also be touched and smelled—he accepts his red hair. The next day, he is driven from Tunis and finds refuge in France, so that the portrait's association of him with Europe was a prophecy, as Françoise Merllié has pointed out ("Histoires" 34-35), and the portrait thus belongs to what Tournier considers the highest art, being a "reflection of the future" (*Tabor* 107). It also has the kind of resemblance Tournier prefers, resemblance to its creator (*Tabor* 12), for the material and the scene reflect Kerstine's origins as well as Barberousse's future.

"Barberousse" concerns several kinds of images. First is the image Barberousse and his contemporaries have of his red hair: they apply their cultural values and read it only as an indicator of his shameful origin, reducing an image (his hair) from a symbol to a sign. In contrast, Ahmed's portrait includes more of Barberousse's past and his present and reveals Ahmed's conception of Barberousse's personality. In Sartre's terms, the portrait is a real object (black lines on white paper) which is a "material analog" (*Psychology* 275) of Ahmed's mental image, a symbol which is Ahmed's way of thinking about Barberousse.

In contrast to both physical appearance and portrait, the tapestry is both sign and symbol. It is a sign because, like a written message, it needs to be read or decoded, and it is a symbol because it appeals in a complex way to the senses, evoking different readings. Its complexity is shown partly by the fact that it can be touched and smelled; as Merllié has pointed out, Barberousse's reaction to it is like Colombine's response to her image in *brioche* dough in

Pierrot ou les secrets de la nuit ("Histoires" 35). Barberousse leans his cheek against the wool and says, "What a beautiful, deep smell!" (53) just as Colombine says of her image in bread, "How beautiful I am, how good I smell!" (*Sept* 30). The tapestry has shown Barberousse a new way to read the symbol of his red hair; at first it seemed to be only a sign of his origin, but his hair also symbolizes his future: royal abundance, a culmination of experience, and a life in Europe.

IMAGES OF IDRISS IN ALGERIA

What Idriss retains from the story, however, is the fact that Barberousse's picture was made by a blond European woman and that Barberousse subsequently went to France, and Idriss hopes someday to do the same thing. That he is protected by destiny seems to be shown when, the next morning, he discovers the golden drop on the ground and takes it for a lucky charm. He will later learn from a goldsmith that such amulets date to Etruscan times and were worn by free-born children, who sacrificed them to the household gods on reaching adulthood (117-18). The charm thus signifies Idriss's innocence and his freedom; it is not after all a sign with no meaning, for that would be a contradiction in terms, but a sign whose meaning must be learned, like all the other conventional abstract signs Idriss knows.

Idriss values this abstract sign, but images dominate his story even before he leaves home. Although the promised photograph never comes, a practical joker amused by Idriss's eager waiting sends him a postcard of a laughing donkey and, as Idriss stares thunderstruck at it, asks if it is a photograph of him (59). This symbolic representation of his seeming stupidity is the first image of himself Idriss receives because of the blond woman.

He sees a different image of himself on his journey to Paris to recover or rejoin his photograph, after apparently two years' time (Tournier, *Petites proses* 156). At the oasis of Béni Abbès he visits a museum of Saharan life, where the daily utensils of Tabelbala are displayed to the amusement of a group of French tourists, who see the Sahara through their own distorted images of Africa, and Idriss realizes that customs and objects which he has never questioned are symbols of his culture. As he leaves, he sees his own image reflected in one of the glass cases as if it also forms part of the display of endangered life (90). In Béni Abbès he also has his first experiences of being treated as a stranger, most forcefully when he and the truck driver he has ridden with are questioned in connection with a theft, and the police, however briefly, see Idriss as a thief (81).

At his next stop, Béchar, Idriss meets Mustapha, a nearsighted studio photographer who poses his subjects in front of garishly painted backdrops; he photographs a French couple, for example, standing in front of a painted Sahara, even though Béchar is in the real Sahara (95). The backdrops conform to the most sentimental and stereotypical mental images possible, as does the mood music Mustapha provides on a wind-up phonograph. Mustapha's photographic portraits are Ahmed's kind of portrait painting reduced to its lowest level, for Mustapha's photo of a workingman dressed as a sultan and posing before a backdrop representing "a crowd of chastely undressed women" (93-94) inevitably suggests Ahmed's painting of Barberousse's sickly predecessor, Moulay Hassan, "surrounded by his favorites fainting with love" (39).

The difference between Ahmed's portraiture and Mustapha's is that Ahmed tries to represent the inner essence of his subject, whereas Mustapha creates false images, letting his clients realize their "wildest fantasies" (94), while the similarities reflect Tournier's belief that the perfection of photography made realistic painted portraits not only unnecessary but impossible (*Petites proses* 174-76). Mustapha's nearsightedness symbolizes the limitations of commercial photography, but he provides real insight when he poses Idriss in front of a painting of Paris illogically including in a single perspective all its hackneyed visual symbols: the Eiffel Tower, the Arc de Triomphe, the Moulin Rouge, the Seine, and Notre Dame (99). The grayish image of Idriss, who is reduced to insignificance by this violently colored environment, actually does prefigure his future in Paris.

On the bus to Oran, Idriss finds a different image of himself when Lala Ramirez, an elderly widow, takes him for a reincarnation of her son Ismaïl. In Oran she shows Idriss Ismaïl's tombstone with his photograph on it, but although Idriss thinks that the boy might look somewhat like himself (106), he is not tempted by Lala's offer to support him luxuriously. He rejects the photographic image and trusts to the verbal sign of his identity: "I'm not Ismaïl. I'm Idriss" (107). The power of words has helped save him from a maleficent image. Still in Oran, Idriss has another misadventure with photographs when the automatic machine he uses to get a snapshot for his immigration document gives him instead a photograph of a bearded man (108). Idriss calmly puts it on his papers, thinking that it is not up to him to resemble his photograph, but up to the photograph to resemble him (114). Nobody notices the lack of resemblance, perhaps because the authorities do not really look at

Idriss because they already have their own image of him, perhaps because the paperwork has the right words to go with the wrong picture.

LOOKING AT FRANCE

Idriss must struggle not only with his own image but also with images he has of France. On the ferry to Marseille, the first sight of France the passengers have is through television, when they watch stereotypical images in ads for insurance, soap powder, and toothpaste, or frightening ones in the news, which seems to be the student demonstrations of May 1968 (119). The fact that Idriss and the other North African travelers do not understand these images shows clearly that images need to be read in terms of one's culture. After disembarking in Marseille, Idriss is disoriented by a travel poster showing an oasis far more lush than any he has ever seen (121-22), but he classifies it, correctly, with other false images of himself, dimly sensing the maleficence of powerful images which distort the world.

Before leaving Marseille, however, Idriss is taken in by another image. He could stay in his room at the Hotel Radio, to which he has been sent by a group of Mozabite grocers whose conversation seemed to reduce physical life to "numbers, to signs, to abstract figures" and whose company gave Idriss a "bitter lesson in mastering things" (92) by reducing life to symbols. But Idriss does not want words alone, although their power is suggested by the Hotel Radio's name. Instead, he ventures into the busy streets, treats himself to dinner at McDonald's, and finds himself in the red-light district, where he loses his golden drop and his virginity to a blond prostitute who reminds him of the blond Frenchwoman who snapped his picture.

This incident, coming approximately at the book's center, is the "hinge" event. Until now, Idriss has been a free child, as symbolized by his possession of the gold fetish; now he is no longer a child and no longer free, as symbolized by its loss, for he has succumbed to the woman's appearance and so, by implication, to the images which surround him and to which he is susceptible because he has not learned their meaning. Unlike the lines and spots used in face painting in Tabelbala, which are abstract signs reflecting a woman's social position (126-27), the prostitute's lipstick and mascara not only symbolize her profession but also exaggerate her natural appearance; and because they imitate nature, Idriss confounds them with nature. The verdant oasis in the travel poster, the brilliant smile in the toothpaste commercial, and the prostitute's lipstick all appear to be real things, whereas, to use Sartre's terms, the real things are ink on paper, electronic impulses on a screen, and paint, while the things evoked—an ideal place, love, exaggerated sexuality—are unreal. Even the prostitute's blond hair is bleached (131).

The incident with the prostitute introduces a subordinate theme, which is that most of the images Idriss sees in France are visual only—not, like Barberousse's tapestry, images which can be touched and smelled. Some, like the travel poster or television pictures, are visual by nature; others are visual only because Idriss is poor. Thus, when Idriss first tries to touch the prostitute, she tells him "hands off" because he looks broke (126). Later, on the train to Paris, Idriss is befriended by a young man, Philippe, but when Idriss sees a picture of Philippe's blond fiancée, he feels immediately that the fiancée and Philippe belong to a different world (133). This is also the world of expensive Paris shops with their closed-in shop windows. This closed world reflects what Tournier calls a northern French "horror of physical contact" that he attributes to Anglo-Saxon Puritanism, in contrast to Africa, which he calls "a continent where one never sleeps all alone, people sleep in groups, they keep each other warm," adding, "There is no doubt that we live in a 'civilization of images': everything is to be seen, nothing to be touched" (Pasternak).

FRENCH IMAGES OF IDRISS

In Paris, Idriss settles into a *foyer* for guest workers in an area dominated by African immigrants, the Goutte d'Or district, called after a street which was in turn named for the "golden drops" of a white wine once made and sold nearby (Tournier, *Golden Droplet* 204). Idriss's golden drop has thus prefigured his arrival in the Goutte d'Or district; losing the literal drop, he has found it in another, impure and figurative, form. Rooming with his older cousin Achour, who has lived in Paris for several years, Idriss begins to learn about the images the French have of North Africans. He gets more education from the young Marquis Sigisbert de Beaufond, a "mythomaniac" (262) who treats Idriss to dinner at a restaurant serving supposedly typical North African food including couscous and tagine, all of which is new to Idriss. Sigisbert wants to teach, not to learn, and undertakes to explain the Sahara to Idriss in a hilarious reversal of logic which brings out the conviction of some French people that they understand North Africa because they have seen movies like *La Bandera* and *L'Atlantide* (152), people for whom, Tournier says, "the

Sahara corresponds to a whole set of images" based on myths which are totally alien to a North African (Rollin 42).

More important than Sigisbert is a director of television commercials, Achille Mage, whose attention Idriss has caught while working as a street sweeper. Like the blond woman who photographed Idriss at the book's opening, Mage, a homosexual with some of the dilettantish qualities, egoism, and wit of Alexandre Surin in *Les Météores*, also photographs Idriss, making him an extra in a commercial. Instead of a promise to send him the photo, Mage gives Idriss his perfumed lavender visiting card and an invitation to telephone (147). Idriss is too intimidated to do so, but later when he runs into Mage in a pinball arcade, he naively accepts Mage's invitation to his apartment. Mage explains to Idriss his sexual arrangements with the boys from the arcade, who have been organized by one of them, "le grand Zob" ("Big Cock"), so that one or another young man shows up regularly on a noisy motorscooter, providing "a harmonious succession of explosive visits, as varied as regular" (162). Idriss does not understand the sexual allusions, but it soon develops that Mage wants something more than sex from Idriss: he wants Idriss to be Saint-Exupéry's Little Prince and rescue Mage from the pointlessness of his life. Mage even reads to Idriss from *Le Petit Prince* (164). Mage's image of Idriss has little to do with Idriss himself; like Sigisbert, he is too busy looking at Idriss through his own cultural biases and too busy talking to see the real Idriss.

Mage is a complex creation. On the one hand, he represents French intellectuals generally, for he amusingly but ostentatiously displays his literary education; on the other, he is one more artist of the debased, like the photographer at Béchar. His name and appearance help show his significance. Like Achilles, his Greek namesake, Achille Mage is homosexual, and he, too, has an Achilles' heel, his willingness to be exploited by the boys from the arcade. He even seems to enjoy being humiliated, since he says that giving someone money can substitute for having sexual relations with him (168). His last name, Mage, can mean either wise man (magus) or magician. Like the Magi in *Gaspard, Melchior et Balthazar* he is looking for a boy to save him, but his search is a parody of theirs; he does not want true enlightenment. And like a magician, he creates fantasy in his television ads. "Mage" also suggests the word *image*, appropriate because he makes images for television. But he cannot accept the image of himself he sees in the boys' eyes, that of a "fat sentimental auntie" (168), nor does he literally see well, for his eyes do not track together, making him either cross-eyed or wall-eyed. His eyes' inability to work together symbolizes his divided nature; a cultured, even overeducated man, he devotes himself cynically to the debased popular culture of advertising. Tournier has said that he loves commercials because they are a "celebration of life, of the body, of beauty" (Pasternak), and he contrasts news photography, which usually suggests "a hellish world," with advertising photos, which "lead one to Heaven" (*Tabor* 166). This is not as unusual a judgment as it may seem, at least in regard to French television advertising, which is generally agreed to be much more aesthetically appealing than the programs. Nevertheless, the ends must be considered as well as the means; these images can be used to sell useless or even harmful products, and the means themselves may be derisory, as we see when watching Mage film a commercial for a soft drink, Palmeraie ("palm grove"). The commercial is a complex of clichés about the desert, and the props are paper palm-leaf skirts and plastic flowers (171-73). Mage insists that the actors must believe what they say, but when someone gives him some Palmeraie to drink, he spits it out in disgust and calls for beer (174). He illustrates Tournier's belief that advertising is seduction (*Tabor* 165), for Mage as potential seducer of Idriss, and Mage as the "Eisenstein of advertising" (175) are the same person; both attempt to create images of themselves and of the listener/viewer in order to seduce. Mage fails with Idriss because they do not have enough culture in common, but his commercials succeed because he and his French viewers have similar cultural preconceptions.

But if Mage's commercial is saturated with hypocrisy, the chapter's end, which recalls Idriss's life in the desert, is an enchanted tale. When the production is through with the camel, Idriss must take it to a slaughterhouse on the other side of Paris, so he calmly leads the beast through the streets, naps with it in the Montmartre Cemetery, and then goes through early morning traffic into the heart of Paris, even crossing the Place de la Concorde. Finally he finds the slaughterhouse, where, in a section which is a miniature descent into Hell, the narrator describes the killing in electrifying detail. But the workers reject both Idriss and his camel—"We've seen everything here: a Bedouin with his camel! Now you can really say France is done for!" (183)— and, through the purest chance, Idriss wanders into the Jardin d'Acclimatation, where his camel finds a new home in the children's rides. Despite the happy ending, in the process of this journey Idriss has seen a whole new series of deformed images of himself: to the sophisticated city dwellers, he and his camel seem invisible; to the slaughterhouse workers, Idriss is a stereotype of a Bedouin; to himself, looking in the funhouse mirrors of the Jardin d'Accli-matation, he is distorted into weird shapes to the accompaniment of children's laughter (184-85).

FANTASY AND IMAGERY

As Mage's commercials suggest, everyone may be misled by false images, although Westerners are more resistant to such images than Idriss because they have the cultural knowledge to interpret them if they choose to do so. The falseness of many images in contemporary Western culture is shown when Idriss discovers peep shows, which Tournier has called in an interview "unmixed frustration" and, sarcastically, a "triumph of our antiphysical and antiseptic civilization" (Rollin 43). Idriss is fascinated by a nearly naked, leo-nine blond writhing in ecstasy or pain on a stage surrounded by the one-way mirrors of the tiny booths for clients, but when he goes looking for her during the day, he finds an unattractive, middle-aged, nearsighted cleaning lady who would look just like the lion-woman in the right wig and make-up. Achour tells Idriss later that the women in the peep show are not real but exist only for one's eyes (191); this is close to what Sartre would have said, that there is a real person who creates an unreal image, that of the lion-woman. Since an image is a way of thinking about the world, Idriss is a passive spectator (is not thinking) when he takes simplified, commercial images for the truth or sub-stitutes them for his own images—that is, interpretations—of the world.

Comic books, another source of such stereotypes and to Tournier "a worse source of illiteracy than television" (Magnan, "Vers la concision"), are also satirized. Deaf to the violent songs written in the slang of the underclass (193), which are at least attempts to interpret and perhaps so control the world, Idriss, sitting in a bar, is reading a comic about a Berber shepherd being photographed by a young blond tourist—his very story. This *mise en abyme* seems to destroy the barrier between illusion and reality, a collapsing which ironically happened in real life when Harlem Désir, the head of the French antiracist movement S.O.S. Racisme, told Tournier that he was certain he had read that same comic somewhere (Magnan, "Vers la concision"). Because of the power of the image, Idriss loses hold on the difference between the comic and reality when the conversation in the comic appears to be continued by a couple sitting at the bar near him. Certain that the woman is the one who photographed him near Tabelbala (and she may be), Idriss tries to save her from her companion, a pimp. She is alarmed, there is a fight, and Idriss is again photographed, this time by the police. Because of Idriss's black eye and bloody nose, these photos represent him falsely, but Tournier believes that anthropometric photographs are always false because they are demeaning (*Tabor* 103). (To further illustrate this point, Tournier's interview with Rollin about *La Goutte d'or* is accompanied by anthropometric photographs, most of which are of turn-of-the-century workers. The largest pair, however, is of Tournier.)

Image and reality continue to collapse as Idriss becomes entangled in odd adventures involving department-store dummies—commerce's answer to sculpture, or, to the window dresser Bonami, the "exact opposite" of sculpture, since statues are primarily nude, while mannequins are designed to be dressed. Bonami does not even consider them images, but "ectoplasms of three-piece suits" (204). But they are images to Etienne Milan, a puppetmaker who considers dummies more real than people and the sight of a basement of old mannequins "breathtakingly erotic" (203). The eroticism is narcissistic, for he likes only mannequins that represent ten-year-old boys and were made around 1960, when he himself was ten (202-03).

In indirect reference to his previous self-absorbed protagonists, Tournier gives Milan various of their traits; like Robinson, Milan values superficiality rather than depth (208) and lives in self-chosen isolation; like Tiffauges, he wants to be surrounded by "adolescents" whom he controls, and his two-room apartment full of pieces of mannequins resembles "the Ogre's pantry" (207); like Alexandre Surin, he is interested in twins, but in the form of identical mannequins (207). Just as Milan blurs into other of Tournier's characters, he blurs the line between reality and man-made image by photographing his dummies on picnics, with real children mixed in. As a result, the real scenery looks slightly fake, for a picture of mannequins "is an image of an image, which has the effect of doubling their dissolving power" and undermining reality (211). It is fitting that Milan's last name means a bird of prey, the kite, for he is a sort of predator. The character is based, it seems, on real-life photographer Bernard Faucon, whose last name means "falcon" (Davis, *Michel Tournier* 94).

Mass production of mannequins is the starting point of Idriss's other adventure with store-window images, when he serves as a flesh-and-blood model for polyvinyl mannequins. The method is the three-dimensional equivalent of taking a snapshot, for art has been replaced by technology, as pointed up by Idriss's first sight at the workshop, a talentless sculptor carrying out a life-sized Christ for which he himself has served as model—a twofold imposture, for he is posing not only as Christ but also as an artist. To make the mold, Idriss must be submerged to above his mouth in a sticky alginate. The feeling of being buried alive reminds Idriss of Ibrahim, who was buried when the well collapsed beneath him (218), but Idriss is being buried merely to earn some money, unlike Ibrahim, who died asserting his strength and intelligence. Idriss's burial is both his low point and the catalyst for his recovery, as indicated by the fact that his extraction from the hardening alginate suggests birth (219), and he makes his first step to health by resisting Bonami's offer of a job pretending to be a mannequin and posing in the store window in the midst of the real mannequins to be made from the mold of his body (a further blurring of false image with reality). Instead, he enters a period of reappraisal. Because it now seems to be around 1975, as is suggested by some comments Milan makes about his own age (203, 212), Idriss would have been in Paris for seven years, more than enough time for him to make a change.

READING, WRITING, AND INTERPRETING

Idriss has a number of guides on this new path, which will take him back to a world of signs related to his Tabelbala culture. An Egyptian, Amouzine, introduces Idriss to the songs of the famous Egyptian singer Oum Kalsoum, whose words give Idriss the first clue of the healing power of language. This power is reinforced through a story Amouzine tells of a concert at which Oum Kalsoum made a blind man see the color green (228). From Oum Kalsoum it is only a step to Idriss's memory of Zett Zobeida and her obsessive song of the cricket's wing being a piece of writing and the dragonfly's wing being a document.

To understand these songs, Idriss turns to the written signs of his Moslem culture: he begins to study Arabic calligraphy, which "celebrates the freedom of the mind" (*Tabor* 130). Through learning to make his own ink and write with a reed pen, Idriss immerses himself in abstract signs, finding the equivalent of the seemingly limitless time he enjoyed at Tabelbala (232). No longer preoccupied with the stereotyped and limiting images on television, in shop windows, or in advertising, he is concerned only with interpreting the written word. Writing gives him the equivalent of his golden drop, for, like that jewel, written words are pure signs whose meaning must be learned. Because reading involves triple deciphering—decoding the written signs to find the words, decoding the words to find their meaning, then interpreting

the symbols produced by those meanings—it serves as a model for deciphering images as well. Fittingly, his destiny has been hidden all the time in Idriss's
name, his own verbal symbol, for *Idris* is the Moslem name of Enoch, the
father of Methuselah, and in Moslem tradition Idris is the inventor of the pen
and of written language, and his name means "educated."

Idriss is now ready to hear from his calligraphy teacher the novel's second
tale, "La Reine blonde." Like "Barberousse," the blond queen's story is about
a ruler with hair whose color reflects the parents' sexual sin, for the woman's
hair is blond because she was conceived in sunlight, contrary to law. As
Françoise Merllié explains in a thorough exploration of this tale ("La Reine"),
because everyone reads the queen's hair as a sign of sexuality, it incites
uncontrollable passion in all who see her, and she can escape only by living
an austere life and hiding her hair beneath a veil. Like Barberousse, she is
represented in a portrait, but because it is a realistic one that simply reproduces
her image, after her death it sows as much uncontrolled passion in all who see
it as she herself did during her lifetime. After devastating the lives of a series
of possessors, it finally obsesses a poor fisherman, but he is saved by his son,
Riad. The boy learns not only to read and write (to decode signs), but to
interpret word-symbols, including figures of speech, and to decode visual
symbols, after which he saves his father by interpreting the queen's portrait to
him through reproducing in pen and ink the separate parts of the queen's face,
then reading those lines as words (248-50). He interprets most of her face, not
just the hair, so he makes conscious all the parts of the image which others
were responding to without knowing it, and he brings out the many meanings
of the queen's image, not just the sexuality. At the same time, he is presumably
creating *his* image of the queen; that is, he is writing his image of her, which
is his way of thinking about her, rather than submitting passively to the
influence of her unanalyzed portrait.

Both this story and "Barberousse" contrast a realistic portrait (Ahmed's
sketch and the original portrait of the queen) with a symbolic portrait
(Kerstine's tapestry and Riad's interpretation of the queen's portrait). The
novel's epigraph, ascribed to Thomas Jefferson, "You are so exactly what you
seem that I can't hear what you say" (Tournier, *Golden Droplet*), expresses the
mistake of those who reduce Barberousse and the queen to their hair or Idriss
to an image of a Berber; the viewers see their stereotypes so fully incarnated
that other signals are lost. By now Idriss has, presumably, understood Zett
Zobeida's song which said that the dragonfly's wing is a document, the
cricket's wing a piece of writing: like the blond queen's portrait, nature—

including dragonflies and crickets—can be read, or interpreted. That is how one "thwarts death's tricks" and "unveils life's secrets," for to look analytically at an image, whether natural or created, is to interpret, to share with the author (or with God) the power of creation, whereas to look passively at an image is to succumb to its presentation of life, to take it as reality. Idriss now has been taught that the image belongs to and reflects the person who has made it, not the person or thing it seems to represent.

In the novel as published, Idriss misses at least one lesson in the relationship between signs and symbols that Tournier had planned for him, and although Tournier eliminated this chapter from the book because it had the wrong tone, the fact that he published it separately seems to mean that he stands by its ideas. In this chapter, "Le Peintre et son modèle," a painter called Charles Frédéric de l'Epéechevalier (based on Carl Fredrik Reuterswärd) explains the history of modern painting, a lesson apparently coming at a late stage of Idriss's education, as it is set after Sartre's death in 1980 (*Petites proses* 164). L'Epéechevalier, first seen drawing the pyramids at Gizeh although his easel is set up in front of the Cathedral of Notre Dame, later shows Idriss a drawing representing at once the interior plan of Notre Dame and the design of a gambling table, above the legend "What men think is chance is God's design" (*Petites proses* 164). Like Kerstine's portrait of Barberousse, which is both the king and a European forest, this drawing conflates two apparently unrelated images to reveal a hidden visual congruence of church and gambling table underscored by the pun on "design," which means both drawing and plan.

L'Epéechevalier also shows Idriss two different portraits of Sartre. The first, like the literal portraits of Barberousse or the blond queen, is a copy of reality, "a portrait of the traditional sort which photography has made worse" (*Petites proses* 165); the second is a symbolic portrait consisting of a beech tree and its shadow, with Sartre's face suggested in the space between. The drawing puns on the title of Sartre's *L'Etre et le Néant* (*Being and Nothingness*), with being (*l'être*) symbolized by the beech (*le hêtre*) and nothingness by the shadow. L'Epéechevalier insists, however, that it is not just a pun, since there are linguistic links between words for books and words for trees, and says that his aim is to bring out those connections, making his drawings "sparkle with meanings" (*Petites proses* 166).

The episode shows that *La Goutte d'or* is not exploiting a simplistic contrast between visual art and language but rather is contrasting stereotypical, flat, and mechanical images, which may seduce one into accepting their view of life, with representations which must be interpreted because they use symbols. Tournier considers simple copying of reality the lowest form of painting (*Tabor* 129), while art which must be interpreted (whether it appears to be representational or not) is the summit. He even denies that true art is ever representational: "there is only abstract painting, but part of abstract painting is hidden under a figurative mask" (*Tabor* 130). In other words, we may think that we are responding to a painting of a lush countryside; in fact, we are responding to a pattern of shapes and colors which the painter, as a ruse, presents in the form of a landscape.

Idriss acts on his new insights in the rather ambiguous last chapter of *La Goutte d' or*. He is in the Place Vendôme, where everything exudes an air of "show, dough, and Old France" (254), part of a crew about to begin work on an underground parking garage. Surrounded by elegant jewelers' shops, Idriss tries out a jackhammer. This tool, which to the French has come practically to symbolize the workers from the Maghreb (253), is a huge pen with which Idriss can "write" on Paris, and, as the other workers tell him, it is also "a giant's cock. With that, you're . . . balling France" (255). This potent pen(is) symbolizes the intellectual and emotional maturity Idriss has gained through his study of calligraphy, and it also represents his consequent new power. One cannot avoid the sexual implications of this scene, for Idriss has first seen his golden drop on a woman, Zett Zobeida; he has lost it to a woman, the prostitute; but he is about to rediscover it in an entirely masculine world: not only is he holding a pneumatic drill which is explicitly compared to a giant penis, but he is surrounded by other workmen and is standing in the Place Vendôme, whose center is the undeniably phallic brass column surmounted by Napoleon's statue. Idriss finds freedom only when he frees himself of his interest in women, one more protagonist in Tournier's fiction who has had to learn to sublimate his sexuality.

Because he has now become a real adult, it is fitting that Idriss should rediscover his golden drop, which began as a sign with no known referent, became a sign referring to his freedom and childhood, and has gradually been transformed into a symbol of innocence, beauty, value, and abstract meaning (for it symbolizes all abstract signs). Seeing it in an expensive jewelry store's display window protected by seismic detectors, Idriss begins to dance crazily with his pneumatic hammer. Out of control, he begins to peel up the Paris pavement, while the reverberations crack the shop window, set off the alarms, and summon the police. Interpreting this, the book's last event, is crucial, but the scene is ambiguous. William Cloonan is inclined to see in it Idriss's succumbing to "the seduction of the image" ("Word, Image and Illusion" 473) but also says that the reader must decide. It seems to me that, given everything that has led up to this scene, the dance must be a triumphant celebration of power. Idriss's dance reflects Zett Zobeida's dance and Ibrahim's dance on the wellhead, and so suggests that Idriss is returning to his roots and can at last understand and imitate Zett Zobeida's and Ibrahim's joy in life. His dance, however, has diabolical overtones, as the jackhammer sounds like an "infernal" sleigh bell and the pavement rises like a snake's skin (257). The jackhammer itself is "Zett Zobeida changed into an enraged robot" (257)—hardly a reassuring image.

Still, the dance is a breakthrough, even on a literal level, where the vibration breaks the shop window. He has not attacked the window, but his very celebration of his intellectual and physical force has broken it, as if to suggest that even the holy of holies of French capitalism and privilege will crumble once the immigrants learn to interpret their lives and take charge of them. In the last view of Idriss, he is dancing, "deaf and blind," in front of the golden drop as police vans begin to block off the street (257). Idriss will find himself once more in a police station, perhaps even in jail, but that must be seen as a small price for dancing with, in his head, a "fantasmagoria of dragonflies, crickets, and jewels shaking with a frenzied vibration" (257). Idriss knows that he no longer needs that golden jewel, for he is no longer a child, and we realize that the window cracks as if to give it up to him because he is at last free of the power of visual images, free of his childish timidity, free of the power of others to make him see life as they want him to.

Idriss's rediscovery of the drop of gold at the end suggests that, in the second part of the novel, he has been retracing his journey in the first half. This is true; from the incident of the prostitute onwards, each subsequent event tends to recapitulate a still earlier event from the first half. The goldsmith Idriss meets on the ferry to Marseille corresponds to Philippe, whom he meets on the train to Paris, each explaining the relations between Algerians and the French; Lala Ramirez and Achille Mage both want to take Idriss into their lives and turn him into the image they have of him; the photographer at Béchar is like Etienne Milan in that they both take photographs that mix real people with cheap, man-made images; the museum at Béni Abbès puts oasis life into sealed cases, as the peep show does with sexuality; the police incident in Béni Abbès parallels the one in Paris; the story of "Barberousse" is echoed in "La Reine blonde," and Ibrahim's and Zett Zobeida's dances prefigure Idriss's final dance. Idriss's discovery at the end is a discovery of himself and his origins, but he returns to them with liberating knowledge he has gained on his journey.

THE ROLE OF THE ARTIST

The emphasis on images in *La Goutte d'or* and in the related essays in *Le Tabor et le Sinaï* brings into sharper focus than ever before Michel Tournier's ideas about artistic creation. He has long insisted on the role of the reader in creating fiction, speaking of "co-creation" between author and reader (*Vol* 19) and saying that though a novel must have a "message . . . it must be the reader who puts it there" (Rollin 43). One need not take this statement entirely at face value, since Tournier also says that he writes because he has something to say, a message to convey, but his claim that he believes in "co-creation" is reinforced by his insistence on interpretation in *La Goutte d'or*, whose very theme is deciphering images.

Although it seems natural that the novel would value written words over images—Tournier is after all a writer—it may seem strange that realistic images are presented as harmful, and symbolic ones as life-giving, because Tournier's own fiction has a realistic surface. However, he is like the painter described by Valéry: "If the painter wants black, he puts in a black person; if he needs the color rose, a rose" (*Tabor* 129). The realistic surface is a conventional covering which the audience expects; for the painter the meaning is in the play of colors and shapes, and for Tournier it is in the play of ideas and patterns. In the philosophical journey I have been tracing, *La Goutte d'or* is Tournier's study of aesthetics, for it focuses on the nature and function of art. Since Tournier believes that art should *create* a world which resembles it, through the influence of art on its audience, it is obvious that his consideration of art must include ethics; bad art turns people into stereotypes, reduces their freedom, and limits their creativity, but good art frees them by making them think for themselves. This means that an author should seek not agreement from a reader but dialog; to be argued with should be as satisfying as to have one's propositions accepted, providing that the argument is on the issues.

Michel Tournier's fiction invites such discussion, but one must understand what he is doing. He is not finally a realistic novelist. Like the painter who uses a realistic landscape as an excuse to create shapes and colors, Tournier has created literature which appears to mirror the world but which exists on its own bases, derives from its own *données*, and fulfills its own intellectual and aesthetic demands. At the same time, he is not an aesthete, but a reformer, for all of his fiction aims at reconceiving some aspect of the world and at changing people's attitudes or acts. Although he began writing fiction as a way to explain his philosophy, he gives his concerns with ontology, ethics, mysticism, Christian theology, and aesthetics immediacy through the contemporary issues in which he embeds them, including sexuality, racism, and economic exploitation, for he knows that a novel is not a philosophical treatise but a fiction which will succeed or fail according to the reader's imaginative participation. Each of his major works thus combines a realistic surface, an aesthetic pattern, a philosophical issue, and an exploration of social problems. If Michel Tournier is a great writer, as I think he is, it is because he satisfies the intellect and the heart at the same time, providing a reader with cerebral adventures evoked by the physical and emotional adventures of his protagonists.

8
An Interview with Michel Tournier:
"I Write Because I Have Something to Say"

On July 11, 1987, late on a warm Saturday afternoon, I spent three hours with Michel Tournier at his house in Choisel, discussing his work and ideas. We settled into the first-floor living room, adjacent to a library with filled floor-to-ceiling bookshelves and more books in boxes on the floor, and, to the accompaniment of the church clock striking the hour, songs of birds outside, and a visit from a neighbor boy, Tournier spoke with great animation of his ideas and his work. Following is a translated and edited version of our conversation.

Susan Petit: It's been 20 years since the publication in 1967 of your first book, *Vendredi ou les limbes du Pacifique*. What changes have there been since then in your goals as a writer?

Michel Tournier: I don't think my goals have changed, and the proof is that, although I didn't write my ideal book right away, I did so almost from the start—with *Vendredi ou la vie sauvage*. *Vendredi ou les limbes du Pacifique* was so far from what I wanted that I rewrote it to create *Vendredi ou la vie sauvage*. After that, I wrote books in their first version and didn't rewrite them. I'm speaking of *Le Roi des aulnes* and *Les Météores*, which aren't very close to *Vendredi ou la vie sauvage* but which gradually get closer. And I really think that eleven-year-old boys and girls can read *La Goutte d'or*, my latest novel, which for me is the criterion of success.

That doesn't mean at all that I write for children. But it's a criterion, because it means I can write clearly and briefly, and be concrete—which is very hard, especially because I started out as a philosopher. I was trained on Kant and Hegel, who are really the height of difficulty. But it's just that difficulty that I'm looking for. So you could say that my goal hasn't changed in 20 years, but I hope I've gotten a little closer to reaching it.

SP:	Up until *La Goutte d'or* your novels made use of problems and structures based on Christianity, but your protagonist in that book is a Moslem. Is it an Islamic book?

MT:	There's only one passage where Islam and Christianity are contrasted. And, unfortunately—because I'm a Christian—Islam comes out ahead. It's at the end, in this sentence, which I took from the quotations attributed to Mohammed: "There is more truth in the scholar's ink than the martyr's blood." That's an incredibly important sentence, and it condemns a whole aspect of Christianity, the part which glorifies pain and suffering, the bloody part, which, unfortunately, plays so large a role in Christianity. You just have to look at the crucifix, which is the major sign of Christianity. I wish it weren't.

In addition, you mustn't think that when I contrast the sign and the image I'm contrasting Islam and Christianity. Absolutely not—because, luckily, the West (and I belong to the Western world) has even more signs than images. I could give you countless examples. Take a book of photographs. All the publishers will tell you, at least in France, but I think it's the same everywhere, that it won't sell unless there's a good-sized text with it. The public doesn't buy images; images are free. It buys signs. One can sell signs because they represent work, but the image is given for free.

Television is another example. The televised image doesn't interest anyone unless there are words to listen to. If you turn off the sound, or if you listen to television in a language you don't understand, the pictures don't interest you. This proves that the image can't win out over the sign. You don't have to go to the Islamic world to see the victory of the sign.

SP:	When you've written about Christianity, you seem to get most of your inspiration from heresies and heretics. Why is that?

MT:	Western civilization is largely the work of heretical Jews—even renegades. Jesus, Spinoza, Marx, and, in France, Henri Bergson and Simone Weil were all Jewish renegades. And they're all obviously influential. And I believe—as I've written in *La Goutte d'or*—that a prison isn't only a lock, but a roof as well. That is, a prison deprives me of freedom but protects me. And that's the great temptation, to lock oneself up in orthodoxy, to give away one's freedom, to lose all one's creative power, but to be sheltered. The opposite is to break down the prison door and go outside where you have to take risks, but where you're able to create something.

That's why I'm interested in heretics. The heretic is someone who breaks the lock and does without the roof.

SP: In an essay called "Le Baroque," you contrast baroque art with classical art, curves with straight lines.[1] If we can apply the terms to literature, would you call your novels baroque or classical?

MT: I don't know how to answer that, because those ideas were invented for visual arts—painting, sculpture, architecture. It's very hard to apply them to literature. People often ask me, "Do you think you're a classical author?" I say, "Yes, because I'm read in class!" I think that's a good definition.

But it's clear that I admire most the values related to life: strength, flesh, warmth, and food are fundamental in my thinking. Well, are they baroque values? Probably. Smell—is smell baroque? What I resent most in today's society is its fight against smells; it thinks that every smell is a bad one. I object! I hate the word *deodorant*, which is one of those pseudo-French words that come from England or the United States and that aren't really French.

Speaking of smells, let me mention a novel by Patrick Süskind, *Perfume*.[2] For a whole year, any number of people said to me, "It's your kind of book, you really should read it, you should have written it!" And one day, a critic who hates me was talking on the radio with some other people and I was listening, just by chance, in my car. They were talking about Süskind's book, and this gentleman said, "Oh, don't talk to me about that book, it's even worse than Tournier's stuff!" Well, right away, I bought it, read it, and I thought it was wonderful! And I think it's really a baroque book. If you haven't read it, I recommend it. It's a masterpiece.

SP: I'll do that. As to your own books, I would have said that they're classical in outline but with baroque details.

MT: That's a good way to look at it. I like that description. You know, I do like applying dichotomies, especially to literature. For example, in *Le Vol du vampire*, in an article about André Gide, you may remember that I did that at the start, divided writers into two kinds in various ways: "There are writers who—" and "There are writers who—." But you have to be careful, because there are always some you can't divide up like that. I said, for example, that some writers write about themselves and others can't write about themselves. Jean-Jacques Rousseau and André Gide couldn't write

---

[1] *Petites proses* 129-30.
[2] *Das Parfum*, published in Germany in 1985.

about anything but themselves. Balzac and Zola couldn't write about themselves. It's a game. So baroque and classical art—why not? But it's difficult, because in French literature, classical means Racine. And, really, so many of Racine's lines are exciting because they are, as it were, twisted, complex—"Ariane, ma sœur, de quel amour blessée / Vous mourûtes aux bords où vous fûtes laissée!"[3] I'm not at all sure that *that's* classical. On the other hand, I owe a great deal to Paul Valéry. And he's truly classical, isn't he? Yes.

SP: When you contrast signs and images, you seem to be contrasting movies, where the spectator is passive, with books. But you have written for television, haven't you? Isn't *La Goutte d'or* going to appear on television?

MT: No. Let me tell you what happened. A television producer, Marcel Bluwal,[4] asked me for a scenario. So I wrote a scenario, *La Goutte d'or*. He scouted locations, costed it out, and then the proposal was rejected by the television company. I had half expected that might happen. From the scenario, then, I wrote the novel. The same thing happened with *Gilles et Jeanne*; it started as a scenario. But I'm not completely against television—or the movies. I think television is a medium, not an art. Movies are an art, but a mediocre one, because of the viewer's passivity.

SP: What about plays?

MT: They're a little better, but theater is still a minor art. The very fact that you're in a hall, in a chair, in the dark, that you can't move for two hours while you're being bombarded by a message—that shows that you're in a lesser condition. And that's even more true for the movies than for theater; the theater isn't as dark as the movie house, where people are actually hypnotized. That's my quarrel with movies.

But with a book, I'm in charge; I'm the boss. I had a terrible dispute with Claude Lanzmann, who is more than a friend, he's like a brother to me. He sent me an invitation to see the premier of *Shoah*: nine hours and a half! I wouldn't go. I told him, "I can't do it. I can't sit down for nine and a half hours in a hall! I'll die! You don't want me to die!" He was

---

[3] *Phèdre*, lines 253-54.

[4] Bluwal's connection to *La Goutte d'or* is indirectly acknowledged in the novel when Achille Mage tries to impress Idriss by telling him, "I know everyone important in Paris. I'm on a first-name basis with Yves Montand, Jean Le Poulain and Mireille Mathieu. I have lunch with Marcel Bluwal and Bernard Pivot" (165).

furious. And then I sent him *La Goutte d'or*. He called me up and he said, "You've got a lot of nerve! You send me your books and you won't see my films!" I said to him, "But it's not at all the same! I didn't ask you to stand up on a chair in your bathroom and read my book out loud without stopping, did I? Well, that's what you asked with your movie! You don't have to read my book, you can take it or leave it, you can take it with you on a trip, you're free. It's not a movie. Movies make one into a slave." For me there's one image which symbolizes a person watching a movie. It's from *A Clockwork Orange*. There's a man in a straitjacket, tied to a chair, his head fastened facing the screen, his eyes held open so he has to look. That's a person watching a movie. I can't accept that.

SP: In *Le Vol du vampire* you spoke of the reader's freedom and even of what you called the reader's "co-creation." Do you see any contradiction between your desire to teach something and the reader's freedom?

MT: I don't try to teach anything in my books—not in my fiction. We mustn't confuse fiction and nonfiction. When I wrote *Le Vent paraclet* or the *Petites proses*, that was nonfiction, and there I did want to teach something. But in *La Goutte d'or*, or *Le Roi des aulnes* or *Vendredi*, in the fiction, I'm not teaching anything. I'm telling a story, and the reader does whatever he wants with it. He interprets it in his own way. I can't tell how he's going to interpret it.

I *can* tell a little if he's alive today and if he comes from a background like my own, but suppose by some chance my book might still be read in two thousand years. How can I tell what it would mean to a reader then? Think about Defoe's *Robinson Crusoe* and what I did with it. Two hundred fifty years earlier, Defoe couldn't have anticipated one one-hundredth of what I saw in it, or what you see in it, because we read it with the eyes of people at the end of the twentieth century, conscious of the problems of the Third World, modern sports, the Club Med—all those things add to our vision, and they didn't exist in Defoe's day.

SP: All the same, you have things you want to say. There aren't just events in the novels; there are ideas as well.

MT: Don't you think it's the reader who has the ideas? The reader always thinks that the ideas he has are in the text he's reading. In the Gospels, Jesus says, "Suffer the little children to come unto me." Well, we have Lewis Carroll, Victor Hugo, a whole mythology about childhood behind us which dates from the nineteenth century, and we read the Gospel verse in light of that mythology. But let's go back to the seventeenth century.

Bossuet interpreted that sentence this way: he said, "You see that Jesus wasn't afraid of contamination. He allowed himself to be approached by the Roman soldier, who was part of the occupying troops and whom you weren't supposed to hang around with, and by the woman taken in adultery, who was going to be stoned, by the prostitute, and he even descends so low that he associates with children, who are the most vile beings, the most repugnant members of humanity because of their dirtiness, their stupidity, their sin! And he goes all the way down to their level!" And Bossuet adds, "And Jesus accepted the two greatest humiliations of human life, dying on the cross and becoming a child!" So, you see, the reader is always right. Can you say that Bossuet didn't know what he was talking about? That Jesus actually admired children, that they're pure little angels? Jesus didn't say that—it was Victor Hugo! [He laughs.] You see?

SP: But if we're talking about something written in our own society, in our own century—

MT: Yes, but maybe in a hundred years, two hundred years, Europeans will have vanished for demographic reasons and the Chinese, or the Arabs, who will be living in France, England, and so on, will read Michel Tournier's books—maybe. And they'll have their own interpretations.

SP: Speaking of different cultures, I wonder why your books haven't had more success in the United States. Do you think that perhaps English doesn't convey your style well?

MT: I don't know. My greatest success has been my books for young people. Well, unfortunately, in every country in the world, including France, there's a major barrier to new books for young people. An ordinary publishing house wants authors to have talent, to be original—they don't mind if they're surprising and shocking, because they know that's part of being creative.

But publishers of children's books *do* mind. They insist on complete conformity! And each country has its own kind of conformity. For example, in the United States it's conformity to the Walt Disney model. I first wrote *Vendredi ou les limbes du Pacifique*, which was published in the United States by Doubleday. Doubleday has a big children's department, so when I wrote *Vendredi ou la vie sauvage*, I offered it to them also. They rejected it. And finally *Vendredi ou la vie sauvage* was published by Knopf, which doesn't put out children's books. Knopf published it as a sort of curiosity, something odd to amuse the intellectuals—which wasn't my idea at all! In France, a million and a half copies of *Vendredi ou la vie sauvage* have been sold. In the United States two thousand copies were printed, and they didn't sell at all. You see? I simply can't reach my major public, which is young people, in foreign countries.

I've had problems in France. But I'm here; I fight. I go to the schools all the time, and classes come here. Last week, two schools came because it's the end of the school year and they take trips. One came from Besançon in a bus. They had a picnic here, and then they spent two hours with me and I talked with them. Let me show you a book from a *lycée* at Courbevoie. I went there to see them, and then they came to see me here. You see, it says "A meeting with Michel Tournier," "Michel Tournier greets us"—and so on. There's a drawing by a student. Here's a photo; you can see, they're here in my living room, and here I am in their class.

SP: What had they read?

MT: They'd read a little of everything, because they're older students. But I go to kindergartens, too. I can keep the attention of a class of 30 five-year-old girls and boys for 20 minutes! I can assure you that takes something. I've broken down the doors to reach this public. But that doesn't keep conservative magazines from publishing articles all the time accusing me of perverting young people.

SP: Why do they say that?

MT: Why? Well, for example, in "La Fugue du petit Poucet," there's a little boy who drinks alcohol, smokes marijuana, and sleeps with the ogre's little girls. Those are the three cardinal sins for children: alcohol, drugs, and sex. I've never said that I recommend them. But I write about them— and one isn't supposed to. Children's literature can't have any sex, politics, or money in it. That's funny because that corresponds to the three vows of monks and priests—vow of chastity, vow of poverty, and vow of obedience. But I can't see why books for children have to follow the vows of monks and priests. In any case, sex, money, and politics are things that children care about.

The translation of *Vendredi ou les limbes du Pacifique* into English makes an interesting story. Norman Denny was with my English publisher, Collins, and he translated *Vendredi*. But he changed everything, made really staggering changes. I don't mind, I'm broad-minded; I got a good laugh out of it. Then, when I offered the manuscript of *Le Roi des aulnes* to Collins, they had Norman Denny read it. He wrote a horribly negative report, which I've seen. Collins took it anyway, but Norman Denny didn't do the translation. I think Norman Denny's translation of *Vendredi* is excellent, but completely unfaithful. But that's not important. I prefer an unfaithful but good translation to a faithful but bad one. But it was crazy; you can't tell why he did those things, there isn't any explanation. For example, the boat at the end is named the *Whitebird*, but he called it the *Heron*.[5] I don't know why. He just didn't like the *Whitebird*.

SP: In *Le Vent paraclet*, you write that you made changes, too, when you translated novels from German into French.

MT: Yes, that's right; that's why I'm not upset. It's so boring to translate; you have to have a little fun. You know, I've done a lot of translating, and the problems I had weren't ever with the German text but with French, which I didn't know well enough. In your case, if you translate, you'd be translating from French into English. That means you need a passive knowledge of French but an active knowledge of English. You're given the French. But the English you'll turn the text into, you're writing it, and there's the problem! It's not a problem with French for you, but a problem with English.

SP: Speaking of problems, let me ask you a little about philosophers, because your use of philosophy in your novels may present a problem for most readers, who don't know much about philosophy. Leibniz, for example—did he influence *Vendredi*?

MT: I myself am very Leibnizian, but I don't think *Vendredi* is. I've said before that it's mainly Spinozan because Robinson goes through three stages which resemble Spinoza's three kinds of knowledge. First there's the pig wallow, then the administered island, and the solar life, which somewhat resemble Spinoza's three kinds of knowledge, which are passion, scientific knowledge, and direct intuition of essence.

But there's also a theory of knowledge in that book which is entirely my own and which I published—the very first thing I ever published—in

---

[5] In the version called *Friday, or The Other Island* and published in England as a King Penguin in 1984, the ship is indeed called the *Heron* (184), although in the American 1985 paperback published by Pantheon and called simply *Friday*, the ship is called the *Whitebird* (217). Although both are the Norman Denny translation, and although both have copyright information implying that they are identical, there are numerous other small differences between the American and the English text. If the ship is indeed meant to represent the Holy Spirit, changing the name to the *Heron* would certainly destroy the symbolism. The change is the more surprising since the ship's name was in English to begin with.

1950, in a magazine. The magazine was called *Espace* and doesn't exist any more; in fact, I think that my article was in its very last issue. The article had a theory of knowledge which I used in *Vendredi* and which I'll summarize briefly for you. The problem of knowledge is deciding how the subject arrives at knowledge of the object. There's idealism, which says that the object is produced by the subject, and there's realism, which says that the object exists independently of the subject.

I solved the problem differently by saying that they're the same thing at two different stages. I said that the world exists without a subject who observes it but that it's full of contradictions and that it tries to get rid of those contradictions, and each time it makes an effort to get rid of them, it produces a by-product, a kind of waste matter, which is the subject. I'll use a simple example. I wake up in the morning and I see my mother in my chair. But that's absurd, because my mother can't be in my chair, either because she's dead, or she's gone to the country—she's not there; she can't be there. So, I wake up, I shake myself, and I see that it's just my bathrobe that I've put on the chair which made me think there was someone there, a woman—my mother.

That's a simple story. I'll describe it according to my system. First stage, my mother is in my chair and nobody else is in the room. She's really there. But that causes a crisis because it's impossible. It can't be, either because my mother is in the country or because she's dead. So the world makes an effort to get rid of the contradiction, and following that effort everything makes sense again, my mother isn't in the chair but my bath-robe is. And what remains of the first stage, where my mother was in the chair? I do—I, who thought I saw my mother in the chair, you see? I, the subject, have been thrown into the world! No mother in the chair, a bath-robe on the chair, and me!—who thought I saw my mother in the chair.

So, in the first stage, there's an absurd world with no subject; then, there's an effort to achieve rationality, and from this effort, the former absurd world has fallen away—my mother in the chair—and has *become* *me*, who thought I saw my mother in the chair. So you could say that the subject is the absurd object which has been expelled from the world. *That's* the theory of knowledge that you'll find in *Vendredi ou les limbes du Pacifique*! But it's my theory; it's not from Leibniz. You'll find the theory in the book—unless Norman Denny threw it out.[6] My theory says that the

---

[6] The relevant passage is on pages 94-95 of *Friday*.

world needs to get rid of an absurdity. It's like the stomach which can't digest something and which spits it out. And when the world rids itself of the absurdity, the thing which falls to the ground is the subject. That's a philosophical theory; one has to approach it that way. [He laughs.] It's easier, anyway, than Hegel, or Spinoza, or Kant.

SP: Let's go further back in the history of philosophy. You seem to prefer Aristotle to Plato when you write, "The value of form begins when a little matter weights and distorts it."[7]

MT: I know Plato much better. I wrote an essay on Plato.

SP: The thesis for your *diplôme*.

MT: That's right. But I can't stand Plato. I concluded from my work on him that he's a bad master, and everything bad attributed to Christianity doesn't actually come from Jesus but from Plato. Christianity became Platonized because Christian doctrine was worked out in Alexandria and because the Gospels were written in Greek. What I hate in Plato is his morality. The theory of knowledge I think is wonderful, *Parmenides* is wonderful—but he has a morality which I think is hateful and harmful and which thinks of the body as a prison for the soul and which hopes that the soul can escape from that prison.

And that's one of the major ideas of Christianity—but it's not in the Gospels. It's in *Phaedrus*, where Plato says that when a man loves a boy— that's the only kind of love he speaks of—he mustn't love his body, he must love his soul, which is nonsense, isn't it? It doesn't mean anything. It's totally opposed to the Gospels. The Gospels aren't concerned with the soul, but the body. The major difference, I think, between the Old and the New Testaments is shown in the opposition between Moses on Mount Sinai and Jesus on Mount Tabor.

Remember, Moses goes up Mount Sinai and doesn't see God. He hears God, and God gives him the tablets of the law. We're in the realm of signs, disincarnated signs. That's the Old Testament. In the New Testament, Jesus comes and rehabilitates the flesh—and at the same time he rehabilitates the image! When he goes up on Mount Tabor with his Disciples there's literally a divine striptease show: he shows himself to them in his fleshly splendor, just the opposite of Sinai, you see? The Disciples are completely dazzled. They want to stay there forever, they find it so delightful. It's actually voluptuous.

---

[7] In the essay "L'Image abîmée," found in *Petites proses* 137.

Tabor is the opposite of Sinai. And it continues. "Eat my flesh, drink my blood"—and when Jesus dies he comes back to life, it's victory over death, and he goes to Heaven in the flesh, he speaks, his body doesn't rot, his body goes to Heaven! So, you see, Jesus is the victory of the flesh.

SP: Could we apply that to *Les Météores*? Alexandre seems to be a follower of Plato; he says that the idea is worth more than the thing.

MT: Yes, and he says that the idea of the idea is more than the idea. That's Leibnizian, very much Leibnizian. But I'm not Alexandre. I create a character like Alexandre and he does what he wants to and says what he wants to. You mustn't identify me with one of my characters.

SP: I was thinking of the opposition in the book between Alexandre, who cares about ideas, and the twins, who care more for things, for bodies. Alexandre lives mostly in his head.

MT: Alexandre, you know, has only a very, very short meeting with the twins, but they kill him, in a sense. You could say that *Les Météores* is constructed this way: there is in the center an absolute, eternal, and unchangeable couple, the twins Jean and Paul, eternal because they're identical. And then around them is a whole circle of couples who, unlike them, are dialectical, nonidentical, men and women who have to change, who live in time, like Edouard and Maria-Barbara, the German painter and his Japanese girlfriend, the American and his English wife in Djerba, and so on. And then between the twins at the center and the periphery of mixed couples, there's Alexandre who makes a sort of bridge because he's not a twin so he should belong to the periphery, but he refuses to do so. He claims the privileges of a twin although he isn't entitled to them.

That's why Paul compares him to Molière's bourgeois gentleman, a member of the middle class who tries to be a gentleman. And all his problems come from that fact. If he'd been satisfied with belonging to the middle class he wouldn't have had those problems, but we wouldn't have had Molière's comedy, either. Well, Alexandre is the bourgeois gentleman. He doesn't have a twin but wants the privileges of a twin.

SP: Koussek, too, speaks of the bourgeois gentleman when he complains of heterosexuals trying to have what he considers the privileges of homosexuals.

MT: Yes, he says that they claim the freedom of homosexuals, which they're not entitled to. I could add something else to that now. Homosexuals claim AIDS as their own disease, they're proud of it, to have such a horrible and dramatic disease. But AIDS is the disease of people who have a sex life.

And the more sex they have, the more they're exposed to AIDS, as people were a hundred years ago to syphilis. A hundred years ago, syphilis was a problem only for people who had an active sex life. Well, who has an active sex life? Not very many people. Take our society—there are only about ten percent who have an active sex life. There are the people who are too young, those who are too old, and those who are too lazy. If you eliminate all of them, you're left with ten percent.

SP: That's a low figure—

MT: Fifteen percent, if it makes you happy! But not one more! Well, from that point of view, AIDS doesn't seem so dramatic. It's not like the plague—or tuberculosis! Everyone used to catch tuberculosis, just breathing the air, it was dreadful.

The other day I saw a television broadcast about AIDS, and they were asking people in the street about it, and one fellow said, "I don't have relations with homosexuals or with heterosexuals, so I'm not worried about AIDS!" It made everybody laugh! But that fellow was saying something that's true for nearly everyone.

AIDS is a venereal disease, and venereal diseases are horrible. You know, a hundred years ago, my grandfather was twenty and was doing his military service. Later, when I was a child, he said to me, "Oh, some of those idiots used to go to prostitutes! But I was studying pharmacy, and I knew what syphilis was, and you can be sure that I didn't go!" You could say the same thing about AIDS. But because AIDS began with homosexuals, two things have played a part. For one, the homosexuals claimed for themselves something which was horrible, dramatic, and which gave them prestige, and, on the other hand, there was an antihomosexual racism which wanted to see AIDS as being God's fire destroying Sodom. Homosexuals claim AIDS as the Jews claim the gas chambers. That's right! Because it's terrible, the end of the world. Homosexuals don't like heterosexuals to get AIDS, just as the Jews hate it when one says that it wasn't only Jews who died in the gas chambers. They want to claim the greatest horror for themselves.

SP: Why is that?

MT: From pride! Because misfortune is overwhelmingly huge and beautiful!

SP: Let me change the subject to *bricolage*—not tinkering around the house, but what the literary critics and "new novelists" mean by *bricolage*. They *bricolent*—play around, tinker—with sentences, with words. In your books, you seem to play in much the same way with ideas.

MT: Yes.

SP: This use of the term *bricolage* comes from Lévi-Strauss, in *La Pensée sauvage*, where he said that primitive societies tinker with ideas, reusing the same ideas in different ways. In your title *Vendredi ou la vie sauvage* were you hinting at a connection with Lévi-Strauss's ideas?

MT: No. You could call the similarity of titles a coincidence. You know, when I took courses from Lévi-Strauss at the Musée de l'Homme I knew him personally, but he wasn't the only person who influenced me. There was also André Leroi-Gourhan, who, in the area of *bricolage* was astounding because he invented primitive technology. He wrote several books which I have here, which I could show you, where he describes, for example, how one closes the doors, how one makes locks, in the entire world! [He goes into the library, takes down books, opens them.]

He tells you how people carry babies all over the world—on their back, on their arm, on their leg. It's wonderful! That's primitive technology. You mustn't forget that *bricolage* isn't just tinkering with ideas, it's also tinkering with things. He taught me how to use a bow and arrow. He gave me boomerang lessons! That was the material side of *bricolage*, which fascinated me because I didn't know how to use my hands. Leroi-Gourhan had another specialty, which was prehistory, especially stone tools. He made stone tools, he made arrowheads.

SP: What about the character Vendredi? Would you say that he tinkers, as Lévi-Strauss would say people in primitive cultures do?

MT: No, because Vendredi is an inventor. And nobody invents less than people in what are called primitive societies. They're very restricted by their traditions. They make bows, they make fire, just in the ways Leroi-Gourhan says. In contrast, Vendredi weans Robinson from his slavish reproduction of English civilization and makes him create and invent. So, for example, he invents the wind harp. The wind harp wasn't a part of Araucanian civilization; it was a romantic invention. They had wind harps in the nineteenth century, people had them in their gardens, it was the fashion. He invents the kite, the kite dance. When I think that they filmed *Vendredi ou la vie sauvage* for television—*five hours*—and that they left out the kite![8] What a shame!

---

[8] Perhaps the kite was not in the final cut. A version of *Vendredi ou la vie sauvage* published by Gallimard/Flammarion in 1981 and illustrated with photographs taken by Pat York during filming, however, shows Vendredi, played by

SP: Was that the production with Michael York?

MT: Yes, that was it.

SP: Were you satisfied with the production in other ways?

MT: Naturally, I prefer my book. There are some very, very rare cases where a movie adaptation is better than the book. For example, Hitchcock's *Rear Window*. It was made from a story by William Irish. I read it. It was very bad—amazing—an amazing case—where a writer has a splendid subject and doesn't know it. And Hitchcock saw it! Do you know what the difference is? You can read the story, and not once does he mention the noise, the sound. You remember, the man is in his room, with his leg in a cast, and all the windows are open because it's hot, and across the way is a building with all the windows open. What does he hear? He hears a murmur. And that murmur is important—it's life! Everyone speaks at once—something comes from every window—music, cries—and that murmur runs throughout the film. That's what the film is made from, that's what gives it texture. Irish's story doesn't say one word about noise, about sound. You can't forgive a mistake like that! Whereas Hitchcock—oh, it's wonderful, the noise is wonderful!

SP: Maybe it's just third-rate books that can be improved by movies.

MT: That's true, that's true. For example, Simenon's books. The Maigret books make good movies, because they're not important Simenon works. But the great Simenon books, *Trois Chambres à Manhattan*, *L'Aîné des Ferchaux* and the others, you can't make movies from them.

SP: I'd like to ask you about your duties as a member of the Académie Goncourt. The Goncourt is very important in France, but most Americans don't know much about it.

MT: I'll tell you about it briefly. It started with Edmond de Goncourt, who was a good writer and and an excellent judge of the literature of his own time. His friends who were writers, Baudelaire, Balzac, Flaubert, Maupassant, Alphonse Daudet, Zola, Turgenev, Huysmans, and others, used to get together with him in his attic. These writers couldn't belong to the Académie Française and didn't want to. Goncourt said, "It's a scandal that the Académie Française is betraying its function. *I* am the Académie Française!" And when he died, he wanted his own academy to continue, so he left his money to form a literary society, the Académie Goncourt, to

---

Gene Antony Ray, preparing to fly a kite (64), though one cannot tell what the kite has been made from.

be composed of ten professional writers, whereas the Académie Française has forty members and there are all kinds of people who belong—doctors, priests, generals, everything. So, Goncourt wanted only professional writers, and there was a woman from the start,[9] but the Académie Française waited until six years ago to have its woman, Marguerite Yourcenar. And the Académie Goncourt meets every month in a restaurant, their official place of business, and every year they give the Prix Goncourt for the year's best novel.

So, you could say that from the start there was a sort of opposition to the Académie Française. If you apply to be a member of the Académie Française and you're rejected, you can't ever become a member of the Académie Goncourt. It's a sort of original sin; you're finished. If you're elected to the Académie Française, you can't become a member of the Académie Goncourt, and if you're elected to the Académie Goncourt, you can't ever be a member of the Académie Française.

And in addition, the writers whose names I've mentioned—Flaubert, Balzac, Maupassant, Zola, Huysmans, Alphonse Daudet—they form a school, the school of Realism and Naturalism. The Académie Goncourt has always been faithful to that heritage. For example, it rejected Symbolism and Surrealism, rejected the "new novel," because they weren't compatible with the Realist-Naturalist approach which is the Goncourt heritage.

You're elected to the Académie Goncourt without applying—you're not permitted to ask to join. You're elected for life, except that you can resign, and we meet every month, we know each other, we become friends, we yell at each other, the atmosphere is—like a café. That's it, the atmosphere of the Académie Française is like a *salon*, and the Académie Goncourt's is like a café. We're great eaters. And we each have our silver place setting, with the names of our predecessors engraved on it.

The first Prix Goncourt was given in 1903, the year in which the very first Tour de France was held! There, that's everything about the Académie Goncourt, the main points.

SP: What do you think of your duties as a member of the Académie Goncourt? Do you feel that the point of the prize is to encourage writers?

MT: The main duty is to make a good choice for the annual prize. And that's very, very hard. You can't be influenced by friendship, family, publishers.

---

[9] Judith Gautier, elected in 1910.

The publishers don't exert pressure on the members of the academy, but there is a shared standard, because if you've chosen to be published by Gallimard, or by Grasset, that's not a matter of chance. It's because you feel you share the views of that publisher. So, you naturally have a tendency to favor his books. That's not corruption, or you could call it the highest kind of corruption, corruption by friendship, by shared values.

SP: I really was asking whether you think you should choose certain writers to encourage them to continue to write.

MT: No, not encourage—we should rather discourage them. There are far too many. They write too much. [He laughs.]

SP: It must be a lot of work for you if you have to read them all.

MT: There are about 50 to 100 a year. But you don't have to read them all, from start to finish. Right from the start you can often tell that they can't be candidates for the Goncourt.

SP: Isn't the academy also giving prizes for short story collections?

MT: Yes, we're giving monetary prizes. We give them for short stories, historical accounts, biography. We're going to give one for poetry. But it's not as serious. The Prix Goncourt is horrible. You have to take into account what's at stake. A young writer publishes a novel, and if he can sell two thousand copies, that's the maximum. If he wins the Prix Goncourt, he might have four hundred thousand. His whole life is changed! Four hundred thousand copies—think of how much money that represents! He might earn three dollars for each copy sold—multiply that by *four hundred thousand* copies. That's one million, two hundred thousand dollars! [He laughs.] That's incredible! His whole life is changed! And we—*we're* the ones who make the decision. We hate each other on the day we vote for the prize.

We each come with the name of our favorite candidate hidden in our pockets [he pantomimes] and look at each other angrily. It's terrible! The day of the Prix Goncourt is horrible! That's the only day when we hate the Académie Goncourt.

SP: You must have problems when you can't get a majority to vote for your first choices and have to go to everyone's second or third choice.

MT: I'm very proud that I'm the one who began to get Marguerite Duras the prize for *L'Amant*.[10] When I read the book, I telephoned her publisher, Robert Landon, and I said to him, "Do you think that Marguerite Duras

---

[10] In 1984.

would accept the Prix Goncourt?" He said, "I'll ask her and call you back." Fifteen minutes later he called back and said, "She'll be delighted to have a prize which was once given to Marcel Proust."

From then on, I campaigned for her. And when we voted, on the first ballot, she had only one vote, mine. On the second ballot, she had three. On the third ballot, she had six votes, so she had won the Prix Goncourt, and I said, "Let's vote once more and give her the prize unanimously, because of her age and because she's so well known." And the four others refused.

And I deserve credit for trying to get her the Prix Goncourt unanimously because I had won it unanimously, and I'm the only one.[11] And when I became a member of the Académie Goncourt, somebody said, "I know why he became a member, it's to be sure that nobody else will ever have the Prix Goncourt unanimously."

SP: I remember when the prize for Duras was announced, you were the only one to discuss your choice.

MT: Yes, because it was my decision. [He laughs.] The others didn't have anything to say.

You were mentioning the "new novel" earlier. I'd like to tell you about a discussion I had one day on the radio with some people concerned with the "new novel." I was saying, "I write because I have something to say." And Robbe-Grillet, who was there, was jumping around, saying, "And I write because I don't have anything to say!" So we kept on talking, and I said, "I start from a big subject. I need World War II—*Le Roi des aulnes*. Immigrant workers—*La Goutte d'or*. Christianity—*Gaspard, Melchior et Balthazar*. Sex and couples—*Les Météores*. I always have to have a big subject. So I have to have something to say!" And Robbe-Grillet was saying, "I can't have any subject! Nothing! The absolute minimum!" I said, "I write to be read, I write for my readers," and he shouted, "As for me, I write against my readers!"

I wound up saying, "Robbe-Grillet, you think you're very original and that our discussion is unusual, but it could have taken place a little over a

---

[11] According to Jacques Robichon, there had been three previous unanimously awarded prizes: the 1909 prize, given to Marius and Ary Leblond, for *En France*; the 1915 prize, given to René Benjamin, for *Gaspard*; and the 1940 prize, which because of the war was not given until 1946, to Francis Ambrière for *Les Grandes Vacances* (356-57, 362).

hundred years ago between Mallarmé and Zola. They were the same age, the same generation. Zola wrote because he had something to say. He wrote to be read. And Mallarmé wrote because he didn't have anything to say. He wrote against his readers. And I think that in every century one could find that contrast. I'm Zola's grandson, and you're Mallarmé's! And this debate will go on in the next century. There will be a future Robbe-Grillet and a future Tournier to take up the discussion again."

SP: You've compared yourself to Flaubert as well. I've read that you've claimed to be the Flaubert of your generation.

MT: That's true. [He laughs.]

SP: What did you mean by that?

MT: Oh, I was just trying to get a reaction. There was a sort of panel discussion, and somebody started out by saying, "What remains today of Flaubert?" and I said, "Me!"

SP: But there's some truth, you're influenced by Flaubert—

MT: Oh, yes, I admire *Salammbô* above everything. I think that there are two Flauberts, Flaubert in color and Flaubert in black and white. Flaubert in black and white is *Madame Bovary, L'Education sentimentale, Bouvard et Pécuchet*, and "Un Cœur simple." Flaubert in color is *La Tentation de Saint Antoine*, "Saint Julien l'Hospitalier," "Hérodias," and *Salammbô*. You see?

And there's no question that I'm in favor of Flaubert in color, with, at the very top, *Salammbô*, which I think is the crowning achievement of the nineteenth-century novel.

SP: It seems to have influenced your *Gaspard, Melchior et Balthazar*.

MT: Yes. I was very influenced by it. And I should say that the dinner of the Magi with Herod in that book has a huge resemblance, not to the banquet of the barbarians at the start of *Salammbô* but to Herod's reception in "Hérodias." The comparison terrifies me. No one can surpass the banquet in "Hérodias."

SP: I've also been told that, like Flaubert, you plan to write your own "trois contes" and that *Gilles et Jeanne* is one of them.

MT: No, that's not right. I did publish a little book for young people called *Sept contes*. It includes *Pierrot ou les secrets de la nuit,* which I think is my very best writing. I do have work in progress. If you like, I'll tell you about it.

SP: I'd be delighted.

MT: Right now I have three things I'm working on. First, a life of Saint Sebastian. There is a play about Saint Sebastian by D'Annunzio, which he wrote in French and which is excellent, *Le Martyre de Saint Sébastien*, for which Claude Debussy wrote an oratorio. So, now, it's become a ballet.[12]

It's strange, because D'Annunzio was more or less a professional heterosexual, a great seducer, and the text he wrote is so equivocal that it's been danced three times, staged three times, and the first two times the role of Saint Sebastian was danced by a woman, Ida Rubinstein and someone else.[13] And the third time, finally, a year or two ago, Béjart staged it, and for the first time a boy danced it.[14] Well, I would like to write the story, Saint Sebastian's life, which I'm very interested in, because it's a key period. It's the end of the pagan Roman Empire, just before the Christian Roman Empire. One could consider Saint Sebastian the last Christian martyr.

Saint Sebastian was the head archer at Diocletian's court, and also at the court there was a nephew of Diocletian's named Constantine, who was the same age as Sebastian. So one could imagine that they were friends. That's made up, because it's likely that he never spoke with Sebastian, but that doesn't matter, it's a legend. Well, Diocletian, the last pagan emperor, has at his court Sebastian, who has secretly converted to Christianity, and

---

[12] D'Annunzio commissioned Debussy to write the incidental music—including preludes, choruses, and solo passages—for *Le Martyre de Saint Sébastien*, which combined dance and song and was based on medieval mystery plays.

[13] D'Annunzio had been inspired to write the play by Rubinstein, a Russian dancer, whose "lithe and slender body, long straight limbs, and absolutely flat chest" suggested the perfect androgynous Saint Sebastian (Gullace 84). She danced the role in the original production, May 22, 1911, which was an almost unqualified disaster, and in 1926, in an unsuccessful production in Italy (Lockspeiser 165, n. 1). There was a somewhat more successful revival at the Paris Opéra in 1957 (Gullace 84; Lockspeiser 162).

[14] More recently, in the summer of 1988, *Le Martyre* was performed by the Paris Opéra Ballet using totally new choreography by Robert Wilson, a "freewheeling adaptation" of D'Annunzio and Debussy's work in which the saint was danced by both a man, Michaël Denard, and a woman, Sylvie Guillem. The new production, which was first performed near Paris, then at the Metropolitan Opera House in New York (Dupont), seems also to have been unsuccessful (Kisselgoff).

his nephew, Constantine. Sebastian is martyred, and Constantine becomes emperor, and Constantine establishes Christianity in the Empire. Also, he leaves Rome, which for him is necessarily pagan, which can't be cleansed of its paganism, and he goes to Byzantium, which becomes Constantinople. There's the book. You can see it's a big subject, and in the same vein as *Gaspard, Melchior et Balthazar*.

My second subject is a novel to be called *Eva ou la république des corps* and which will have three themes. First, East Germany, with Prussia in the background, because East Germany is thought of as the heir to Prussia. Second, sports, which are very important in East Germany. And third, women athletes.

SP: Haven't you been working on this novel for a long time?

MT: Yes. And last year I spent all of June in East Germany.

SP: Is it going to be a big book?

MT: I don't know. I don't even know if I'll write it. You can't ever tell what will happen with work in progress.

SP: I ask because, since *Les Météores*, your novels—

MT: They keep getting shorter, yes. I'm slimming down. There are two ways of aging, getting fatter and drying out.

SP: You also write more short pieces, more tales.

MT: Yes. I like tales more and more all the time. And do you know what irritated me about *La Goutte d' or*? If you read the reviews—and some are horrible, nasty, full of hate, anger—nobody, not even the best ones, talked about the two tales, "Barberousse" or "La Reine blonde," which I think are the essence of the book!

SP: I liked them very much. I also liked a chapter that didn't appear in the book, that you published separately in *Petites proses*.

MT: You see that it couldn't be part of the book. There was something about it that didn't sound right. Idriss struck a false note. It was too clever, artsy. Too Saint-Germain-des-Près. Just what I wanted to avoid.

SP: I liked it very well—

MT: It amused you because there was wordplay, cleverness—

SP: What I liked best was the painter who painted the pyramids—

MT: —while he was in front of Notre Dame! [He laughs.]

SP: The idea was funny—

MT: [He laughs.] Well, then, my third project, which is the furthest along, is called *Le Médianoche amoureux*. You might think of it as a remake of the *Decameron*. There's a couple who decide to separate, and they invite their friends to a *médianoche*, a midnight meal, to tell them that they're going to separate. The friends come, and one of them tells a story. They discuss the story, and then a second one tells a story. They discuss this second story. And so on. These stories have an impact on the couple because the couple has a problem talking to each other, because when you live together for a long time you run out of things to say. What can you say when you've been together for 10, 15, 20, 30 years? So, the tales, the stories, come and fill up this emptiness.

They tell two kinds of stories. There are stories based on real life, or *nouvelles*, and there are tales, or *contes*. The *nouvelles* tend to separate the couple, and the *contes* tend to bring them together. As the evening wears on, the *contes* become more and more beautiful, stronger and stronger, becoming insurpassably, irresistibly beautiful. And the last *conte* is the most beautiful tale which has ever been told. Everyone has left except one guest, the last one, who is alone in front of the couple and tells this last story. And then he leaves. Then the curtains are opened, the sun comes up in front of the cluttered table, and the couple sit there, look at each other, and realize that they aren't going to separate because their problem has been solved, their problem of not having anything to say to each other.

That will be the next thing I publish.[15]

---

[15] Before the interview started, Tournier had spoken of a shorter project. He had just finished *Angus*, based on Victor Hugo's "L'Aigle du casque," and showed me his finished handwritten version, yet to be typed. He said he objected to Hugo's sentimentalizing of children and their supposed purity; Tournier's version of the story would correct Hugo's poem.

Works by Michel Tournier

The works are listed in chronological order under each heading.

FICTION: NOVELS

Vendredi ou les limbes du Pacifique. Paris: Gallimard, 1967. Rev. ed. Paris: Gallimard–Folio, 1972.
Le Roi des aulnes. Paris: Gallimard, 1970. Paris: Gallimard–Folio, 1980.
Les Météores. Paris: Gallimard, 1975. Paris: Gallimard–Folio, 1981.
Gaspard, Melchior et Balthazar. Paris: Gallimard, 1980. Gallimard–Folio, 1982.
La Goutte d'or. Paris: Gallimard, 1985. Gallimard–Folio, 1987.

FICTION: SHORT FICTION

Vendredi ou la vie sauvage. Paris: Flammarion, 1971. Illus. Pat York. Paris: Gallimard/Flammarion, 1981. Illus. Georges Lemoine. Paris: Gallimard–Folio Junior, 1984.
Le Nain rouge. Illus. Anne-Marie Soulcié. Montpelier and Paris: Fata Morgana, 1975.
Amandine ou les deux jardins. Paris: G. P. Rouge et Or, 1977.
L'Aire du Muguet. 1978. Illus. Georges Lemoine. Paris: Gallimard–Folio Junior, 1982.
Le Coq de bruyère. Paris: Gallimard, 1978. Paris: Gallimard–Folio, 1982.
La Fugue du petit Poucet. Paris: G. P. Rouge et Or, 1979.
Pierrot ou les secrets de la nuit. Illus. Danièle Bour. 1979. Paris: Enfantimages/Gallimard, 1982.
Barbedor. Illus. Georges Lemoine. Paris: Enfantimages/Gallimard, 1980.

Que ma joie demeure. Paris: Enfantimages/Gallimard, 1982.
Gilles et Jeanne. Paris: NRF and Gallimard, 1983. Gallimard–Folio, 1985.
Les Rois mages. Paris: Gallimard, 1983. Illus. Michel Charrier. Paris: Gallimard–Folio Junior, 1985.
Sept contes. Illus. Pierre Hézard. Paris: Gallimard–Folio Junior, 1984.
"La Mère Noël." *Contes et nouvelles de Noël*. Ed. Marie-Claudette Kirpalani. Paris: Hachette, 1987. 49-51.
Angus. Illus. Pierre Joubert. [N.p.]: Signe de Piste, 1988.
Le Médianoche amoureux: Contes et nouvelles. Paris: NRF and Gallimard, 1989.

FICTION AVAILABLE ON AUDIOTAPE

Vendredi ou la vie sauvage. Read by Michel Tournier. Gallimard–Jeunesse, GJ 001, 1983.
Sept contes. Read by Michel Tournier. Gallimard–Jeunesse, GJ 020, 1985.
"La Fugue du petit Poucet." Read by Raymond Gérome. *Bonnes nouvelles, grands comédiens*. Includes "Au crèpe anglais" by Daniel Boulanger. Cassettes Radio France, K 1090; distrib. Auvidis, AD 035, n.d.
La Goutte d'or. Read by François Chaumette. Auvidis, AD 804, 1987.

NONFICTION: BOOKS

Canada: Journal de voyage. Ottawa: La Presse, 1977.
Le Vent paraclet. Paris: Gallimard, 1977. Paris: Gallimard–Folio, 1980.
Des clefs et des serrures: Images et proses. Paris: Chêne/Hachette, 1979.
Rêves. Photographs by Arthur Tress. Brussels: Complexe, 1979.
Vues de dos. Photographs by Edouard Boubat. Paris: NRF and Gallimard, 1981.
Le Vol du vampire: Notes de lecture. Paris: Mercure de France,1982.
Introduction. *François Mitterrand*. Photographs by Konrad R. Müller. Paris: Flammarion, 1983.
Journal de voyage au Canada. [Augmented ed. of *Canada: Journal de voyage*.] Paris: Laffont, 1984.
Le Vagabond immobile. Drawings by Jean-Max Toubeau. NRF and Gallimard, 1984.
Petites proses. Paris: Gallimard–Folio, 1986.
Le Tabor et le Sinaï: Essais sur l'art contemporain. Paris: Belfond, 1988.

NONFICTION: UNCOLLECTED PIECES

"Treize clés pour un ogre." *Figaro Littéraire* 30 Nov.-6 Dec. 1970: 20-22.

"Les Petites Boîtes de nuit." *Nouvel Observateur* 26 July-1 Aug. 1971: 25-28.

"Le Tribunal international de Nuremberg condamnait à mort les principaux chefs nazis." *Monde* 1 Oct. 1971: 1-2.

"Les Enfants dans la bibliothèque." *Nouvel Observateur* 6-12 Dec. 1971: 56-57.

"Quand Michel Tournier récrit ses livres pour les enfants." *Monde* [*des Livres*] 24 Dec. 1971: 13, 20.

"La Prusse était-elle vraiment le berceau du militarisme?" *Figaro Littéraire* 26 Feb. 1972: 13, 16.

"Lucien Clergue." *Sud* 7 (1972): 141-44.

"Point de vue d'un éducateur." *Monde* 20 Dec. 1974: 20.

"L'Homme de l'absolu." *Monde* 24 Oct. 1975: 26.

"Pour un retour à Byzance." *Monde* 16-17 Nov. 1975: 9.

"Lewis Carroll au pays des petites filles." *Point* 5 Jan. 1976: 74-75.

"Dans l'ancienne Prusse Orientale—la réalité dément le rêve du romancier." *Réalités* Oct. 1976: 66-75.

"L'Ile et le jardin." *Monde* 31 Oct. 1976: 9.

"Le Micro et la plume." *Brûler tous les livres?* Spec. issue of *La Nef* Oct.-Nov.-Dec. 1976: 75-82.

"Les Voyages initiatiques." *Monde* 19-20 Jan. 1977: 1, 22.

"L'Espace canadien." *Ecrire.* Spec. issue of *Nouvelle Critique* June-July 1977: 51-52.

"Les Voyages initiatiques." *Ecrire.* Spec. issue of *Nouvelle Critique* June-July 1977: 106-07.

"Faut-il, peut-on 'changer la mort'?" *Monde* 15 Oct. 1977: 1, 14.

"Michel Tournier fasciné par l'Allemagne de l'Est." *Monde* 10 Feb. 1978: 15, 20.

"Le Sacre de l'enfant." *Monde* 7 Apr. 1978: 21.

"Une Epaisseur glauque." *Monde* [*des Livres*] 9 Mar. 1979: 22.

"Comment écrire pour les enfants." *Monde* [*des Livres*] 21 Dec. 1979: 19.

"Le Vampire de papier." Spec. issue of *Incidences* 2-3.2-3 (1979): 5-8.

"L'Etrange cas du Dr Tournier." *Michel Tournier.* Spec. issue of *Sud* (1980): 11-16.

"La Logosphère et les taciturnes." *Michel Tournier.* Spec. issue of *Sud* (1980): 167-77.

"Qui a peur de la biologie?" *Monde* 8-9 Nov. 1981: 1, 7.

"Extraits: 'Pages extimes.'" *Monde* [*des Livres*] 6 Aug. 1982: 11, 13.

"Sébastien, archer de Dieu." *Nouvel Observateur* 13 Jan. 1984: 14-15.

"A la place de Dieu." *Monde* [*d'Aujourd'hui*] 1-2 July 1984: xiv.

"Gustave et Marguerite." *Sud* 55 (1984): 68-77.
"Les Mots sous les mots." *Débat* Jan. 1985: 94-109.
"L'Imagerie de Michel Tournier." *Magazine Littéraire* Jan. 1986: 13.
"Quand Raymond Queneau 'lisait' Tournier." *Michel Tournier.* Spec. issue of *Sud* 16 (1986): 7-10.
"Préface à l'édition en braille [de *Vendredi ou la vie sauvage*]." *Michel Tournier.* Spec. issue of *Sud* 16 (1986): 11-13.
"Ecrire à l'âge nucléaire." *Michel Tournier.* Spec. issue of *Sud* 16 (1986): 170-72.
"L'Europe, une révolution nécessaire." *Michel Tournier.* Spec. issue of *Sud* 16 (1986): 173-77.
"Journal extime (suite)." *Michel Tournier.* Spec. issue of *Sud* 16 (1986): 178-89.
"Egypte: Du rêve à Mokhatam." *Michel Tournier.* Spec. issue of *Sud* 16 (1986): 190-94.
"Sois belle ou tais-toi." *Nouvel Observateur* 27 Mar.-2 Apr. 1987: 93.
"Un Homme à femmes." *Lucien Clergue.* Spec. issue of *Sud* (1989): 11-12.

NONFICTION: VIDEOCASSETTE

Michel Tournier. By Gérard Blain. Témoins, 1983. 50 min.

NONFICTION: MAJOR INTERVIEWS IN FRENCH

"De Robinson à l'ogre: Un Créateur de mythes." By Jean-Louis de Rambures. *Monde* 24 Nov. 1970: 28. Rpt. as "Michel Tournier: Je suis comme la pie voleuse." *Comment travaillent les écrivains.* By Jean-Louis de Rambures. Paris: Flammarion, 1978. 163-67.
"Michel Tournier." By Jean-Louis Ezine. *Nouvelles Littéraires* 2-8 June 1975: 3. Rpt. as "Michel Tournier." *Les Ecrivains sur la sellette.* By Jean-Louis Ezine. Paris: Seuil, 1981. 223-28.
"Une Logique contre vents et marées: Entretien avec Michel Tournier." By Alain Poirson. *Ecrire.* Spec. issue of *Nouvelle Critique* June-July 1977: 47-50.
"L'Ogre Tournier." By Michel Braudeau. *Express* 29 May-4 June 1978: 80-89.
"Michel Tournier s'explique." By Gilles Lapouge. *Lire* Dec. 1980: 29-46.
"Michel Tournier." *Gai-Pied* Feb. 1981: 12-14.
"Qu'est-ce que la littérature?" By Jean-Jacques Brochier. *Magazine Littéraire* Dec. 1981: 80-86.
"Rencontre avec Michel Tournier." By Alain Sanzio, Katy Barasc, and Jean-Pierre Joecker. *Masques: Revue des Homosexualités* Autumn 1984: 8-26.

"Tournier face aux lycéens." By Arlette Bouloumié. *Magazine Littéraire* Jan. 1986: 20-25.
"Michel Tournier." By Pierre Boncenne. *Lire* Nov. 1987: 61-66.

FICTION AVAILABLE IN ENGLISH: NOVELS

Friday. Trans. Norman Denny. New York: Doubleday, 1969. New York: Pantheon, 1985. Published in England as *Friday, or The Other Island.* London: Collins, 1969. London: King Penguin, 1984. Trans. of *Vendredi ou les limbes du Pacifique.*
The Ogre. Trans. Barbara Bray. New York: Doubleday, 1972. New York: Pantheon, 1984. Published in England as *The Erl-King.* Trans. of *Le Roi des aulnes.*
Gemini. Trans. Anne Carter. New York: Doubleday, 1981. London: Methuen, 1985. Trans. of *Les Météores.*
The Four Wise Men. Trans. Ralph Manheim. New York: Doubleday, 1982. London: Methuen, 1983. Trans. of *Gaspard, Melchior et Balthazar.*
The Golden Droplet. Trans. Barbara Wright. New York: Doubleday, 1987. Trans. of *La Goutte d'or.*

FICTION AVAILABLE IN ENGLISH: SHORT FICTION

Friday and Robinson: Life on Speranza Island. Trans. Ralph Manheim. Illus. David Stone Martin. New York: Knopf, 1972. Trans. of *Vendredi ou la vie sauvage.*
The Fetishist. Trans. Barbara Wright. New York: Doubleday, 1983. New York: Plume–New American Library, 1985. Trans. of *Le Coq de bruyère.*
The Fetishist. Trans. Barbara Wright. New York: Ubu Repertory Theater Publications, 1983. Trans. of *Le Fétichiste.*
"Blandine, or The Father's Visit." Trans. Penny Hueston and Colin Nettelbeck. *Scripsi* 2.4 (1984): 7-12. Rpt. *Partisan Review* 54 (1987): 247-54. Trans. of "Blandine ou la visite du père."
Pierrot, or The Secrets of the Night. Trans. Margaret Higonnet. *Children's Literature* 13 (1985): 169-79. Trans. of *Pierrot ou les secrets de la nuit.*
"The Music of the Spheres: A Biblical Tale." Trans. Ralph Manheim. *Winter's Tales.* New Series: 2. Ed. Robin Baird-Smith. New York: St. Martin's, 1986: 207-09. Trans. of "La Légende de la musique et de la danse."
Gilles and Jeanne. Trans. Alan Sheridan. London: Methuen, 1987. New York: Grove Weidenfeld, 1990. Trans. of *Gilles et Jeanne.*

NONFICTION AVAILABLE IN ENGLISH

"Writing for Children is No Child's Play." *UNESCO Courier* June 1982: 33-34.
"Five Keys for André Gide." Trans. Penny Hueston and Colin Nettelbeck. *Scripsi*
2.4 (1984): 25-41. Trans. of "Cinq clefs pour André Gide."
"Writer Devoured by Children." Trans. Margaret Higonnet. *Children's Literature* 13
(1985): 180-87.
"Experience." Trans. Ninette Bailey and Michael Worton. *Paragraph* 10 (1987):
1-3.
"The Flight of the Vampire." Trans. Ninette Bailey and Michael Worton. *Paragraph*
10 (1987): 4-11. Trans. of "Le Vol du vampire."
The Wind Spirit: An Autobiography. Trans. Arthur Goldhammer. Boston:
Beacon, 1988. Trans. of *Le Vent paraclet.*

NONFICTION AVAILABLE IN ENGLISH: INTERVIEWS

"The Offal Truth." By Nina Sutton. *Guardian* [Manchester, Eng.] 10 Feb. 1971: 8.
"An Interview with Michel Tournier." By Penny Hueston. *Meanjin* 38 (1979):
400-05.
"Philosophy in Frills." By Hugh Hebert. *Guardian* [Manchester, Eng.] 12 Nov.
1983: 8.
"A Grand Scale: Ronald Hayman Talks to Michel Tournier." By Ronald Hayman.
Literary Review Jan. 1984: 40-41.
"An Interview with Michel Tournier." By Maura A. Daly. *Partisan Review* 52
(1985): 407-13.

Works Consulted

The works are in alphabetical order under each heading.

WORKS BY MICHEL TOURNIER

"Barberousse ou le portrait du roi." *Nouvelle Revue Française.* July-Aug. 1984: 1-16.

Canada: Journal de voyage. Ottawa: La Presse, 1977.

Le Coq de bruyère. Paris: Gallimard–Folio, 1982.

Des clefs et des serrures: Images et proses. Paris: Chêne/Hachette, 1979.

"Les Enfants dans la bibliothèque." *Nouvel Observateur* 6-12 Dec. 1971: 56-57.

"L'Espace canadien." *Ecrire.* Spec. issue of *Nouvelle Critique* June-July 1977: 51-52.

"Extraits: 'Pages extimes.'" *Monde [des Livres]* 6 Aug. 1982: 11, 13.

Friday. Trans. Norman Denny. New York: Pantheon, 1985.

Friday, or The Other Island. Trans. Norman Denny. London: King Penguin, 1984.

Gaspard, Melchior et Balthazar. Paris: Gallimard, 1980.

Gilles et Jeanne. Paris: NRF and Gallimard, 1983.

The Golden Droplet. Trans. Barbara Wright. New York: Doubleday, 1987.

La Goutte d'or. Paris: Gallimard, 1985.

"Lewis Carroll au pays des petites filles." *Point* 5 Jan. 1976: 74-75.

Le Médianoche amoureux: Contes et nouvelles. Paris: NRF and Gallimard, 1989.

Les Météores. Paris: Gallimard–Folio, 1981.

Petites proses. Paris: Gallimard–Folio, 1986.

"Point de vue d'un éducateur." *Monde* 20 Dec. 1974: 20.

"Préface à l'édition en braille [de *Vendredi ou la vie sauvage*]." *Michel Tournier.* Spec. issue of *Sud* 16 (1986): 11-13.

Présentation. *La Goutte d'or.* Read by François Chaumette. Auvidis, AD 804, 1987.

Le Roi des aulnes. Paris: Gallimard–Folio, 1980.
Les Rois mages. Paris: Gallimard–Folio Junior, 1985.
Sept contes. Illus. Pierre Hézard. Paris: Gallimard–Folio Junior, 1984.
Le Tabor et le Sinaï: Essais sur l'art contemporain. Paris: Belfond, 1988.
Le Vagabond immobile. Drawings by Jean-Max Toubeau. NRF and Gallimard, 1984.
Vendredi ou la vie sauvage. Paris: Gallimard–Folio Junior, 1984.
Vendredi ou les limbes du Pacifique. Paris: Gallimard–Folio, 1972.
Le Vent paraclet. Paris: Gallimard–Folio, 1980.
Le Vol du vampire: Notes de lecture. Paris: Mercure de France,1982.
"Writer Devoured by Children." Trans. Margaret Higonnet. *Children's Literature* 13 (1985): 180-87.
"Writing for Children is No Child's Play." *UNESCO Courier* June 1982: 33-34.

OTHER WORKS CONSULTED

Alberès, R.-M. "A la manière de . . ." Rev. of *Vendredi ou les limbes du Pacifique.* *Nouvelles Littéraires* 6 Apr. 1967: 5.
Allen, Bruce. "Vision Quest." Rev. of *The Golden Droplet.* *Chicago Tribune* 25 Oct. 1987. Sec. 14: 3.
Andersen, Hans [Christian]. *Hans Andersen: His Classic Fairy Tales.* Trans. Erik Haugaard. Illus. Michael Foreman. Garden City, NY: Doubleday, 1978.
Arrouye, Jean. "Paraboles photographiques." *Michel Tournier.* Spec. issue of *Sud* 16 (1986): 154-60.
Baine, Rodney M. Rev. of *Friday.* *Georgia Review* 23 (1969): 420-21.
Baroche, Christiane. "La Matière première." *Michel Tournier.* Spec. issue of *Sud* (1980): 74-102.
———. *"Les Météores* ou l'enfer et le paradis." *Magazine Littéraire* June 1978: 18-21.
———. "Michel Tournier ou l'espace conquis." *Critique* Nov. 1975: 1178-84.
———. "Michel Tournier par lui-même." Rev. of *Le Vent paraclet. Quinzaine Littéraire* 16-31 Mar. 1977: 4-6.
———. "Vieux mythes et habit neuf." Rev. of *Le Coq de bruyère. Quinzaine Littéraire* 16-31 May 1978: 7.
Baroche, Christiane, et al., eds. *Michel Tournier.* Spec. issue of *Sud* (1980). 1-183.
———, et al., eds. *Michel Tournier.* Spec. issue of *Sud* 16 (1986). 1-194.
Baumbach, Jonathan. "But Taor Had a Sweet Tooth." Rev. of *The Four Wise Men.* *New York Times* 24 Oct. 1982, natl. ed.: 7.32.

Berger, Yves. "Une Nouvelle Version de Robinson Crusoé." Rev. of *Vendredi ou les limbes du Pacifique*. *Monde* [*des Livres*] 18 May 1967: II.

Bevan, D[avid] G. *Michel Tournier*. Amsterdam: Rodopi, 1986.

————. "Tournier's Photographer: A Modern Bluebeard." *Modern Language Studies* 15 (1985): 66-71.

Bevernis, Christa. "Michel Tournier—l'œuvre et son message." *Philologica Pragensia* 26 (1983): 197-203.

Birkerts, Sven. "Ogres and Oracles." *New Republic* 11 Feb. 1985: 39-42.

Boisdeffre, Pierre de. Rev. of *Gilles et Jeanne*. *Revue des Deux Mondes* July-Sept. 1983: 424-25.

————. Rev. of *La Goutte d'or*. *Revue des Deux Mondes*. Jan.-Mar. 1986: 715-19.

Boncenne, Pierre. "Michel Tournier." Interview. *Lire* Nov. 1987: 61-66.

Bonnefis, Philippe. "L'Excentrique du texte." *Les Sujets de l'écriture*. Ed. Jean Decottignies. Lille: Presses Universitaires de Lille, 1981. 23-39.

Bonnefoy, Claude. "Le Roman classique perverti." Rev. of *Les Météores*. *Nouvelles Littéraires* 21-27 Apr. 1975: 4.

Borges, Jorge Luis. "Pierre Menard, autor del *Quijote*." *Ficciones*. By Jorge Luis Borges. Buenos Aires: Emecé, 1956. 45-57.

Bosquet, Alain. "Michel Tournier et les mythes renouvelés." *Nouvelle Revue Française* June 1975: 82-86.

Bougnoux, Daniel. "Des Métaphores à la phorie." *Critique* June 1972: 527-43.

Bougnoux, Daniel, and André Clavel. "Entretien avec Michel Tournier." Interview. *Silex* 14 (1979): 12-16.

Boullier, Henry. Rev. of *Le Vol du vampire*. *Commentaire* 5 (1982): 508-09.

Bouloumié, Arlette. "Deux thèmes chers au romantisme allemand: La Mandragore et la harpe éolienne dans *Vendredi ou les limbes du Pacifique* de Michel Tournier." *Recherches sur l'Imaginaire* 17 (1987): 163-78.

————. "Icone et idole dans *La Goutte d'or* de Michel Tournier." *Recherches sur l'Imaginaire* 17 (1987): 145-62.

————. *Michel Tournier: Le Roman mythologique*. [Paris]: Corti, 1988.

————. "Mythologies." *Magazine Littéraire* Jan. 1986: 26-29.

————. "Onomastique et création dans *Les Météores* de Michel Tournier." *Revue d'Histoire Littéraire de la France* 88 (1988): 1096-112.

————. "Tournier face aux lycéens." Interview. *Magazine Littéraire* Jan. 1986: 20-25.

Bourbonnais, Nicole, et al., eds. Spec. issue of *Incidences* 2-3.2-3 (1979): 1-102.

Bourgeade, Pierre. Rev. of *Gilles et Jeanne*. *Nouvelle Revue Française* 1 Sept. 1983: 136-37.

Bourniquel, Camille. Rev. of *Les Météores*. *Esprit* Sept. 1975: 333-35.

Boyd, William. "The Earthly Twins." Rev. of *Gemini*. *Sunday Times* [London] 29 Nov. 1981: 42.

Brahimi, Claude. "Une Enivrante Expérience de la liberté." *Magazine Littéraire* June 1978: 14-15.

Brassell, Tim. *Tom Stoppard: An Assessment*. New York: St. Martin's, 1985.

Braudeau, Michel. "L'Ogre Tournier." Interview. *Express* 29 May-4 June 1978: 80-89.

Bray, Barbara. "Heavenly Twins." Rev. of *Les Météores*. *Times Literary Supplement* 22 Aug. 1975: 950.

Brenner, Jacques. *Tableau de la vie littéraire en France d'avant-guerre à nos jours*. N.p.: Luneau Ascot, 1982.

Brochier, Jean-Jacques. "Dix-huit questions à Michel Tournier." Interview. *Magazine Littéraire* June 1978: 10-13.

————. "Qu'est-ce que la littérature?" Interview. *Magazine Littéraire* Dec. 1981: 80-86.

Brogniet, Eric. "Michel Tournier: De l'initation au salut." *Revue Générale* Dec. 1983: 51-59.

Buzbee, Lewis. "Images as an Enslaver." Rev. of *The Golden Droplet*. *San Francisco Chronicle* 8 Nov. 1987, home ed., book sec.: 11.

Caute, David. "Diary of a Giant." Rev. of *The Erl-King*. *Guardian* [Manchester, Eng.] 5 Oct. 1972: 16.

Cesbron, G. "L'Imagination terrienne du corps dans *Vendredi ou les limbes du Pacifique* de Michel Tournier." *Francia* 64 (1980): 9-16.

"Chaldean Rite." *A Catholic Dictionary*. Ed. Donald Attwater. 3rd ed. New York: Macmillan, 1961. 86-87.

Chancel, Jacques. "Michel Tournier: Le Secret d'un livre c'est la patience." Interview. *Figaro Dimanche* 9 Dec. 1979: 29.

Châtelet, François. "Bep, tu joues?" Rev. of *Les Météores*. *Quinzaine Littéraire* 16-30 Apr. 1975: 3, 5.

————. "Robinson délivré." Rev. of *Vendredi ou les limbes du Pacifique*. *Nouvel Observateur* 12-18 Apr. 1967: 41-42.

Clavel, André. "Le Corps Météo." *Michel Tournier*. Spec. issue of *Sud* (1980): 118-35.

————. "Un Nouveau Cynique: Tournier le jardinier." Rev. of *Le Vent paraclet*. *Critique* June-July 1977: 609-15.

Cloonan, William. "The Artist, Conscious and Unconscious, in *Le Roi des aulnes*." *Kentucky Romance Quarterly* 29 (1982): 191-200.

————. *Michel Tournier*. Boston: Twayne, 1985.

————. "Michel Tournier." *Dictionary of Literary Biography: French Novelists since 1960*. Ed. Catherine Savage Brosman. Detroit: Gale, 1989. 83: 295-305.

————. "The Spiritual Order of Michel Tournier." *Renascence* 36 (1983-84): 77-86.

————. "Tournier's *Salammbô: Gaspard, Melchior et Balthazar*." Special Session on Michel Tournier, MLA Convention. New Orleans, 29 Dec. 1988.

————. "Word, Image, and Illusion in *La Goutte d'or*." *French Review* 62 (1989): 467-75.

————. "World War II in Three Contemporary Novels." *South Atlantic Review* 51.2 (1986): 65-75.

Cluny, Claude Michel. "Michel Tournier de *Vendredi* au *Roi des aulnes*." Rev. of *Le Roi des aulnes*. *Magazine Littéraire* Oct. 1970: 37-38.

Contival, Isabelle. "Versions et inversions de l'ogre dans *Le Roi des aulnes*." *Recherches sur l'Imaginaire* 13 (1985): 333-49.

Coulaud, Pierre. "Michel Tournier parle de son nouveau livre: *Le Coq de bruyère*." Interview. *Dépêche du Midi* 23 Apr. 1978.

Cross, F. L., and E. A. Livingstone, eds. *The Oxford Dictionary of the Christian Church*. 2nd ed. London: Oxford UP, 1974.

Daly, Maura. Rev. of *Gaspard, Melchior et Balthazar*. *MLN* 96 (1981): 949-51.

————. "An Interview with Michel Tournier." Interview. *Partisan Review* 52 (1985): 407-13.

Dante Alighieri. *The Divine Comedy*. Trans. H. R. Huse. New York: Holt, 1963.

David, Catherine. Rev. of *Le Coq de bruyère*. *Nouvel Observateur* 29 May-4 June 1978: 74.

Davis, Colin. "Art and the Refusal of Mourning: The Aesthetics of Michel Tournier." *Paragraph* 10 (1987): 29-44.

————. "Identity and the Search for Understanding in Michel Tournier's *Les Météores*." *French Forum* 12 (1987): 347-56.

————. "Michel Tournier between Synthesis and Scarcity." *French Studies* 42 (1988): 320-31.

————. *Michel Tournier: Philosophy and Fiction*. New York: Oxford, 1988.

Delcourt, Xavier. "Michel Tournier: 'Dans le mythe se conjuguent roman et philosophie.'" Interview. *Quinzaine Littéraire* 1-15 Mar. 1977: 25-26.

Deleuze, Gilles. "Une Théorie d'autrui (autrui, Robinson et le pervers)." *Critique* June 1967: 503-25. Revised as "Michel Tournier et le monde sans autrui." Postface to *Vendredi ou les limbes du Pacifique*. Paris: Gallimard–Folio, 1980. 257-83.

Desarzens, Véronique. "Michel Tournier et les rois mages." Interview. *Genève Home Informations* 22 Jan. 1987: 32.

Dey, Tarcis. Rev. of *La Goutte d'or. Nouvelle Revue Française* 1 Apr. 1986: 91-93.

Dieckman, Suzanne. Rev. of a stage production of *The Fetishist.* Perry Street Theatre, [New York?]. 1984. *Theatre Journal* 37 (1985): 123-24.

d'Ivernois, Roger. "Michel Tournier: 'J'ai pris ma plume et j'ai inventé la vérité.'" Interview. *Journal de Genève* 9 Jan. 1981: 13.

Dort, Bernard. "Faire théâtre de tout." Rev. of the stage production of *Vendredi ou la vie sauvage.* Adapt. and dir. Antoine Vitez. Théâtre National de l'Enfance, Paris. 1973. *Théâtre en jeu.* By Bernard Dort. Paris: Seuil, 1979. 231-35.

Dumur, Guy. "Des petites filles modèles." Rev. of the stage production of *Vendredi ou la vie sauvage.* Adapt. and dir. Antoine Vitez. Théâtre National de l'Enfance, Paris. 1973. *Nouvel Observateur* 21-27 May 1973: 76-77.

Dupont, Joan. "The Paris Opéra Ballet Seeks Innovation." *New York Times* 19 June 1988, natl. ed.: H19, 21.

Eminyan, M[aurice]. "Extra Ecclesiam Nulla Salus." McDonald 5: 768.

————. "Necessity of the Church for Salvation." McDonald 12: 995-97.

Engel, Marian. Rev. of *The Ogre. New York Times Book Review* 3 Sept. 1972: 7, 14.

"Entretien avec M. Tournier." Interview. *Recherches sur l'Imaginaire* 5 (1979): 6-29.

Escoffier-Lambiotte. "L'Ecrivain et la société: Un Entretien avec Michel Tournier." *Monde [d'Aujourd'hui]* 8-9 Oct. 1978: 32.

"Eucharist." Cross and Livingstone 475-77.

Ezine, Jean-Louis. "Lettres de mon jardin." Rev. of *Le Vol du vampire. Nouvelles Littéraires* 3-10 Dec. 1981: 29.

————. "Michel Tournier." Interview. *Les Ecrivains sur la sellette.* Paris: Seuil, 1981. 223-28.

————. "Qui sème le vent récolte le Saint-Esprit." Rev. of *Le Vent paraclet. Nouvelles Littéraires* 17-25 Feb. 1977: 5.

————. "Le Temps des nomades." Rev. of *Gaspard, Melchior et Balthazar. Magazine Littéraire* 6-13 Nov. 1980: 37.

Fabre-Luce, Anne. Rev. of *Vendredi ou les limbes du Pacifique. French Review* 41 (1968): 900-01.

Fairlie, Henry. *The Seven Deadly Sins Today.* Washington: New Republic, 1978.

Fergusson, Kirsty. "Le Rire et l'absolu dans l'œuvre de Michel Tournier." *Michel Tournier.* Spec. issue of *Sud* 16 (1986): 76-89.

Fernandez, Marie-Henriette. "Bessons et serors germaine." *Littératures* 9-10 (1984): 23-29.

Rev. of a stage production of *Le Fétichiste*. Théâtre de la Roquette, Paris. 1982. *La Vie Ouvrière* 23 Sept. 1982: n.p.

Fischer, Manfred S. *Probleme internationaler Literaturrezeption: Michel Tourniers "Le Roi des aulnes" im deutsch-französischen Kontext*. Bonn: Bouvier, 1977.

Fleming, Thomas J. Rev. of *Friday. New York Times Book Review* 13 Apr. 1969: 47.

Flower, D. E. "An Exercise in Translation: Michel Tournier's 'Le Dit de l'âne.' " *Modern Languages* 67 (1986): 200-13.

Foote, Audrey C. "Noble Savage." Rev. of *Friday. Chicago Tribune Book World* 6 July 1969: 12.

Freustié, Jean. "Le Jumeau de soi-même." Rev. of *Les Météores. Nouvel Observateur* 7-13 Apr. 1975: 68-69.

Friedländer, Saul. *Reflections of Nazism: An Essay on Kitsch and Death*. Trans. Thomas Weyr. New York: Harper, 1984.

Fumaroli, Marc. "Michel Tournier et l'esprit de l'enfance." *Commentaire* 3 (1980-81): 638-43.

Galey, Matthieu. "L'Ange noir né des flammes." Rev. of *Gilles et Jeanne. Express* 10 June 1983: 33-34.

————. "La Guerre initiatique du soldat Abel." Rev. of *Le Roi des aulnes. Express* 7-13 Sept. 1970: 66.

————. "Un Oratorio pervers." Rev. of the stage production of *Le Roi des aulnes*, by Irène Lambelet and Jean-Philippe Guerlais. Théâtre de la Tempête-Cartoucherie, Paris. 1983. *Nouvelles Littéraires* 20-26 Jan. 1983: 34.

Gantrel, Martine. "Les Romans de Michel Tournier: Une 'Folie raisonneuse et systématique'?" *French Review* 63 (1989): 280-89.

Garcin, Jérôme. "L'Art de faire du neuf avec du vieux." Rev. of *Gaspard, Melchior et Balthazar. Nouvelles Littéraires* 6-13 Nov. 1980: 37.

Gardner, Edmund G. *Dante and the Mystics*. New York: Octagon, 1968.

Garreau, Joseph. "Réflexions sur Michel Tournier." *French Review* 58 (1985): 682-91.

Geiringer, Karl, with Irene Geiringer. *Johann Sebastian Bach: The Culmination of an Era*. New York: Oxford UP, 1966.

Rev. of *Gemini. New Yorker* 10 Aug. 1981: 106.

Genette, Gérard. *Palimpsestes: La Littérature au second degré*. Paris: Seuil, 1982.

Gilby, Thomas. "Prudence." McDonald 11: 925-28.

Glendinning, Victoria. "Living with Legends." Rev. of *The Four Wise Men. Sunday Times* [London] 14 Nov. 1982: 44.

Glenn, Catherine. "La Robinsonnade de Michel Tournier: Quelle réécriture?" *French Studies in Southern Africa* 15 (1986): 90-100.

Godard, Colette. Rev. of the stage production of *Vendredi ou la vie sauvage*. Adapt. and dir. Antoine Vitez. Théâtre National de l'Enfance, Paris. 1973. *Monde* 28 Nov. 1973: 25.

"Good Friday." Rev. of *Vendredi ou les limbes du Pacifique*. *Times Literary Supplement* 27 July 1967: 659.

Gorin, J.-P. "Le Grand Prix du roman est décerné à M. Michel Tournier." *Monde* 18 Nov. 1967: 10.

Gorra, Michael. "A Rich but Flawed Novel of the Magi." Rev. of *The Four Wise Men*. *San Francisco Chronicle Book Review* 31 Oct. 1982: 3.

Grainville, Patrick. "Tournier au lycée." Spec. issue of *Sud* (1980): 42-47.

Gramond, Agnès de. "Les Romans de Michel Tournier ou les ruses de Narcisse." *Michel Tournier*. Spec. issue of *Sud* (1980): 103-17.

Gripari, Pierre. Rev. of *Gaspard, Melchior et Balthazar*. *Ecrits de Paris* Dec. 1980: 124-25.

————. "Michel Tournier et le mythe de la phorie." *Critique et autocritique*. By Pierre Gripari. Lausanne: Age d'Homme, 1981: 144-50.

Guichard, Nicole. *Michel Tournier: Autrui et la quête du double*. Paris: Didier Erudition, 1989.

Gullace, Giovanni. *Gabriele D'Annunzio in France: A Study in Cultural Relations*. Syracuse, NY: Syracuse UP, 1966.

Häring, Bernard. "Justice." McDonald 8: 68-72.

Harris, Frederick J. *Encounters with Darkness: French and German Writers on World War II*. New York: Oxford UP, 1983.

Hayman, Ronald. "A Grand Scale: Ronald Hayman Talks to Michel Tournier." Interview. *Literary Review* Jan. 1984: 40-41.

————. "Underwear and Tear." Rev. of a stage production of *The Fetishist*. 1983. *Times Literary Supplement* 25 Nov. 1983: 1322.

Heins, Paul. "Stories for the Older Readers." Rev. of *Friday and Robinson*. *Horn Book Magazine* 49 (1973): 59.

Herbst, Winfrid John. "Envy." McDonald 5: 451.

Higonnet, Margaret R. "Marguerite Yourcenar and Michel Tournier: The Arts of the Heart." *Triumphs of the Spirit in Children's Literature*. Ed. Francelia Butler and Richard Rotert. Hamden, CT: Library Professional Publications, 1986. 151-58.

Hue, Jean-Louis. "Gilles et Michel." Rev. of *Gilles et Jeanne*. *Magazine Littéraire* July-Aug. 1983: 48-49.

Hueston, Penny. "An Interview with Michel Tournier." Interview. *Meanjin* 38 (1979): 400-05.

Jardine, Alice. "Woman in Limbo: Deleuze and His Br(others)." *SubStance* 44-45 (1984): 46-60.

Jay, Salim. *Idriss, Michel Tournier et les autres.* [Paris]: Différence, 1986.

—————. "Les Plumes du *Coq de bruyère.*" *Michel Tournier.* Spec. issue of *Sud* (1980): 144-48.

Jeffress, Lynn Carol Bird. *The Novels of Michel Tournier.* Diss. U of Oregon, 1981. Ann Arbor: UMI, 1981. 8123599.

Johnson, Phyllis, and Brigitte Cazelles. "L'Orientation d'Abel Tiffauges dans *Le Roi des aulnes.*" *Rocky Mountain Review* 29.3-4 (1975): 166-71.

Josephus, Flavius. *The Works of Flavius Josephus* . . . . Trans. William Whiston. 2 vols. Philadelphia: J. B. Lippincott, 1888.

Joxe, Sandra. "Michel Tournier: 'Je suis un monstre qui a réussi.' " Interview. *Autre Journal.* Nov. 1985: 50-54.

Kakutani, Michiko. Rev. of *The Golden Droplet.* *New York Times* 24 Oct. 1987, natl. ed.: 13.

Kane, Thomas Cornelius. "Fortitude." McDonald 5: 1034.

Kanters, Robert. "Creux et plein d'ordures." Rev. of *Les Météores.* *Figaro Littéraire* 5 Apr. 1975: [I], 15+.

—————. "Le Temps des ogres." Rev. of *Le Roi des aulnes.* *Figaro Littéraire* 23-29 Nov. 1970: 17-18.

Kirpalani, Marie-Claudette. "Usages possibles d'un texte littéraire." *Français dans le Monde* Jan. 1984: 86-91.

Kisselgoff, Anna. "Robert Wilson's Stunning Images: Do They Add Up?" *New York Times* 24 July 1988, natl. ed.: H16.

Koster, Serge. "Eléments de Tournierologie: En suivant *Gaspard, Melchior et Balthazar.*" *Michel Tournier.* Spec. issue of *Sud* 16 (1986): 35-51.

—————. *Michel Tournier.* Paris: Veyrier, 1986.

—————. "Tournier, mode d'emploi." Rev. of *Petites proses.* *Monde* 26 Dec. 1986: 8.

Kovacs, Laurand. Rev. of *Gaspard, Melchior et Balthazar.* *Nouvelle Revue Française* 1 Apr. 1981: 131-32.

Kramer, Jane. "Letter from Europe." *The New Yorker* 22 Feb. 1988: 87-95.

La Bardonie, Mathilde. Rev. of the stage production of *Le Roi des aulnes.* Adapt. Irène Lambelet. Dir. Irène Lambelet and Jean-Philippe Guerlais. Théâtre de la Tempête-Cartoucherie, Paris. 1983. *Monde.* 15 Jan. 1983: 20.

Lapouge, Gilles. "Michel Tournier s'explique." Interview. *Lire* Dec. 1980: 29-46.

Laureillard, Rémi. "Une Nouvelle Histoire de Robinson." Rev. of *Vendredi ou les limbes du Pacifique.* *Quinzaine Littéraire* 1-15 June 1967: 10-11.

Lavine, T. Z. *From Socrates to Sartre: The Philosophic Quest.* New York: Bantam, 1984.

Lévi-Strauss, Claude. *Anthropology and Myth: Lectures 1951-1982.* Trans. Roy Willis. New York: Basil Blackwell, 1987.

Lévi-Strauss, Claude. *Myth and Meaning*. New York: Schocken, 1979.

————. *The Savage Mind*. Chicago: U of Chicago P, 1973.

Lockspeiser, Edward. *Debussy: His Life and Work*. Vol 2. New York: Macmillan, 1965.

Lubac, Henri de. *La Postérité spirituelle de Joachim de Flore*. 2 vols. Paris: Lethielleux, 1978 and 1980.

Luccioni, Gennie. Rev. of *Le Roi des aulnes*. *Esprit* Dec. 1970: 987-90.

————. Rev. of *Vendredi ou les limbes du Pacifique*. *Esprit* Dec. 1967: 1041-45.

Lyman, Stanford M. *The Seven Deadly Sins: Society and Evil*. New York: St. Martin's, 1978.

Maclean, A[rthur] J[ohn]. "Nestorianism." *Encyclopedia of Religion and Ethics*. Ed. James Hastings et al. Edinburgh: T. and T. Clark: 1917. New York: Scribner's, 1962.

Maclean, Mairi. "Michel Tournier as Misogynist (or Not?): An Assessment of the Author's View of Femininity." *Modern Language Review* 83 (1988): 322-31.

————. "Human Relations in the Novels of Tournier: Polarity and Transcendence." *Forum for Modern Language Studies* 23 (1987): 241-52.

Magnan, Jean-Marie. "L'Amour-ogre." Rev. of *Le Roi des aulnes*. *Quinzaine Littéraire* 1-15 Oct. 1970: 5-6.

————. "Un Passionnant Roman sur la vie des livres." Rev. of *Le Vol du vampire*. *Sud* 12 (1982): 196-200.

————. "Les Rois mages ou la première eucharistie selon Michel Tournier." Rev. of *Gaspard, Melchior et Balthazar*. *Sud* 41-42 (1981): 231-33.

————. "Le Roman philosophique de Michel Tournier—système et bande dessinée." *Michel Tournier*. Spec. issue of *Sud* (1980): 60-73.

————. "Saint Gilles de Rais ou Tournier hagiographe." *Michel Tournier*. Spec. issue of *Sud* 16 (1986): 30-34.

————. "Vers la concision et la limpidité." Interview. *Quinzaine Littéraire* 1-15 Feb. 1986: 16.

"Malabar Christians." Cross and Livingstone 860-61.

Marissel, André. Rev. of *Le Roi des aulnes*. *French Review* 45 (1971): 218.

Marty, Catherine. "Du corps rhétorique de Roland Barthes au corps érotique de Michel Tournier." *Michel Tournier*. Spec. issue of *Sud* 16 (1986): 90-96.

Maulpoix, Jean-Michel. "Des limbes à la vie sauvage." *Michel Tournier*. Spec. issue of *Sud* (1980): 33-42.

————. "L'Or, l'encens, la myrrhe . . . et l'imaginaire." Rev. of *Gaspard, Melchior et Balthazar*. *Quinzaine Littéraire* 16-30 Nov. 1980: 7.

McDonald, William J., et al., eds. *New Catholic Encyclopedia*. 15 vols. New York: McGraw, 1967.

McDowell, Danièle. Rev. of *Gaspard, Melchior et Balthazar. World Literature Today* 55 (1981): 428-29.

McMahon, Joseph H. Rev. of *Le Coq de bruyère. French Review* 52 (1979): 801.

―――. "Michel Tournier's Texts for Children." *Children's Literature* 13 (1985): 154-68.

―――. Rev. of *Le Vent paraclet. French Review* 51 (1978): 918-19.

Merllié, Françoise. Rev. of *La Goutte d'or. Esprit* Mar. 1986: 116-17.

―――. "Histoires de barbes." *Magazine Littéraire* Jan. 1986: 29-35.

―――. *Michel Tournier.* Paris: Belfond, 1988.

―――. "La Reine blonde. De Méduse à la muse, ou comment les mots délivrent de l'image." *Michel Tournier.* Spec. issue of *Sud* 16 (1986): 14-29.

"Michel Tournier." Interview. *Gai-Pied* Feb. 1981: 12-14.

Mignone, Patricia. "Michel Tournier, une symbolique initiatique." *Cahiers Internationaux de Symbolisme* 45-47 (1983): 185-95.

Miller, Karl. "The Cyclopean Eye of a European Phallus." Rev. of *The Ogre. New York Review of Books* 30 Nov. 1972: 40-43.

Mitchell, Kendall. "Tales Introduce Fresh, New French Voice." Rev. of *The Fetishist. Chicago Tribune* 25 Nov. 1984, home ed., book sec.: 36.

Monès, Philippe de. "Abel Tiffauges et la vocation maternelle de l'homme." Postface to *Le Roi des aulnes.* Paris: Gallimard–Folio, 1980. 587-600.

Montalbetti, Jean. "Le Piège de l'image." Rev. of *La Goutte d'or. Magazine Littéraire* Jan. 1986: 18-19.

Montrémy, J.-M. "Michel Tournier: 'Je me suis toujours voulu écrivain croyant.'" Interview. *La Croix* 9-10 Nov. 1980: 8.

Morita-Clément, Marie-Agnès. *L'Image de l'Allemagne dans le roman français de 1945 à nos jours.* Nagoyashi, Jap.: Presses Universitaires de Nagoya, 1985.

Musil, Robert. *The Man without Qualities.* Trans. Eithne Wilkins and Ernst Kaiser. Vol 1. London: Secker & Warburg, 1953.

Nettelbeck, Colin. "Getting the Story Right: Narratives of World War II in Post-1968 France." *Journal of European Studies* 15.2 (1985): 77-116.

―――. "The Return of the Ogre: Michel Tournier's *Gilles et Jeanne.*" *Scripsi* 2.4 (1984): 43-50.

Nourissier, François. "Les Pentecôtes de Michel Tournier." Rev. of *Le Vent paraclet. Point* 21 Mar. 1977: 138.

―――. Rev. of *Le Roi des aulnes. Nouvelles Littéraires* 1 Oct. 1970: 4.

―――. Rev. of *Vendredi ou les limbes du Pacifique. Nouvelles Littéraires* 23 Nov. 1967: 2.

Nyssen, Hubert. Rev. of *Le Roi des aulnes. Synthèses* Jan.-Feb. 1971: 53-56.

O'Hearne, D. J. "Michel Tournier: Symbols and Stories." *Scripsi* 2.4 (1984): 13-23.

P.-D., B. Rev. of *Le Vent paraclet*. *Monde* 18 Feb. 1977: 1.

Pancrazi, Jean-Noel. "Idriss 'aux semelles de vent.'" Rev. of *La Goutte d'or*. *Quinzaine Littéraire* 1-15 Feb. 1986: 15-16.

Parmisano, Stanley Fabian. "Pride." *McDonald* 11: 765-66.

[Pascal, Blaise]. *Pascal's Pensées*. New York: Dutton, 1958.

Pasternak, Guitta Pessis. "Tournier le sensuel." Interview. *Monde* 12-13 Aug. 1984: xiv.

Pécheur, Jacques. Rev. of *Gilles et Jeanne*. *Français dans le Monde* Oct. 1983: 13.

Pérusat, Jean-Marie. "*Le Roi des aulnes*: Une Ecriture sinistre ou adroite?" *Français dans le Monde* Jan. 1980: 62-66.

Petit, Susan. "The Bible as Inspiration in Tournier's *Vendredi ou les limbes du Pacifique*." *French Forum* 9 (1984): 343-54.

————. "Fugal Structure, Nestorianism, and St. Christopher in Michel Tournier's *Le Roi des aulnes*." *Novel* 19.3 (Spring 1986): 232-45.

————. Rev. of *Gilles et Jeanne*. *French Review* 59 (1985): 342-43.

————. "*Gilles et Jeanne*: Tournier's *Le Roi des aulnes* Revisited." *Romanic Review* 76.3 (May 1985): 307-15.

————. Rev. of *La Goutte d'or*. *French Review* 60 (1987): 731.

————. "Joachim de Fiore, the Holy Spirit, and Michel Tournier's *Les Météores*." *Modern Language Studies* 16.3 (1986): 88-100.

————. "Psychological, Sensual, and Religious Initiation in Tournier's *Pierrot ou les secrets de la nuit*." *Children's Literature* 18 (1990): 87-100.

————. "Salvation, the Flesh, and God in Michel Tournier's *Gaspard, Melchior et Balthazar*." *Orbis Litterarum* 41 (1986): 53-65.

Piatier, Jacqueline. "Entretien: 'Je suis un métèque de la littérature.'" Interview. *Monde* [*des Livres*] 28 Mar. 1975: 16.

————. "Une Idée diabolique de Michel Tournier: L'Ecrivain au miroir." *Monde* [*des Livres*] 12 June 1973: 17-18.

————. "Michel Tournier et le voyage d'Idriss." Rev. of *La Goutte d'or*. *Monde* [*des Livres*] 10 Jan. 1986: 11, 14.

————. "Michel Tournier, romancier chrétien?" Rev. of *Gaspard, Melchior et Balthazar*. *Monde* 1 Nov. 1980: 1, 20.

————. "Michel Tournier sur la courte distance." Rev. of *Le Coq de bruyère*. *Monde* [*des Livres*] 26 May 1978: 17.

————. "Ramon Fernandez et Michel Tournier: Du philosophe au conteur." Rev. of *Le Vol du vampire*. *Monde* [*des Livres*] 11 Dec. 1981: 15, 18.

————. Rev. of *Le Roi des aulnes*. *Monde* [*des Livres*] 12 Sept. 1970: 1.

————. "Le Roman et les mythes: Michel Tournier entre le ciel et l'enfer." Rev. of *Les Météores*. *Monde* [*des Livres*] 28 Mar. 1975: 16.

————. "Vu: L'Homme en question." Rev. of *Le Vent paraclet. Monde* 28 June 1977: 27.

Pieper, Joseph. *The Four Cardinal Virtues: Prudence, Justice, Fortitude, Temperance.* Trans. Richard Winston and Clara Winston et al. Notre Dame, IN: U of Notre Dame P, 1966.

Plato. *The Republic of Plato.* Trans. Francis MacDonald Cornford. New York: Oxford UP, 1962.

————. *Symposium.* Trans. Benjamin Jowett. Indianapolis: Library of Liberal Arts, 1956.

Pluymène, Jean. "Un Objet captivant." Rev. of *Le Vent paraclet. Magazine Littéraire* June 1978: 22-23.

Podipara, P[lacid of St.] J[oseph]. "Malabar Rite." McDonald 9: 92-96.

Poirier, Jacques. *Approche de . . . "Le Roi des aulnes" (Michel Tournier).* Dijon: Alei, 1983.

Poirson, Alain. "Une Logique contre vents et marées: Entretien avec Michel Tournier." Interview. *Ecrire.* Spec. issue of *Nouvelle Critique* June-July 1977: 47-50.

Poulet, Robert. "Michel Tournier, romancier hors série." *Ecrits de Paris* Sept. 1975: 93-101.

Prescott, Peter S. "Monsters in Love." Rev. of *The Ogre. Newsweek* 1 Sept. 1972: 84.

Prévost, Claude. *Les Ogres de l'histoire: Littérature, politique, idéologie.* Paris: Sociales, 1973. 247-52.

Pudlowski, Gilles. "Saint Tournier, priez pour nous!" Interview. *Nouvelles Littéraires* 6-13 Nov. 1980: 36.

Purdy, Anthony. "The Essential Michel Tournier: Paradigm or Paradox?" *Dalhousie French Studies* 12 (1987): 54-67.

————. "From Defoe's *Crusoe* to Tournier's *Vendredi*: The Metamorphosis of a Myth." *Canadian Review of Comparative Literature* 11 (1984): 216-35.

————. "*Les Météores* de Michel Tournier: Une Perspective hétérologique." *Littérature* Dec. 1980: 32-43.

————. "Michel Tournier, lecteur de Stendhal." *Stendhal Club* ns 26 (1983-84): 86-88.

Raban, Jonathan. "Inventing Worlds." Rev. of *Friday, or The Other Island. New Society* 6 Feb. 1969: 217-18.

Rambures, Jean-Louis de. "Michel Tournier: Je suis comme la pie voleuse." Interview. *Comment travaillent les écrivains.* Paris: Flammarion, 1978. 163-67.

Ramirez Dulanto, Jacobus M. "Hope." McDonald 7: 133-41.

Redfern, W. D. "Approximating Man: Michel Tournier and Play in Language." *Modern Language Review* 80 (1985): 304-19.

Reeves, Marjorie. *Joachim of Fiore and the Prophetic Future.* New York: Torchbooks–Harper, 1977.

Regan, Augustine Richard. "Lust." McDonald 8: 1081-85.

Ricaumont, Jacques de. "De Jeanne d'Arc à Mata-Hari." Rev. of *Gilles et Jeanne. Spectacle du Monde/Réalités* Feb. 1984: 78-81.

Richard, Lionel. "La Tentation faustienne." *Magazine Littéraire* June 1978: 16-17.

Rinaldi, Angelo. "Connaissez-vous Pompignan?" Rev. of *La Goutte d'or. Express* 10 Jan. 1986: 56.

————. "Donnez-moi des nouvelles." Rev. of *Le Médianoche amoureux. Express* 21 Apr. 1989: 62-63.

————. "Michel Tournier: Cours du soir." Rev. of *Le Vol du vampire. Express* 11 Dec. 1981: 87.

————. "Michel Tournier dans le miroir." Rev. of *Le Vent paraclet. Express* 21-27 Feb. 1977: 58.

Ritzen, Quentin. "Plaidoyer pour un ogre. Entretien avec Michel Tournier." Interview. *Nouvelles Littéraires* 26 Nov. 1970: 6.

Rivadulla Pazos, Alfonso. "L'Imaginaire dans *Gilles et Jeanne* de Michel Tournier." *Recherches sur l'Imaginaire* 19 (1989): 239-48.

Robichon, Jacques. *Le Défi des Goncourt.* Paris: Denoel, 1975.

Rodríguez Monegal, Emir. Notes. *Borges: A Reader.* Ed. Emir Rodríguez Monegal and Alastair Reid. New York: Dutton, 1981. 339-64.

Rohou, Guy. Rev. of *Le Roi des aulnes. Nouvelle Revue Française* 1 Nov. 1970: 107-09.

Rollin, André. "*La Goutte d'or* par Michel Tournier au peigne fin." Interview. *Lire* Jan. 1986: 41-43.

Ronse, Henri. "Un Robinson solitaire." Rev. of *Vendredi ou les limbes du Pacifique. Lettres Françaises.* 19-25 July 1967: 10.

Rosello, Mireille. *L'In-différence chez Michel Tournier.* Paris: Corti, 1990.

Rushdie, Salman. "The Stuff of Marvels." Rev. of *Gemini. New York Times Book Review* 4 Oct. 1981: 12+.

Sankey, Margaret. "Meaning Through Intertextuality: Isomorphism of Defoe's *Robinson Crusoe* and Tournier's *Vendredi ou les limbes du Pacifique.*" *Australian Journal of French Studies* 18 (1981): 77-88.

Sanzio, Alain, et al. "Rencontre avec Michel Tournier." Interview. *Masques: Revue des Homosexualités* Autumn 1984: 8-26.

Sartre, Jean-Paul. *Being and Nothingness: An Essay on Phenomenological Ontology.* Trans. Hazel E. Barnes. New York: Philosophical Library, 1956.

————. *Critique of Dialectical Reason.* Trans. Alan Sheridan-Smith. Ed. Jonathan Rée. London: NLB, 1976.

————. *Huis clos. Théâtre*. Paris: Gallimard, 1947. 111-68.

————. *Imagination: A Psychological Critique*. Trans. Forrest Williams. Ann Arbor: U of Michigan P, 1972.

————. *La Nausée*. Paris: Gallimard, 1960.

————. *The Psychology of Imagination*. New York: Citadel, 1966.

Sbiroli, Lynn Salkin. *Michel Tournier: La Séduction du jeu*. Genève: Slatkine, 1987.

Schaper, Edzard. *Die Legende vom vierten König*. Köln: Jakob Hegner, 1961.

Shattuck, Roger. "Why Not the Best?" *New York Review of Books* 28 Apr. 1983: 8, 10-15. Rpt. as "Locating Michel Tournier." *The Innocent Eye: On Modern Literature and the Arts*. New York: Farrar, 1984. 205-18.

Sheppard, R. Z. "Mythomania." Rev. of *The Ogre*. *Time* 21 Aug. 1972: 68.

Showers, Paul. Rev. of *Friday and Robinson*. *New York Times Book Review* 14 Jan. 1973: 8.

Sieburth, Richard. "Enslaved by Plastic, Freed by Calligraphy." Rev. of *The Golden Droplet*. *New York Times* 1 Nov. 1987, natl. ed., book sec.: 37.

Sissman, L. E. "Obversities." Rev. of *The Ogre*. *New Yorker* 30 Dec. 1972: 68-70.

Slonim, Marc. "European Notebook." Rev. of *Le Roi des aulnes*. *New York Times Book Review* 13 Dec. 1970: 34-35.

————. "European Notebook." Rev. of *Vendredi ou les limbes du Pacifique*. *New York Times Book Review* 24 Dec. 1967: 11.

Smith, Stephen. Rev. of *Gaspard, Melchior et Balthazar*. *French Review* 55 (1981): 311-12.

————. "Toward a Literature of Utopia." *Homosexualities and French Literature*. Ed. George Stambolian and Elaine Marks. Ithaca, NY: Cornell UP, 1979.

St. Aubyn, F. C. "Friday and/or Vendredi." *Romanic Review* 79 (1988): 366-76.

Stirn, François. *Vendredi ou les limbes du Pacifique: Tournier*. Paris: Hatier–Profil Littérature, 1983.

Stoppard, Tom. *Dogg's Hamlet, Cahoot's Macbeth*. London: Faber, 1980.

Strauss, Walter. "Toward a Third Testament: Michel Tournier's Attempt to Re-appropriate the Sacred." *South Central Review* 6.1 (1989): 75-83.

Strickland, Geoffrey. "The Latest Tournier." Rev. of *Gaspard, Melchior et Balthazar*. *Cambridge Quarterly* 10 (1980): 238-41.

Sturrock, John. "We Four Kings." Rev. of *Gaspard, Melchior et Balthazar*. *Times Literary Supplement* 13 Feb. 1981: 158.

————. "The Sound of Myth." Rev. of *Le Vent paraclet*. *Times Literary Supplement* 7 Oct. 1977: 1144.

"Superhuman Prospectus." Rev. of *Le Roi des aulnes*. *Times Literary Supplement* 23 Oct. 1970: 1214.

Süskind, Patrick. *Perfume: The Story of a Murder.* Trans. John E. Woods. New York: Pocket, 1987.

Teilhard de Chardin, Pierre. *Let Me Explain.* Ed. Jean-Pierre Demoulin. Trans. René Hague et al. New York: Harper, 1970.

Terry, Charles Sanford. *The Music of Bach: An Introduction.* London: Oxford UP, 1933.

Tindall, Gillian. "New Fiction." Rev. of *Friday, or The Other Island. New Statesman* 7 Feb. 1969: 197.

Updike, John. Rev. of *The Wind Spirit. New Yorker* 10 July 1989: 92-96.

Valéry, Paul. *Monsieur Teste.* New and augmented ed. Paris: Gallimard, 1946.

Van Baelen, Jacqueline. Rev. of *Les Météores. French Review* 50 (1976): 205-06.

van Dyke, Henry. *The Story of the Other Wise Man.* New York: Harper, 1899.

Voll, Walter Urban. "Acedia." McDonald 1: 83-84.

Von Euw, C[harles] K. "Liturgy of Malabar Rite." McDonald 9: 96-97.

Vray, Jean-Bernard. "De l'usage des monstres et des pervers." *Michel Tournier.* Spec. issue of *Sud* 16 (1986): 100-31.

————. "L'Habit d'Arlequin." *Michel Tournier.* Spec. issue of *Sud* (1980): 149-66.

Waelti-Walters, J. "Autonomy and Metamorphosis." *Romanic Review* 73 (1982): 505-14.

Wallace, Ronald S. "Communion, Holy." *The New International Dictionary of the Christian Church.* Ed. J. D. Douglas. Grand Rapids, MI: Zondervan, 1974. 244-45.

Warner, Marina. "The Logic of Decadence." Rev. of *Gilles et Jeanne. Times Literary Supplement* 19 Aug. 1983: 879.

"Washed Up." Rev. of *Friday and Robinson. Times Literary Supplement* 8 Dec. 1972: 1496.

Weightman, John. "Confessions of a Polymorph." Rev. of *The Wind Spirit. New York Review of Books* 8 Dec. 1988: 43-44.

————. "Polymorphic Peter Pan." Rev. of *The Fetishist. New York Review of Books* 8 Nov. 1984: 25-26.

West, Delno C., and Sandra Zimdars-Swartz. *Joachim of Fiore: A Study in Spiritual Perception and History.* Bloomington: Indiana UP, 1983.

West, Paul. "A Gentle, Unjolly Giant with a Savior Complex." Rev. of *The Ogre. Washington Post Book World* 20 Aug. 1972: 3.

White, J. J. "Signs of Disturbance: The Semiological Import of Some Recent Fiction by Michel Tournier and Peter Handke." *Journal of European Studies* 4 (1974): 233-54.

Wisman, Josette. "Idéologie chrétienne et idéologie nazie: Une Lecture herméneutique du *Roi des aulnes* de Michel Tournier." *Romanic Review* 80 (1989): 591-606.

Wolfromm, Jean-Didier. "L'Apocalypse selon Tournier." Rev. of *Les Météores*. *Magazine Littéraire* May 1975: 35-37.

————. "Un Ogre Photographe." *Magazine Littéraire* Jan. 1986: 16-17.

————. "Le Rêveur de mots." Rev. of *Gaspard, Melchior et Balthazar*. *Magazine Littéraire* Dec. 1980: 52.

————. "Tournier le détourneur." Rev. of *Le Coq de bruyère*. *Magazine Littéraire* June 1978: 24-25.

Wordsworth, Christopher. "Late Arrival at Bethlehem." Rev. of *The Four Wise Men. Guardian* [Manchester, Eng.] 18 Nov. 1982: 14.

Worton, Michael J. "Ecrire et ré-écrire: Le Projet de Tournier." *Michel Tournier*. Spec. issue of *Sud* 16 (1986): 52-69.

————. "Intertextuality: To Inter Textuality or to Resurrect It?" *Crossreferences: Modern French Theory and the Practice of Criticism*. Eds. David Kelley and Isabelle Llasera. Leeds: Society for French Studies, 1986. 14-23.

————. "Michel Tournier and the Masterful Art of Rewriting." *PN Review* 11.3 (1984): 24-25.

————. "Myth-Reference in *Le Roi des aulnes*." *Stanford French Review* 6 (1982): 299-310.

————. "Use and Abuse of Metaphor in Tournier's 'Le Vol du vampire.' " *Paragraph* 10 (1987): 13-28.

Wright, Barbara. "Charmingly Unpleasant." Rev. of *Le Coq de bruyère. Times Literary Supplement* 13 Oct. 1978: 1182.

York, R. A. "Thematic Construction in *Le Roi des aulnes*." *Orbis Litterarum* 36 (1980): 76-91.

Zeldin, Theodore. "The Prophet of Unisex." Interview. *Observer* 30 Jan. 1983: 43.

Index

References to the principal treatment of a subject
follow the entry word in boldface type.

 Since its inception in 1980, PURDUE UNIVERSITY MONOGRAPHS IN ROMANCE LANGUAGES has acquired a distinguished reputation for its exacting standards and valuable contributions to Romance scholarship. The collection contains critical studies of literary or philological importance in the areas of Peninsular, Latin American, or French literature or language. Also included are occasional critical editions of important texts from these literatures. Among the authors are some of the finest of today's writers from both the new generation of scholars and the ranks of more established members of the profession. Writing in English, French, or Spanish, the authors address their subjects with insight and originality in books of approximately 200 pages. All volumes are printed on acid-free paper.

INQUIRIES CONCERNING THE SUBMISSION OF MANUSCRIPTS should be directed to the General Editor, Howard Mancing, Stanley Coulter Hall, Purdue University, West Lafayette, Indiana 47907 USA.

Available from

19. Lida Aronne-Amestoy: *Utopía, paraíso e historia: inscripciones del mito en García Márquez, Rulfo y Cortázar*. Amsterdam, 1986. xii, 167 pp. Paper.

20. Louise Mirrer-Singer: *The Language of Evaluation: A Sociolinguistic Approach to the Story of Pedro el Cruel in Ballad and Chronicle*. Amsterdam, 1986. xii, 128 pp. Paper.

21. Jo Ann Marie Recker: *"Appelle-moi 'Pierrot'"*: *Wit and Irony in the "Lettres" of Madame de Sévigné*. Amsterdam, 1986. x, 128 pp. Paper.

22. J. H. Matthews: *André Breton: Sketch for an Early Portrait*. Amsterdam, 1986. xii, 176 pp. Paper.

23. Peter V. Conroy, Jr.: *Intimate, Intrusive, and Triumphant: Readers in the "Liaisons dangereuses."* Amsterdam, 1987. xii, 139 pp. Paper.

24. Mary Jane Stearns Schenck: *The Fabliaux: Tales of Wit and Deception.* Amsterdam, 1987. xiv, 168 pp. Paper.

25. Joan Tasker Grimbert: *"Yvain" dans le miroir: Une Poétique de la réflexion dans le "Chevalier au lion" de Chrétien de Troyes*. Amsterdam, 1988. xii, 226 pp. Cloth and paper.

26. Anne J. Cruz: *Imitación y transformación: el petrarquismo en la poesía de Boscán y Garcilaso de la Vega*. Amsterdam, 1988. x, 156 pp. Cloth and paper.

27. Alicia G. Andreu: *Modelos dialógicos en la narrativa de Benito Pérez Galdós*. Amsterdam, 1989. xvi, 126 pp. Cloth and paper.

28. Milorad R. Margitić, ed.: *Le Cid: Tragi-comédie*. By Pierre Corneille. A critical edition. Amsterdam, 1989. lxxxvi, 302 pp. Cloth and paper.

29. Stephanie A. Sieburth: *Reading "La Regenta": Duplicitous Discourse and the Entropy of Structure*. Amsterdam, 1990. viii, 127 pp. Cloth and paper.

30. Malcolm K. Read: *Visions in Exile: The Body in Spanish Literature and Linguistics: 1500-1800*. Amsterdam, 1990. xii, 211 pp. Cloth and paper.

31. María Alicia Amadei-Pulice: *Calderón y el Barroco: exaltación y engaño de los sentidos*. Amsterdam, 1990. xii, 258 pp., 33 ills. Cloth and paper.

32. Lou Charnon-Deutsch: *Gender and Representation: Women in Spanish Realist Fiction*. Amsterdam, 1990. xiv, 205 pp., 6 ills. Cloth and paper.

33. Thierry Boucquey: *Mirages de la farce: Fête des fous, Bruegel et Molière*. Amsterdam, 1991. xviii, 145 pp., 9 ills. Cloth.

34. Elżbieta Skłodowska: *La parodia en la nueva novela hispanoamericana (1960-1985)*. Amsterdam, 1991. xx, 219 pp. Cloth.

35. Julie Candler Hayes: *Identity and Ideology: Diderot, Sade, and the Serious Genre*. Amsterdam, 1991. xiv, 186 pp. Cloth.

36. Aimée Israel-Pelletier: *Flaubert's Straight and Suspect Saints: The Unity of "Trois contes."* Amsterdam, 1991. xii, 165 pp. Cloth.

37. Susan Petit: *Michel Tournier's Metaphysical Fictions*. Amsterdam, 1991. xvi, 224 pp. Cloth.

38. María Cristina Quintero: *Poetry as Play: "Gongorismo" and the "Comedia."* Amsterdam, 1991. xviii, 260 pp. Cloth.